ALL
OTHER
DUTIES
AS
ASSIGNED

THE **ASSISTANT PRINCIPAL'S** CRITICAL ROLE IN SUPPORTING SCHOOLS INSIDE AND OUT

RYAN DONLAN

Solution Tree | Press

a division of
Solution Tree

555 North Morton Street
Bloomington, IN 47404
800.733.6786 (toll free) / 812.336.7700
FAX: 812.336.7790

email: info@SolutionTree.com
SolutionTree.com

Visit **go.SolutionTree.com/leadership** to download the free reproducibles in this book.

Printed in the United States of America

Library of Congress Cataloging-in-Publication Data

Names: Donlan, Ryan A., 1967- author.
Title: All other duties as assigned : the assistant principal's critical
   role in supporting schools inside and out / Ryan Donlan.
Description: Bloomington, IN : Solution Tree Press, 2022. | Includes
   bibliographical references and index.
Identifiers: LCCN 2021054259 (print) | LCCN 2021054260 (ebook) | ISBN
   9781952812613 (paperback) | ISBN 9781952812620 (ebook)
Subjects: LCSH: Assistant school principals--United States. | School
   management and organization--United States.
Classification: LCC LB2831.92 .D67 2022 (print) | LCC LB2831.92 (ebook) |
   DDC 371.20973--dc23/eng/20220124
LC record available at https://lccn.loc.gov/2021054259
LC ebook record available at https://lccn.loc.gov/2021054260

Solution Tree
Jeffrey C. Jones, CEO
Edmund M. Ackerman, President

Solution Tree Press
President and Publisher: Douglas M. Rife
Associate Publisher: Sarah Payne-Mills
Managing Production Editor: Kendra Slayton
Editorial Director: Todd Brakke
Art Director: Rian Anderson
Copy Chief: Jessi Finn
Production Editor: Miranda Addonizio
Content Development Specialist: Amy Rubenstein
Acquisitions Editor: Sarah Jubar
Copy Editor: Kate St. Ives
Text and Cover Designer: Fabiana Cochran
Associate Editor: Sarah Ludwig
Editorial Assistants: Charlotte Jones and Elijah Oates

☑ ACKNOWLEDGMENTS

I would like first to acknowledge two admired educational leaders and opportunity makers, Principal Leonard Trudeau and Superintendent Franklin D. Ronan, for hiring me into an assistant principalship, my inaugural opportunity to influence lives beyond the classroom. I am also grateful to Assistant Principal Bill Rivest, who took me under his wing with wise counsel to guide my energy. As I move through my career, I won't ever forget the strong leadership, heartfelt compassion, and tactful wisdom of Sharon Stockero-Ryden, who believed in me and encouraged my own unique and unconventional ways of growing into my leadership and management. Also deserving mention are amazing educational confidants who were pivotally influential to me and remain so—they embody all that is special about the profession of education and thus, have influenced what this book is all about. So, to Bob Gulash, Rick Sochacki, and Cindy VanSumeren: a heartfelt thanks. Most of all, I wish to acknowledge three who know me best—as I have spent so much time and energy on what I do while not at home, and often while I'm there—my wife Wendy, son Sean, and daughter Katelyn. Above all else, I love you.

Solution Tree Press would like to thank the following reviewers:

Rolando Casado
Assistant Principal
Parkway Middle School
Kissimmee, Florida

Deanna Herrera
Assistant Principal
Bosque Farms Elementary
Bosque Farms, New Mexico

Peter Marshall
Education Consultant
Burlington, Ontario

Annie Orsini
Assistant Principal
Jordan Creek Elementary
Westridge Elementary
West Des Moines, Iowa

Jennifer Steele
Assistant Principal
Northside High School
Fort Smith, Arkansas

Ringnolda Jofee' Tremain
PK3–8 Principal
Trinity Basin Preparatory
Fort Worth, Texas

Visit **go.SolutionTree.com/leadership** to download
the free reproducibles in this book.

☑ TABLE OF CONTENTS

Reproducible pages are in italics.

☑ ABOUT THE AUTHOR

Ryan Donlan, EdD, professor in the Department of Educational Leadership in the Bayh College of Education at Indiana State University, served for twenty years in traditional and charter schools in K–12 education—in teaching as well as school and district leadership. Ryan has taught for years at the college and university level in the areas of leadership, communication, and education, and he conducts and offers school program reviews, a variety of training opportunities, consulting services, and professional presentations for educators, stakeholder groups, and organizational leaders.

Ryan is a member of various professional organizations and enjoys robust teaching, scholarship, and service and has been awarded the Holmstedt Distinguished Professorship and the Faculty Distinguished Service Award. He has presented throughout the United States and around the world on topics such as adaptive communication, leadership agility, and leveraging relationships for professional and personal success. He has also served on numerous boards, committees, and task forces, and is a frequent faculty sponsor for doctoral dissertations.

Ryan has published articles in a variety of magazines and professional journals and has coauthored the books *Minds Unleashed: How Principals Can Lead the Right-Brained Way*, *The Hero Maker: How Superintendents Can Get Their School Boards to Do the Right Thing*, and *The School Board Member's Guidebook: Becoming a Difference Maker for Your District*.

Ryan received a bachelor's degree in social sciences and English from the University of Michigan–Flint, a master's degree in curriculum design and classroom teaching from Michigan State University, an educational specialist's degree from Central Michigan University, and a doctorate of education from Central Michigan University.

Visit www.ryandonlan.com to learn more about Ryan's work.

To book Ryan Donlan for professional development, contact pd@SolutionTree.com.

☑ INTRODUCTION

> Commencement concluded. Families were taking photos at the ceremony's reception. Tears, smiles, and hugs filled the room, along with talk of summer ahead. A mom of a graduating senior approached. Since the fall of her son's ninth-grade year, I had provided him guidance, assistance, and at times redirection. Mom offered me a gift she made in a ceramics class, a teal-colored shelf-top sculpture fashioned as an angel, with flowing wings and the striped tie of a school administrator.
>
> She said, "This is you."
>
> It was one of the most heartfelt gifts I have received for doing what I loved.

I can summarize the power of our profession in one sentence: schools make all professions possible. I think of this when hearing from former students—how they are doing and the lives they lead. Let me also note the challenge of inspiring our young people. Educators ask students to come to school every day and do things that are difficult for them to do—in front of people they wish to impress. Of course all educators take on this challenge, but I'm here to talk about unique ways that our school administrators do so.

School administrators face many demands from all quarters. They understand the complexity of school, as any challenge outside of the school in the community can find its way through the schoolhouse gate and affect the school. Examples include conflicts, inequities, trauma, and the varying levels of academic and behavioral aptitude people have to *do school*, and do it well. It takes deft leadership to invite success from this mosaic. School administrators anticipate the challenges of tomorrow and influence circumstance today, where success is a moving target. In such, they meet those around them *where they are*, and in doing so elevate positively what is happening in their lives at that moment. They leverage productive difference where supply is light. They leave a lasting impression for the good with their efforts. Researchers Katina Pollock, Fei Wang, and Cameron Hauseman (2017), in their work for the Ontario Principals Council, note "the ability to have greater impact on students" as "the highest motivating factor for entering the vice-principalship," with nearly 80 percent of those surveyed choosing this option. For these reasons and more, there is no better time to be in school administration.

1

In this book, I will deconstruct the unique role of the assistant principal as one integral member of the school administration team. But, first, we'll discuss some background, and then we'll talk about what you can expect as you read.

The Opportunity Maker

At the intersection where challenges inside school meet demands from the outside exists a role in school administration long visible as a frontline choreographer of safety, order, discipline, and attendance: the assistant principal. The assistant principal helps students and families navigate citizenship development, academic preparation, and individual expression. The assistant principal is an opportunity maker, a point-person helping others make the best of circumstances when the going gets tough. Assistant principals provide comfort and guidance to students trying to make sense of it all while helping the adults who work with them. Assistant principals take care of the folks.

Have you, like me, heard critics of assistant principalship call for a reinvention of the role? I have heard for years professional developers and professors of educational leadership say the days of school building management are no longer relevant (that is, fashionable), and that instructional leadership should define the position. I disagree. First, if schools leverage the talents of teachers, there *is* enough instructional leadership to go around. Successful principals with their eyes on the ball might appreciate the assistant principal's role right where it is—positioned to help folks with challenges and personal capacity.

Assistant principals have a unique opportunity to examine themselves from the inside out rather than change what they do. Our profession must refrain from downgrading the importance of school management as compared to school leadership. These duties are *both–and*, not *either–or*. *Management* is not a dirty word. Your role as an assistant principal means you are first to ensure proper school management so that school leadership can flourish. While resources and attention given to principal preparation abound, our profession needs more materials devoted to the assistant principal's role. Researchers supported by the Wallace Foundation found consistent evidence that preservice administration preparation programs do not focus specifically on training the assistant principal, even with the twin realities that (1) graduates are more likely to serve as assistant principals than principals upon graduation and (2) there are no unique professional standards for assistant principals (Goldring, Rubin, & Herrmann, 2021).

You may remain in your assistant principalship for a year or two, or you may embrace it as your long-term career. It is not how long you plan to stay in the assistant principalship that counts; rather, what matters is that you embrace the assistant principal role as pivotal for student success. The good news is that consistent evidence shows that assistant principals are generally highly satisfied with their current roles (Goldring et al., 2021). I hope that is the case with you as well; either way, please allow me to offer something that will help in any regard.

As I have long considered the assistant principalship akin to the special forces of education, I often marveled at the general lack of preparatory attention and resources given the role. Especially in university graduate programs, it seemed folks were in principal preparation programs, with only tangential attention given to the thought that many might start as assistant principals. Because of that, this book has been on my mind for the better part of twenty years.

I originally called this book *Assistant Principal University* because of that lack in existing university programs, and found it hard during the writing process and editorial review to pull myself away from this title. My belief in higher education to expand our thinking, and the resulting improvements in our practitioner scholarship and repertoire of talent and skills, steeled my resolve to offer a resource that would find more than a bookshelf as its home. I want it to find partners in those who care incessantly about students and community, those who cannot simply turn off the desire to find the next way to make a connection with someone else. I want this book to be a teaching tool, and even though the title evolved away from the original during the publishing process, you might consider it a series of lessons packaged as chapters. This book is both a thought leader and teaching partner for the best in all of us that aspires to help and serve others. You can think of it as really the most unique of university experiences, wherein I hope that all who read will consider me someone on speed dial, willing to serve as a teacher and co-learner.

What Do We Have Here?

This book is for current and aspiring preK–12 assistant principals. While this is the term I use throughout the book, you may recognize the role as that of the vice principal (as it is often known in Canada and other settings). In fact, those deans, disciplinarians, and devoted frontline building administrators serving as the right arm of their principals, no matter their title, will find it invaluable. I mentioned a few of these individuals in the Acknowledgments section of this book. It can be used in a quarterly book study with aspiring or sitting leaders or as a textbook for those in professional preparation programs at the graduate level. By reading the book, you will gain a comprehensive understanding of what an assistant principalship entails, things assistant principals do that are critical for their students, and how you can achieve success and happiness in the position. *All Other Duties as Assigned: The Assistant Principal's Critical Role in Supporting Schools Inside and Out* offers relevant strategies from front to back. Many of the ideas presented in the book may be new to you, while others that I present in fresh ways may have already proven over the years to be powerful. Some may appear more relevant to secondary school assistant principals, but I do not discount the critical role of elementary school assistant principals or the linkages between these pages and their daily responsibilities.

The book consists of ten chapters comprising job-specific content ready for you to apply. Each chapter begins with an explanation of *what* the topic is—the definitions, research, and background information you need to know. Following that is the *why*—an investigation into the importance of the chapter topic. Then I move on to the *how*, where I provide relevant and immediate application strategies you can use with students, staff, and yourself. Finally, each chapter closes with a section called Toolkit for Tomorrow that features immediate next steps you can take and an in-depth professional development activity to deepen your knowledge and improve your practice. Throughout the chapters, I've included tips that offer immediate, bite-size ideas you can try out right away.

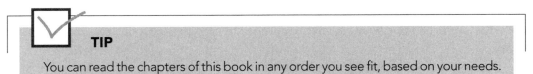

TIP

You can read the chapters of this book in any order you see fit, based on your needs.

If that seems like a lot, it is. Because of the depth and breadth of subjects that comprise the very complex job of an assistant principal, there is indeed a lot to cover. Keep in mind that other than the introduction and chapter 1, you can read the chapters in any order you see fit, based on your needs. In fact, it works well as a reference guide for when the larger issues that each chapter addresses introduce themselves into your particular context. Please enjoy as your schedule allows, and come back to it as often as you would like and find valuable.

Chapter 1 presents information on what inspires professional educators to become assistant principals. It includes perspectives and priorities, as well as a challenge to never lose your identity. It suggests you come first. As a reader, you'll find chapter 1 a bit longer than others in that it provides some foundational information that serves as a platform for later topics.

Chapter 2 argues that any good system of leadership and instruction must sit atop a solid foundation of management. It focuses on prioritizing what you deal with every day in categories: urgent, important, both, and neither.

Chapter 3 widens your perspectives on school, encouraging you to examine your school's climate and community. It shares how assistant principals can foster positive school environments.

Chapter 4 presents relationships as starting points to building effective support systems and making a difference. It shares how you can send and receive communication for successful interactions.

Chapter 5 shows how assistant principals protect and promote priorities and people, including a formula that promotes teaching and learning. Having regard for others is key in the strategies and information presented.

Chapter 6 shows how assistant principals leverage firm and fair discipline. It includes topics of school law and due process. A common theme of dignity is present throughout, and it cautions that discipline is a delicate business.

Chapter 7 shares how assistant principals capitalize on teachable moments. It notes that one's role as a teacher never has to end, and shows how assistant principals can leverage compassionate accountability for positive outcomes.

Chapter 8 discusses safeguarding an appropriate education for all, including societal factors in school performance and students with exceptionalities. It includes a deeper dive into issues of diversity, access, equity, and social justice.

Chapter 9 focuses on taking time for teaching and learning, particularly with the assistant principal spending time in classrooms. This involves gauging fidelity of instruction, as well as ensuring effective supervision and evaluation.

Chapter 10 presents the importance of school improvement and accountability, using data and improvement science to move performance forward. This chapter encourages assistant principals to establish a framework for student empowerment and adult responsibility.

The appendix compiles strategies from chapters 1 through 10 on how assistant principals can implement this book's ideas with students, with staff, and in their own personal or professional development—with corresponding page numbers from the text to serve as a useful tool to quickly find strategies later and identify whether they're for use with students, staff, or yourself.

I wrap up *All Other Duties as Assigned* with a conclusion that mirrors the book's title and helps bring things full circle. Throughout, I offer tips, strategies, and reproducible activities to extend your learning. As each chapter serves as an individual playbook for targeted refinement of skills, the book is ideal for a book study or collaborative learning experience for those preparing for or currently in the role. I hope to garner interest from you as a reader, and also in the assistant principalship as a profession—an opportunity maker, and for some of you, a career destination both fulfilling and impactful.

CHAPTER 1
DECIDING YOU WANT TO BE AN ASSISTANT PRINCIPAL

A sunny day found me on the green of a golf course with administrative colleagues, and with the *ping* of a putter . . . another ball in the cup. I was in my late twenties, a new assistant principal among leaders more senior than I, talking shop and asking how school leaders stay connected to the teacher within them as they assume new roles. Over many years, I have learned our best school leaders never really lose touch; rather, they make decisions with a wider field of attention.

That day, one of my colleagues noted that as we ascend our leadership ladders, we must prioritize our teaching. In fact, we *can* plan for teachable moments as our allotted time to make decisions increases. Teachers make minute-by-minute decisions; assistant principals do so similarly, but as they are free of the obligation to classroom supervision interfering with time to follow up, even more time is allowed for principals and superintendents. At each step of this decisional hierarchy, the impact of such decisions can increase. One point resonated with me: assistant principals' decisions often carry a heavier weight, as they must be made rather quickly, yet in tumultuous situations.

So, with this in mind, you want to be an assistant principal? Let's think about the what and the why of the assistant principal's role first; then I'll present some strategies to use with students, staff, and yourself.

The What and the Why

Assistant principals perform myriad duties as key members of a school's leadership team, and their footprint is growing in schools. The Wallace Foundation reports in a review of seventy-nine empirical research studies that between 1990 and 2016, the number of assistant principals in the United States increased 83 percent from around forty thousand to around eighty-one thousand, with the number of schools employing them moving from around one-third to one-half (Goldring et al., 2021). Elementary schools alone have experienced a dramatic increase in assistant principal employment, moving from around 20 percent in 1990 to around 40 to 50 percent in 2016, depending on the study (Goldring et al., 2021).

In regard to their span of duties, a review of international literature and studies from 1970 to 2011 on "the roles, responsibilities, training, socialization, and typologies of the assistant principal" (Oleszewski, Shoho, & Barnett, 2012, p. 264) notes the assistant principal is a unique entity and critical leader with duties focusing on "student management, instructional leadership, and personnel management" (p. 266), yet with duties within those areas that are neither precise nor exact and that professional literature underrepresents. While particular duties can vary widely from one school or grade level to another, commonalities exist, such as working hand in hand with principals to ensure staff and students are in alignment with the goals a principal sets for all in the learning community. Duties generally center on a combination of education management and administration, student discipline, and instructional leadership (Goldring et al., 2021). You might say assistant principals serve as chief tour guides for staff and students on the daily trip from *mission* (what everyone is expected to do and represent) to *vision* (an ideal state of collaborating for teaching and learning). State policy or rules can also influence the role of assistant principals, particularly with respect to the increased requirements they may place on principals, such as teacher evaluation.

The role of assistant principal typically involves supervising building and grounds; providing for proactive systems, structures, and services to foster positive relationships and pro-social behavior; tracking and holding students accountable for school attendance; handling disciplinary infractions when they arise; serving as leads of specific units in the school (examples might be career and technical education, alternative education, or athletics); chairing school committees (such as curriculum workgroups, school improvement subcommittees, or ad hoc task forces to solve problems); and supervising athletic events and extracurricular activities. In many cases, principals will involve assistant principals in classroom observations and teacher and staff evaluations, as well as the planning and hosting of professional development and staff training. Often, assistant principals will serve directly as the liaison between the school and families and will be a first line of communication in fostering and maintaining positive school-home relations.

Ideally, assistant principals complement and offset the strengths and talents of their principals. They are often expected to carry the principal's expectations for staff and students, and with it, the company line. Some schools have more than one assistant principal, and therefore often share tasks or divvy up responsibilities; some even share tasks with principals, everyone playing to their strengths. It may also be true that assistant principals share duties at the district level among or across schools. Regardless of the local arrangement, you'll find assistant principals serving as confidants and handling many responsibilities the principal wishes to delegate to them, often termed *all other duties as assigned*. In short, assistant principals' roles are highly varied and are largely defined by their principals (Goldring et al., 2021).

Because assistant principals perform numerous duties on a daily basis, they frequently feel there is just not enough time in the day to accomplish everything on their plate. While this is not a unique state of mind among educators, the nature of the assistant principal's role invites all that is happening emotionally in students' lives to end up unpredictably—but consistently—on the assistant principal's desk, no matter what students might have otherwise intended. Pollock and her colleagues (2017) identify overwork, the emotionally draining nature of the job, student discipline, and even the amount of email they receive as substantial reasons to feel overwhelmed. Key to success in this role is prioritizing tasks and keeping a keen focus on what is important. Calls for prioritization are not uncommon in the field of education. In *Focus: Elevating the Essentials to Radically Improve Student Learning*, Mike Schmoker (2011) calls for simplicity, clarity, and priority in teaching. I suggest the same for assistant principals. In an interview published in *Educational Leadership*, Angela Duckworth, noted researcher on the concept of grit, highlights priorities when she talks of focusing on passions over time, choosing particular things to do, and giving up other things to do (Perkins-Gough, 2013). Researchers Grant Clayton and Andrea J. Bingham from the University of Colorado conclude in a 2018 study of first-year assistant principals that necessary ingredients for success are *relearning prioritization* and *letting go*, in that some responsibilities simply must be handled another day. A given for any assistant principal is that constant daily priorities include student discipline and the sheer number of responsibilities on their desks (Clayton & Bingham, 2018). Another given includes the reality that no matter how proactive we are at planning or getting things done, each day brings with it the need to react to what or who visits the office.

When moving from teaching educator to administrating educator, it is natural to ask, "Do I have the right stuff?" and "Am I really moving to the dark side?" as some colleagues quip. Many educators are likely to recognize in this long-standing joke that friends or colleagues who move to administration might seem to switch sides, just as movie villain Darth Vader does in the *Star Wars* series. I have thought much about what runs through educators' minds when moving to administration within their schools or other schools. Any champion of students is doing so with best interests at heart. Commonality exists in what motivates our best to serve, no matter the position: a common desire to touch lives, create opportunity, make an impact, serve beyond ourselves, and embrace challenge in making a difference. Superstar educators shine with confidence in their intersections of passion and purpose.

Those wishing to assume the responsibilities of an assistant principalship might study their why through a look at what motivates them. Cassandra Gaisford (2020), author of *How to Find Your Passion and Purpose: Four Easy Steps to Discover a Job You Want and Live the Life You Love*, notes, "Finding a job you want and living a life you love is impossible without passion, enthusiasm, zest, inspiration and the deep satisfaction that comes from doing something that delivers you some kind of buzz" (p. xvii). I would agree. To accomplish this, it helps to examine two key ingredients that enrich your quality of life and provide the energy to love what you do. The first is what you are passionate about, and the second is the purpose for which you feel you are in your role in the first place. The key is to identify where passion and purpose connect. Let's take a look at each.

For our consideration, I'm focusing on the passion for people, activities, or causes, which is instrumental in leadership developmental readiness (Bronk & McLean, 2016). Passion is what excites you and fills your gas tank. "Real passion is more than a fad or fleeting enthusiasm. It can't be turned on and off like a tap" (Gaisford, 2020, p. 21). It is a present-driven force that consumes you. When you are passionate about something, you crave an immersion into it, where experience of the moment is unintentionally life-giving. When you have passion about something, your connection to it drives your energy through living and doing in a way that interests, empowers, and excites you. It can be profitable for you on many levels, such as revealing your true talents, enhancing your determination, providing a competitive edge, and allowing your work to serve as a vehicle for self-expression (Gaisford, 2020). Passion allows embers of energy inside you to ignite; you live in the moment and wish not to be anywhere else. Passion is a gift that keeps you effortlessly connected to something you love. Are you passionate about your assistant principalship?

The word *purpose* provides us a sense of direction, orienting and guiding our work (Bronk & McLean, 2016). Purpose is something that provides a feeling of obligation in you to make the world a better place. It is a future-driven force that consumes you. Rick Warren (2012), *New York Times* best-selling author of the book *The Purpose Driven Life: What on Earth Am I Here For?*, shares that many people have things around them that drive their lives, but they are the wrong things, such as guilt, resentment and anger, fear, materialism, and the need for the approval of others. Regarding the need for approval, he quips, "I don't know all keys to success, but one key to failure is to try to please everyone" (Warren, 2012, p. 33). He suggests a purpose-driven life instead, and states that knowing your purpose gives meaning to your life, and as well, simplifies, focuses, and motivates your life, and even prepares you for eternity. When you have purpose, you crave involvement in it, where the challenges of the moment are life-enriching. When you have purpose, your connection compels you to expend energy through taking actions to move yourself from where you are currently to a better place. Purpose allows for agency within you, where you drive forward in the moment and focus on making a difference. Purpose is a gift that keeps you effortfully connected to something you feel responsible for and empowered to access, experience, and leverage toward desired ends.

The intersection of passion and purpose superpowers your assistant principalship and gets at your why. Gaisford (2020) calls this intersection a *point of brilliance*: "the intersection of your favorite gifts and talents, your deepest interests and enthusiasms, and all that motivates, inspires and drives you" (p. 55). This is particularly important in that research has shown that passion and purpose are two of four key ingredients to school administrators' well-being and flourishing at work (Cherkowski, Kutsyuruba, & Walker, 2020). Passion and purpose also impact your developmental readiness as a school leader because passion "fosters a critical sense of motivation to grow as a leader" (Bronk & McLean, 2016, p. 30), fuels intrinsic motivation, and models behavior for others. Purpose impacts your developmental readiness; it gives you active engagement to far-reaching goals aligned with your belief system that commit you to causes larger than yourself:

> Individuals with a strong sense of passion and purpose are more likely to seek out opportunities to develop as leaders. They are likely to be highly motivated to find mentors, take on challenging work assignments, and explore formal opportunities to develop leadership skills. (Bronk & McLean, 2016, p. 34)

Additionally, the combination of both passion and purpose serves to support assistant principals in modeling a way of working and being for others that is critical in terms of success and satisfaction. Gaisford (2020) articulates this well: "Passionate people are prepared to give up things to live a more passionate life. Passionate people are prepared to take risks and cope with failure. The compensation is a bigger, fuller, more interesting life with drive and purpose" (p. 4). Where is your intersection of passion and purpose? Who and what resides there?

The How: Strategies to Use With Students

The following strategies—maximizing your visibility, acting with compassion, and reading between the lines—are effective ways to connect passion and purpose and lay the foundation for your work with students.

Maximize Your Visibility

A foundational aspect of your role as an assistant principal in working with students is to ensure each day that you have visibility, as you cannot serve at the intersection of a student's challenges and capacity without being in arm's reach. You might come to work to find large stacks of paperwork on your desk, but resist the temptation to hunker down in your office when your presence is needed elsewhere. This is true each time the passing bell rings, when lunch is served, and before and after school—sometimes even during class.

TIP

When moving from point A to point B in your travels, if time is of the essence and someone wants to chat, be sure to do so, and first say with a smile, "Hey, walk with me."

Visibility includes the notion of both others being able to see you and you being able to see all that is going on. It means being where you need to be when you're most needed. For example, be in the student commons area during the time of day when the most students are present, but don't predictably be there when most students are not. When students are not around in one place predictably, it is best that you are in a variety of places, so that you appear ever-visible. Visibility means getting where you need to go quickly without appearing that you are in a hurry. Use visibility to your advantage by knowing the shortcuts and the corridors. Know which boiler room back doors lead down what hallways to get back to the main thoroughfares. Know which courtyards offer a quick trajectory leading back to a certain destination. In other words, know your building and have master key access to all of it. Often, when you arrive in a location, people feel safer because of it. Prevention requires visibility. With visibility comes great responsibility.

Act With Compassion

Students who visit the assistant principal's office are often uncomfortable and may not present their best selves. What they need in these moments is for you to demonstrate compassion and empathy. This can, of course, be difficult to do. One helpful technique is to envision a place where you feel uncomfortable and connect with those feelings. Connecting to our own insides is critical in building compassion, empathy, and the courage to be there for another who is suffering, notes Kelsey Crowe and Emily McDowell (2017) in *There Is No Good Card for This: What to Say and Do When Life Is Scary, Awful, and Unfair to People You Love*. If you are on the edge of discomfort, then you are probably getting close to where you should be.

Students can tell if you are genuinely concerned for them, so it is important to connect with your own compassion and demonstrate patience and understanding. According to psychologist, author, and organizational developer Nate Regier, *compassion* as defined here has to do with the origins of the word: it's about struggling with something while maintaining dignity (personal communication, January 28, 2020; Regier, 2016; Regier & King, 2013). It is not some pillow-soft construct to describe the feelings of enabling over-adapters or helicopter adults (that is, those who fly in on their metaphorical helicopters and rescue students who would be better off learning from their own mistakes). What this means is that when confronted with conflict, strive to approach things from a *you and me versus the problem* angle, rather than *you versus me*. More meaningful decisions take time and effort to bring about. Again, the key is *struggling with*.

Struggling with can start with connecting equitably. Connecting equitably here means not pretending that you know how students are feeling, as your background may invoke dominance that students cannot muster as a tool. The key is to listen, hear students' voices said their own way, and avoid judgment. Do not be quick to offer prescription, as students are likely to see this as judging and to knowing better; doing this will not position you as an ally. Have cultural humility, and be transparent about power differentials, or at least respect the fact that others perceive them, and don't minimize their presence.

TIP

Sometimes the most compassionate decision is that in which you choose *not* to respond rather than to respond.

Read Between the Lines

Providing a foundation for your assistant principalship also involves developing your skills in reading between the lines of what students say and what they do. Typically what students are presenting to you as the issue is not really the issue, which is important to keep in mind as you work to solve problems students are having with each other. There is a *back* to every *front*, as the saying goes. The professed reason a student is sent to your office is typically because of behaviors such as excessive off-task behavior and noncompliance, but in fact the real reason may more likely be that the student has been pushing the teacher's buttons by questioning the teacher's capabilities, and the teacher may be in fact secretly insecure and observably incompetent. The drama going on between the dance team captains is not because of the selection of songs for competition but rather competition for dates to the homecoming dance. The hostility between two young students is not really about what they said to each other yesterday but instead how their families have interacted for five years. Read between the lines.

TIP

Typically the reported issue is really not the issue, yet it is tangentially related. Don't discount it, but spend some time in intelligence gathering. Once you have done so, you can say, "While we are working to solve [the issue professed], I'd like also to focus on something else that is important to me: [the issue you have uncovered]. May we do both?"

Assistant principals must take time to know what's really going on with students if they are to help solve problems. At times, what students want from you will actually make things worse, not better, and they don't see it. You need to protect students from themselves. Read between the lines in talking to students in dispute so that you can gauge how they wish to frame the problem. Spend time one to one peeling back the layers so that you can see a slightly more vulnerable and open version of the participants, if they allow you in. Contextual cues are necessary, as is the intel from those close to each participant and even students who are disinterested but happen to have their fingers on the pulse of what's going on.

With students' parents, reading between the lines will often reveal something vicarious going on that falls outside the concerns being framed or complaints rendered. It is often something they experienced in school as students themselves, now revisited. It is important to know that you don't have to get folks to fess up on what is between the lines. Often, that would do more harm than good. It is simply that when you fashion a path forward, ensure it applies both to the stated concerns and those that lie unstated.

TIP

Asking the question, "What can we do together to work through this?" rather than "What do you want out of this situation?" is often a safe way to prevent students from being their own worst enemies as they seek your help.

In reading between the lines, know that you must forgive in advance. Students—in fact, all humans—are fallible, and school is hard. As such, the role of the assistant principal is to provide ourselves and others an opportunity to fail, yet fail forward. I once had a mother come to school to yell at me wearing a T-shirt with "F--- you, and the horse you rode in on!" on the front. (Note that the first word wasn't really obscured.) She was irate and thought her son was being singled out because of this or that. The way I ultimately responded to this student's mother reminds me of a tense chance encounter I had outside of my work as an assistant principal. I was returning home one day and discovered a snake on my front porch. It could potentially pack a painful bite, so I needed to remove it or kill it. I chose to remove it to the back of our property where it slithered away. It was a bit of a wrestling match with a grappling tool from the local flea market; nevertheless, I was successful at getting the snake to a place that allowed the humans and it to coexist more harmoniously.

Making the decision to remove rather than kill the snake came with a realization that we all simply want a space, and though the snake was in our space, we were in its space as well. It was the same with the student's mom. While I might have viewed her as a snake getting up in my face, she viewed me as just as much of a snake. This is where forgiving in advance comes in for the assistant principal. The best defense to a jaded perspective is often an affirmation. You can forgive in your head and heart, then listen and read between the lines, while trying to invite others to a different space of thinking if you can. In the case of this parent, I ignored the offensive T-shirt and worked to keep the focus on her son. This may not have changed her perspective of me that day, but it did change the focus of our energies, which was a good thing.

TIP

One of the best affirmations you can offer students is a pause and due consideration for what they have said before you respond to them in word or deed. Let their message soak in, and then share that you appreciate them offering that for you. Then, take things from there.

Noted emotional intelligence expert Daniel Goleman (2013) writes, "The brain is the last organ of the body to mature anatomically, continuing to grow and shape itself into our twenties" (p. 77). This certainly applies to students in school. Why would we not forgive in advance in reading between the lines, if their brains are not fully developed to capacity? As we read between the lines with adults all the time, it is obvious that even the most mature of us can have lapses. Let's show a bit of grace here for those on their way.

The How: Strategies to Use With Staff

The following strategies—deciding through integrity and striving for effectiveness—are useful ways to connect passion and purpose and lay the foundation for your work with staff.

Decide Through Integrity

At the forefront of your role is the need to make tough decisions. You'll experience this from the very beginning of each school year. Decisions and actions travel well through a moral and ethical filter, which helps you decide with integrity. Integrity assists assistant principals when situations of right and wrong are relative rather than absolute. When brokering different paths to an outcome, integrity is a safe bet as an arbiter. A great check is the front-page test. If your decisions were going to be on the front page of the evening newspaper, would you be OK with that? Would you be comfortable with your decision if called out by the crowd in the coffee shop, or the barber shop, or by your family over dinner? If you would, then you have probably acted with integrity.

TIP

Set aside the golden rule—*Do unto others as you would have them do unto you*, and instead use the platinum rule—*Do unto others as they would have you do unto them*. That way, you're considering others' needs and not projecting your own.

Conducting a figurative front-page test is helpful when our performance is being judged, as our decisions often will bring about discontent from staff. You can get a peek into their feelings by doing weekly litmus tests, such as eating lunch once per week in the teachers' lounge, just before or after your cafeteria and commons-area duties. Do the same with the support staff. There will be ample opinions on decisions you have made, and it will keep you honest. One common request from staff for assistant principals is that you provide equal treatment under policy. Colleagues put pressure on assistant principals to treat their students consistently, and in many cases they demand the same consequences each time students are sent from the room. Assistant principals who rigidly adhere to equality fundamentally disrupt fairness and equity. Operating with integrity allows you to rest well on the fact that different people might need different approaches. For example, might the student who has been up all night taking care of siblings in a neglectful home situation need a break if caught sleeping in first period? Most assuredly, and possibly the student also needs a place for a brief nap in your office area as well. Now, not all students might get to snooze in the nurse's office or in the administrator's coffee room, but that's what your integrity allows you to decide. Consider the fact that adults are the same way. Might staff members serving on key committees who are struggling with child care issues need to leave right after the school bell rings rather than attend your curriculum planning session, if they promise to accept a role on the committee that allows them to contribute later in the evening? This does not mean that everyone necessarily can serve any time they wish, virtually or alternatively. Your integrity allows you to make these calls, given context. Integrity provides the strength to do what is right, the right way, and then to be serene in the face of criticism.

Strive for Effectiveness

In working with staff, prioritize effectiveness over justification (Regier & King, 2013). With the daily challenges you face and intermittent pot shots that others take at you, you must have the strength to focus on the next bit of effectiveness you hope to nurture rather than look backward for a better straw poll. Think to yourself, *It is not necessarily about me in terms of how folks perceive things here. It is about getting a desired result.* Model that you can rise above the fray and serve as a beacon of personal excellence. For example, when students and parents try to go over your head to the principal to have your disciplinary decision appealed, don't expend energy worrying about what happens next. It won't do you any good, and it won't help the next situation you'll face. If you receive the opportunity to weigh in, do so. But don't try to preempt what might turn into a political football. Focus instead on your next bit of effectiveness in doing the right thing and making good decisions, and forget about justifying why you did the last thing. You will be better off because of it, and believe me, so will your principal and everyone involved. The system needs your effectiveness, and being effective requires *all* of your energy.

> **TIP**
>
> Teach a focus on effectiveness vicariously by asking teachers and staff to hold you accountable at faculty meetings. Then when they do, listen, thank them, and note you will reflect on their perspective rather than trying to justify what you did.

The How: Strategy to Use With You

The assistant principalship is a calling more than a job, a mission more than a position. Some would say it is a way of life you cannot turn off when leaving school for the day. It is a tough gig. Assistant principals often forego their own needs in the service of others, even to the point of inviting adverse effects upon their own health and happiness. A 2017 report on the role of vice principals to the Ontario Principals' Council notes that 72.3 percent say their work often or always puts them in emotionally draining situations, and that 46.4 percent say that student mental health issues result in days that are emotionally draining (Pollock et al., 2017). Research has found that educators' roles in handling trauma in schools is underexamined; it also suggests that educators can experience secondary traumatic stress and that administrators must assume responsibility for embedding self-care and regulation for the adults (Thomas, Crosby, & Vanderhaar, 2019). This section will explore strategies for practicing self-care.

Tina H. Boogren (2018), in her book *Take Time for You: Self-Care Action Plans for Educators*, stresses *daily* self-care, "not the kind we promise to do during our summer or on the weekends, or when our own children are older, or when we retire" (p. 3). She makes a great point regarding what we do to ourselves as educators: we forego lower-order needs, those psychologist Abraham Maslow (1987) would say are our more basic physiological or psychological needs, while pushing through with our professional responsibilities. Boogren (2018) suggests, instead, we turn inward each day and move out of our heads to live in our bodies—to become more in tune with our warning signs and then do something about them. This is daily self-care.

Often, assistant principals receive pushback and few expressions of gratitude for their good deeds and efforts. Thus, the key is to develop a certain amount of resilience through personal self-care so that stresses of the job do not take root internally. There's no doubt that the challenges that assistant principals face daily include doing the difficult work with those in adversity who need intervention. You are on the front lines.

We cannot take care of others unless we first take care of ourselves. As an example, Boogren (2018) echoes a familiar self-care metaphor—when the oxygen mask drops in an airplane, we must put it on ourselves before those we're caring for. The same holds true in schools. Boogren (2018) applies Maslow's (1987) hierarchy of needs to our own lives as educators (that is, physiological needs, safety, belonging, esteem, self-actualization, and transcendence), and she does so by depicting these needs as rungs on a ladder instead of the typical triangle. She notes:

> It is important to note that at times you can engage in a higher level even though you have some unmet needs. . . . However, if you have a consistently unmet need, the corresponding rung will eventually break completely. That makes the next level unreachable until you repair the rung. (Boogren, 2018, p. 18)

In addition to tending to your basic physiological and psychological needs, it is imperative in self-care that you set aside time to just sit with your thoughts. With all that is on your plate, it is not a guarantee that you think deeply on a daily basis, let alone schedule time for it. You must view thinking as important—important enough to schedule. Doing so allows you to look beyond the surface at the challenges students bring to school. Delve deep. Use your mind to think differently about problems and solutions than you did as a teacher, and make space for ideas that move you forward creatively.

I suggest at least ten to fifteen minutes or more per day of mindful pondering. Mindfulness while thinking is a must. Be aware of what is happening around you and within you. Find your own Walden Pond, just like naturalist, poet, and philosopher Henry David Thoreau (1854), whether it's a place, an activity, or an environmental preference. Mine is on my back deck in the early evenings, overlooking my raised garden beds and wooded lot beyond.

TIP

Schedule a *daily duty* and a *weekly window* for your wonderings. The length of time is really up to you. Ensure you designate this on your official calendar, and protect this time. Don't use it to solve problems or get things done. Just think.

Toolkit for Tomorrow: Next Steps

These next steps provide some suggestions for how you can put the ideas in this chapter into action.

- See figure 1.1 for an example of how you can make note of one thing each you are personally and professionally passionate about. Then, jot down two purposeful goals you would like to accomplish in the next year. From these, create a framework for decision making that will allow you to operate at the intersection of passion or purpose with integrity. I have provided a model in which I have created a tangible formula, pulling both from passion and purpose, one that will center my decision making with integrity. Use the reproducible tool on page 19 to create yours; commit it to memory. You can begin using your framework right away.

This formula strives to honor who I am in the left-hand column, with what I wish to do in the right-hand column.

What I Am Passionate About	Framework for Decision Making	Goals I Am Purposeful About
Personally: *When I walk away from a conversation, I want the person I was just interacting with feeling better than when we began.*	My integrity formula: 1. See the good in others 2. Listen 3. Acknowledge perspective 4. Offer something to help today they will appreciate tomorrow	**Goal 1:** *I wish to establish myself as an assistant principal whose office is one that students visit and get help, even when they are not called down to the office.*
Professionally: *I wish to work with staff to recognize student misbehavior as natural and teachable moments.*		**Goal 2:** *I wish to ensure that teachers respect me and find me relevant and credible, and I want them to know that I have not lost touch with their role.*

FIGURE 1.1: Tool to develop a framework for decision making.

- Schedule ten to fifteen minutes of uninterrupted time on your calendar each day to sit in your office, or somewhere else privately in the school with the door closed, and relax. Take this time to think, or tend in some other way to your oxygen needs.

- Complete the professional development activity on page 20, which invites you to think about your why for your work as assistant principal. Best-selling author and scientist Gregg Braden (2011) shares that a tension between knowledge and wisdom has been a struggle for humanity for quite some time. In fact, he notes that while the 20th century provided us one hundred years of knowledge acquisition, the 21st century will now be seen as the "century of wisdom, as a time when we are forced to apply what we've learned in order to survive the world we've created" (Braden, 2011, p. 38). The same opportunity holds true for assistant principals. We have accumulated quite a bit of knowledge about the role; we have the opportunity to dial inward and develop the necessary wisdom to take the role from where it currently resides, and move it into an even better place in schools. This starts with a personal exploration of you.

Tool to Develop a Framework for Decision Making

This formula strives to honor who I am in the left-hand column, with what I wish to do in the right-hand column.

What I Am Passionate About	Framework for Decision Making	Goals I Am Purposeful About
Personally:	My integrity formula:	Goal 1:
Professionally:		Goal 2:

Professional Development: A Deeper Dive—Deciding You Want to Be an Assistant Principal

Instructions: The purpose of the activity is to spend some time in developing wisdom about your *why* and how it influences your approach to your assistant principalship. Our experiences tend to shape the way we approach professional responsibilities. This activity includes no right or wrong answers; the results do not have to be shared with anyone. It can take as little or long as needed to complete.

STEP 1

Spend a few minutes thinking about the following questions. Answer them all if you can, one at a time. You can do so in any order. Write a few words that capture the essence of each question on the front of an index card; respond to it on the back of the card with a few words regarding what came to mind in answering the question. You'll need twenty-five index cards, one for each question.

- *Why did you pursue a career in education?*
- *Who was your favorite teacher or adult figure in school, and why?*
- *At a time in which you were happiest in life, what made you so?*
- *If you could save the world, what is the first thing you would do?*
- *What do you see when you look in the mirror or in your mind's eye about yourself?*
- *When meeting someone new, what do you try to project?*
- *Do you enjoy being recognized away from school? Why or why not?*
- *What is important to you in terms of finances?*
- *What is your responsibility to those less fortunate than you, and does it depend on whether they are at fault for their circumstances?*
- *When not at school, what do you like to do?*
- *What do you think people say about you when you cannot hear them? Does this matter to you?*
- *When you retire, what will your former students and colleagues say about you?*
- *What does sustainability mean to you?*
- *What would be your gravestone inscription? Would this differ or endure if you wrote it as a high school student, college student, first-year teacher, or now?*
- *If you could fail privately at something, what would it be?*
- *What are two of your favorite memories from teaching?*
- *Does work matter? If so, how much?*
- *What would you be doing if you could have a career do-over?*
- *Who is your hero and why?*
- *What can you share about your most challenging student?*
- *How important is professional autonomy for you, and what does it look like?*
- *When do you feel most like you?*
- *Do you need to have friends at work to be successful?*

- *If you have colleagues you do not respect, why? Do they fit a consistent profile?*
- *How do you find peace?*

Once you have all of your cards, lay them out, response side up, on a big table; begin moving them around, and see if any natural groupings form (thematic coding). See what hangs together. Leave them on the table. Don't hurry. Put a fresh set of eyes on them after a few days away and some reflection. Move them around to modify the groupings as you wish, allowing groups to coalesce if they do.

STEP 2

Prioritize the following statements. Getting to my *why:*

- *Allows others to understand my motives*
- *Allows me to have strength when the job is tough*
- *Brings meaning and purpose to both success and failure*
- *Is a fun thing to do*
- *Allows me to help everyone maintain dignity in difficult conversations*
- *Allows me to re-evaluate perspective and strategies*
- *Allows me to make things happen*
- *Models teachable moments*
- *Feels good to do*
- *Is depressing*
- *Allows me to contribute to an inclusive workplace*
- *Is not important*
- *Is a useful tool in meeting my objectives*

Compare your top three in step 2 to the natural groupings from step 1, put them on index cards, and lay them over or beside any natural groups you find that align. Are there any items that seem to surprise or contradict your current attitude toward ascending in leadership?

STEP 3

Identify the two most difficult things you have done in recent years, and write down on index cards what they were and why you did them.

Identify the two most difficult things you wish to accomplish in the near future, and write down on index cards what they are and why you wish to do them.

Identify two items you will protect at all costs, when doing or planning to do the preceding steps, and write them down on index cards.

Do any of these things seem congruent with your groupings, as they pertain to those from steps 1 and 2? If so, lay these upon or beside the groupings you are developing from steps 1 and 2.

Do any of the items seem to, for any reason, compete or contradict what you have grouped together?

page 2 of 3

STEP 4

Determine which of Maslow's (1987) hierarchy of needs seems to be most prevalent in the groupings you have invited together.

- *Self-actualization (being all you can be, living life to the fullest)*
- *Esteem (earning recognition from others, confidence, self-esteem, feelings of accomplishment)*
- *Love and belonging (family, friendship, connections to others)*
- *Safety (personal, financial, health, security)*
- *Physiological needs (food, water, shelter, air)*

Much has been written about Maslow's (1987) needs, including identifying safety and physiological needs as basic needs, identifying esteem and love and belonging as psychological needs, and identifying self-actualization as a growth need.

How does this resonate with you?

Now . . .

Using what you have collected and sorted from steps 1 through 4, develop a short self-statement. Use the following format.

My why:

The reason *why* I am positioned well as an assistant principal is first that it fulfills my own needs (from step 4) of _____; that my past challenges (from step 3) of _____ have inspired future goals (from step 3) of _____—*and are doable in terms of what I steadfastly protect*—and I bring to the role assets (from step 2) such as _____, and finally, knowing that as my professional and personal lives intersect, I keep things in mind that are important to me (from step 1), such as _____.

Thoughts:

The purpose of this activity could be to help you understand the story you are telling and if it aligns with what others are hearing. There may be some stories that do not complement the role of an assistant principal very well. Some stories may reveal the role as a stepping-stone, as a way to get out of the classroom, as a way to earn respect, or as a way to make more money.

Are there features (disclosed, personal attributes) from the preceding activities that seem to identify those who may become more successful in the role of an assistant principal?

Can you shorten your why to one statement?

Reference

Maslow, A. H. (1987). *Motivation and personality* (3rd ed.). New York: Harper & Row.

CHAPTER 2
MAKING TIME FOR MANAGEMENT

I have long thought the education profession downplays the importance of management in schools. I once had the opportunity to help develop a master of business administration (MBA) program for school leaders, and this experience affirmed my belief. Business professors are much different than those in education. They hold management in high regard. The business professors in this program stretched our learning in course development and delivery in terms of decisive and sometimes combustible action. Some incredibly successful individuals have graduated from that program.

Self-reliance is critical to the assistant principalship. You have to be tough, smart, and forgiving, all at the same time. Your confidence in where you are going, what you are doing, and toward what end you are working is key. That is sound management. You do not wait around for someone to offer you safe passage into the next morning or afternoon. You do not ask for permission every time an opportunity needs seizing. You do it. You make things happen. You leverage the resources you have toward decisions that are both quick and well conceived. This takes one deft operator, an excellent manager. That's you.

This chapter helps you along those pursuits, developing a savvy understanding of how your role in school management often runs in tandem with school leadership, not supplanting it or trying to replicate it. Making time for management means getting the lay of your landscape, embracing and optimizing your role within it, and protecting your best assets: you and the people around you. Let's first focus on the what and the why of management, then we can think about how, with strategies to use with students, staff, and yourself to get you moving ahead.

The What and the Why

The term *instructional leader* is often all the rage at conferences, in books, and in university classrooms. Don't get all caught up in its afterglow. The professed value of instructional leadership dominated our profession from around 1980 to the early 2000s (Loveless, 2016). What was unfortunate in mainstream instructional leadership is that it implied a principal was preeminent among teachers and should be seen as a school's pedagogical expert—like a father or mother who knows best. The principal was to be the *instructional leader*, no longer running in the same circles with less fashionable *building managers*. This began a seeming national urge to move building leaders away from managerial duties, with a naïve assumption that these things will take care of themselves.

The real deal on instructional leadership is that teaching excellence can be fostered most effectively by a more evenly distributed, flatter model. Michael Fullan (2019) notes that the principal:

> . . . does not have to be the best pedagogue in the building but does need to know about developing and leading pedagogues . . . creates a climate for all to learn . . . and enables others to grow to the point where there are many teacher leaders. (p. 80)

Research from Carrie R. Leana (2011) shows that teacher social capital, that which resides in the relationships among teachers, is a predictor of student success. Jenni Donohoo, John Hattie, and Rachel Eells (2018), furthering a meta-analysis of over eight hundred studies related to achievement from Hattie (2009), note teachers' collective efficacy as the top-rated influencer on student learning, with an effect size of 1.57. Effect size, "an objective and (usually) standardized measure of the magnitude of an observed effect" (Field, 2009, p. 785), is considered small at 0.2, medium at 0.5, and large at 0.8 (Ary, Jacobs, & Sorenson, 2009), so 1.57 is significant. What can you do to encourage teacher collaboration? Be the one who supports and cheers their efforts. Hold your confidence high and let teachers know that you believe in them. Charlotte Danielson (2016) has shared that teachers having instructional dilemmas are more likely to approach teaching colleagues than building administrators and that principals should recognize "that much untapped wisdom resides in the knowledge and experience of teachers" (p. 22). Provide them the resources and space to do so. Don't pretend you have all the answers.

 TIP

When gauging the effectiveness of your teacher collaboration in your school building, ask yourself, "Is collaboration *really* collaboration if it is mandated?" Provide time and encouragement, not prescription. Suggest to your most respected and connected teachers that they coordinate and facilitate, and then get out of their way and respond to what they need.

Providing what teachers need to be their own instructional leaders is the hallmark of excellent management. Management is critical, as demonstrated by the work of Gallup Organization researchers Marcus Buckingham and Curt Coffman (1999), who surveyed over eighty thousand managers for their groundbreaking study and apply meta-analytic findings; these findings were updated nearly twenty years later (Gallup Press, 2016). They offer insight into what the best managers do in organizations. The key is that they break the typical rules for managers that exist in conventional wisdom. What they found is that in order to attract and keep the most talented people in your organization, the manager is essential (Buckingham & Coffman, 1999; Gallup Press, 2016). Further, it is not accurate to say managers are lesser versions of leaders, or *leadership lite*, but rather that the roles are foundationally different.

The term *management* has been maligned in education, and there was no official institutional role to take care of the people employed at the school who are taking care of the students. There was certainly not much effort into putting adults first (the oxygen mask metaphor again) so that student caretaking is the natural byproduct of healthy, confident, and energized educators. The takeaway from this is to neither elevate the notion of leadership nor underemphasize the importance of management. Both are necessary, and really, the difference is more a matter of focus than anything else—a focus inward for managers and outward leaders, as I'll detail. Administrative teams in organizations ideally would find the right balance of the two.

Leaders have an outward focus; managers have an inward focus (Buckingham & Coffman, 1999; Gallup Press, 2016). In schools, this would differentiate the roles of principals and assistant principals. Our principals have an outward focus, looking with vision at where the organization could go, then using leadership skills to influence all others to go with them. They offer an invitation to ride the school's mission toward vision, and our best principals get most everyone in the school along for the ride. Conversely and complementarily, assistant principals have an inward focus. Your managerial role allows you to tend to the needs of the people so that all within the organization have their own capacity while following the principal-as-leader. It is really that simple—and that misunderstood. Tending to the needs of those inside means tending more toward your own time management in order to get things done.

The reality of your position is that there are so many responsibilities day to day that it is difficult to conceive of a single person handling them all. Research published by the National Council of Professors of Educational Administration notes additional layers of stress and pressure resulting from countless mandates at the national, state, provincial, and local levels, as well as from testing, school safety, and unfunded mandates (Allen & Weaver, 2014). Ontario research notes that 78.5 percent of vice principals indicate that they never seem to have enough time to get their work done (Pollock et al., 2017). Therefore, time management is critical.

Just what is time management, anyway? Researchers at Vanderbilt and Stanford Universities observe that time management includes formation of short-term and long-term goals, prioritization of things to be done, organizational techniques, and even one's attitudes toward the importance of time (Grissom, Loeb, & Mitani, 2015). Craig Jarrow (2019), author of *Time Management Ninja: 21 Tips for More Time and Less Stress in Your Life*, suggests that for good time management, you make appointments with yourself, not just others, and that "time management should make time, not take time" (p. 19). The notion of making time for yourself demands setting priorities. Jarrow (2019) reminds us, "If you want to be stronger and accomplish more, you have to push your boundaries. Real life is a gym. What lightweight dumbbells are you carrying?" (p. 149). "In fact," he says, "you need to get comfortable with being uncomfortable" (Jarrow, 2019, p. 150).

With that said, let's look at some strategies based on what we've discussed.

The How: Strategies to Use With Students

The following managerial strategies—making class calls as well as inspecting, maintaining, and repairing—are effective ways to lay the foundation for your work with students.

Make Class Calls

Much of what you need to do on your daily itinerary involves ascertaining whether or not you need to take corrective action. It is about a quick, thirty-second conversation with numerous students to gather information regarding their whereabouts, whether or not they have information they can share with you regarding a situation, or if they need your help and assistance in any way. You could accomplish this by setting aside time in your schedule and asking your administrative assistant to call them down, en masse, which would be a time saver; however, this can result in numerous inefficiencies as well. One hazard in this approach is if you are in the middle of this activity and have twenty students lined up, you might get an urgent call that your attention is required elsewhere. If so, you have just inconvenienced twenty students who must be given hallway passes to return to class, and you have interrupted their twenty teachers as well. Further, your assistant will have to manage the frustration of students who are missing instruction and might be angered because of it.

A viable solution is to make class calls. Your assistant provides you a list of students' names and locations for fifteen to twenty brief conversations you need to have, and you walk around the school, asking students to spend only a few minutes just outside the classroom door for your information gathering. Pull students for this brief chat only if other students are not around in the hallway. You can even share with teachers that you request no passes issued during a certain half hour each day because you are on your rounds.

A typical script might be, "Hey [name], thanks for stepping outside. Mr. So-and-So had you marked absent from third class period yesterday, and I'm following up to see if this was the case. Were you in class, or were you somewhere else during that time?" When the student shares briefly, you now know if it was a misunderstanding or if there is disciplinary action needed. Either way, put the responsibility in the student's court to provide confirmation to your assistant later in the day or to show up at your office for the follow-up discussion if consequences are necessary, and then move on to the next student. The key here is to not have conversations that would be of a more private nature regarding disciplinary action in the hallway. The idea here is just to get a quick understanding, and save any serious or private follow-up for later. Let's say out of twenty short conversations, you might end up with a handful of more in-depth ones in your office, later on.

Your class calls provide for sound management in keeping students where they need to be as much as they can and not having students spend inordinate amounts of time traveling to and from the office when false alarms are a possibility. As managers are those with inward focus on the needs of the people in the organization, making class calls allows you to be out and about. While in your travels, you might pass students who are running errands on their own. This provides you an opportunity for a quick, positive comment. You may even see something interesting happening in a classroom and pop in for a closer view. I have found that teachers will often see you walk by, and, before a few seconds pass, wave you in to see something they're doing.

It's important when conducting your class calls to provide homage to the teachers, in full view of the students. This lets teachers know that they are appreciated, and it invites students to share this sense of appreciation. Share that you wish you could stay for a while. This makes teachers feel great, elevating their status with good management, as you are showing them respect publicly. It's a great way to keep your focus on the needs of people and gives you an opportunity to make a daily difference. It's an all-around good time management strategy for you, staff, and students.

Inspect, Maintain, and Repair

The classic science fiction show *Star Trek* offers ample character metaphors for your need to inspect, maintain, and repair not only the school around you but the people within it, including you. You are akin to both Scotty, the starship *Enterprise*'s engineer, and McCoy, the ship's doctor. In these capacities, you have to keep a watch on the overall preventive health and wellness of all in the school, but you also determine treatment when necessary and keep the entire school building moving forward to a shared destination. Goleman (2013) notes the need to keep an eye on the balance of focus: inner focus on ourselves, outer focus on systems, and other focus on people.

I suggest, for the inspection component, you establish a student group every quarter to gauge how things are going with different school processes and offer ideas on whether or not what's happening is optimal. Small groups are best, about four or five in each: one for school climate, one for school safety, and another for student events and activities. These are just ideas to get you started. You may have others in mind that would be useful for you and your situation. Take student events and activities, for example. Get together with your group of students and choose a few key events to focus on, break down the processes involved that are in place purportedly to make them successful from a student standpoint, and then put together a plan to make these key events go more smoothly. Topics for event management analysis in this example might be the typical sporting event logistics, holiday concerts, annual commencement, and seasonal banquets.

For maintenance, you'll want to consider three forms that I often use, which are inspired by the United Kingdom independent research and technology organization TWI (www.twi-global.com), as well as informed more broadly through general overviews of maintenance strategies used in international manufacturing sectors (Gackowiec, 2019): (1) preventive, (2) predictive, and (3) corrective. *Preventive maintenance* is taking steps to do things ahead of time so that you can bring the best possible outcomes of safety, order, discipline, and attendance to teaching and learning. Examples include establishing bullying prevention programs, safe schools training, restorative justice programming, and diversity and inclusivity initiatives. Some of the best preventive maintenance involves quick things you might say to students as they are going about their day to affirm who they are and how they want to be communicated with. *Predictive maintenance* involves being aware of when things are really necessary at certain times of the year, such as providing extra care and attention to the needs of students during winter, when seasonal affective disorder sets in, or in spring, when the stresses of standardized testing are upon everyone. Get out ahead of the things you predict will be a problem without your attention. *Corrective maintenance* is making deft observations of how things are going and then doing your best to right things when they're off course.

For repair, it is typically about what is happening with students emotionally. It is mending a relationship that has gone sour because of conflicts that were not resolved effectively. Yet, it can also be about other things, as well—the building that was vandalized or the poster torn down in the hallway. The more we ignore a quick and careful repair, the more things are going to be invited to get broken, because students see disarray as the norm. Applying this to students means paying attention to every relationship that has gone awry, because every one of them is continually telegraphing that dismay and drama are normal. It is like a call sign for allies in misery or an invitation for someone to kick you. Repair should not be something you see as getting in the way of your job or a distraction; it is a very important part of the upkeep of all things happening with students on your watch.

The How: Strategies to Use With Staff

The following strategies—identifying and empowering your instructional experts, stepping into your casting manager, and embracing and empowering your gatekeeper—are effective ways to lay the foundation for your work with staff.

Identify and Empower Your Instructional Experts

Assistant principals can facilitate leadership at all levels rather than centralizing and dispensing knowledge. This is particularly true in developing teacher leadership; as one Swedish study notes, teachers in leadership roles guide students, support with engagement and care, foster student ideas and autonomy, and encourage the highest outcomes (Oqvist & Malmstrom, 2016). This is where the rubber of performance meets the road: in the classroom, with teachers as a school's true instructional leaders.

To identify your instructional experts, you'll want to include multiple areas of teaching performance excellence. First, your instructional experts should be top performers in their content areas. Don't buy in to the fact that content-area expertise is not as important as other areas of professional responsibility, such as a love for students. Teachers with content expertise know the answers to the oft-asked question, "When will this be important in the real world?" Teachers with content expertise know more than one or two ways to teach important concepts or applications, and thus, they can connect with more students. This results in fewer frustrated students and behavioral problems. This increases motivation and a love for school.

Your instructional experts also have to be experts at pedagogy. They must know both the art and science of teaching, which includes providing and communicating clear learning goals, using formative and summative assessments effectively, conducting direct instruction with practice and deepening application, using strategies for both content and engagement, implementing rules and procedures, building relationships, and communicating high expectations (Marzano, 2017).

Your instructional experts must be diagnosticians of learning. They must embrace the notion that if students are not learning, it is our fault, and if so, they must know what theory, research, and learning science say to do next. Diagnosticians of learning do not exist in isolation; they work in teams, much as medical school surgeons do on rounds, collaborating with other practitioners on what best meets the need of the current prescription. Diagnosticians of learning share what they know with others and make notes to ensure student breakthroughs in the teaching and learning process, as both their obligation and a main reason for doing what they do.

Finally, your instructional experts must be knowledgeable in child development and learning psychology. They must be able to understand and connect with students on a developmentally appropriate level, and understand what makes students tick. In doing so, they are active liaisons with parents and family members to understand things outside the school that may be affecting learning inside the school. They have a deep commitment to family empowerment and agency as student caregivers and use a team approach in leveraging the best assets to help students succeed, aligned with what brain science and psychology says students need developmentally at each stage of their school careers.

TIP

Select your teacher leaders from those who are respected and connected. This will ensure that their influence widens (Gruenert & Whitaker, 2015).

Once you identify staff superstars who exhibit most if not all of these types of expertise, the next step is to work to deploy their talents and empower them as teacher leaders. Establish a wraparound team to help you design and implement strategies for students whom you find struggling in school (Colburn & Beggs, 2020). This team is your think tank, and you seek the members out for guidance and wise council. Meetings can be held as needed, yet not too often; don't waste their time. Hold these experts, and team membership, in high esteem among professional colleagues on site. This team is also a way for teacher leaders at all levels to seek guidance, validation, and professional engagement, and it is encouraged to gather a clearinghouse of resources. These resources for teaching and learning can be available internally and ideally externally as well through professional learning networks and instructional communities. Encourage your instructional experts to work as a guiding team to plan for and deliver professional development to all staff, as well as induction and mentoring for those new to your building and district. Finally, deploy these experts to present alongside you at state and national conferences with a theme of "What Works for Teacher Leadership Teams." Advertise your teacher leaders as the true instructional leaders who not only serve your school but serve as a model for the profession to emulate. In short, practice what you value—that instructional leadership is really the purview of our best teachers who remain focused on that aspect of their professional careers, as surgeons of learning.

Step Into Your Casting Manager

As I often say, someone must take care of the folks. If we wish our most talented educators to come to our schools, stay, and ride the mission toward a shared vision with the principal, it takes great management to do so, and this role of the assistant principal is critical in this human equation. The best assistant principals embrace this role and do not try to be mini-principals, as this would take them away from the inward focus that so aptly works in tandem with the principal's outward focus. An inward focus brings with it a most important role.

TIP

Research from Gallup Press (2016; Buckingham & Coffman, 1999) provides great advice to managers: the folks we work with do not change much, so we should not waste time trying to build on what they lack; instead build on what they bring positively. The latter is hard enough as it is.

As an assistant principal, you'll want to be a casting manager. As such, you are your principal's talent scout. Often, teachers and staff are in the assignments they are in because they have paid their dues and have been in them forever. Some have monetary incentives that impede best fit; in other words, salary or extra-duty compensation keeps them in jobs they're not necessarily well suited for. Make a list of everyone in your school and keep a running tab of their interests, aptitudes, and abilities. Know their wishes and desires, and on a semiannual basis, meet with your principal to discuss best fit. In this way, you can serve as a clearinghouse for talent deployment, and whether or not your principal implements your recommendations, you will still be fulfilling an important role in intel.

Figure 2.1 is a chart starter for a talent bank you can use in order to establish a running list of the talent that you have employed in your school (I used myself as an example here).

Person	
Ryan Donlan	
Content Area and License	• secondary social science and English
Preferred Courses and Grade Levels	• English 10 and developmental English 10 • journalism • advanced composition • current events

Interests	• politics • gourmet foods • charcoal grilling • walking and hiking
Aptitudes and Abilities	• connecting with students who find school difficult and resist authority • entertaining and hosting big events
Extracurriculars Past or Present	• high school debate team • student newspaper • middle school track and field coaching
Bucket List Wishes	• learning to tap dance like Gregory Hines • owning property in Alaska and visiting annually • skydiving more regularly • sampling exotic foods, coffees, and cigars from around the world • starring in a local community theater role that involves singing
Something You Noticed	• Ryan often starts a conversation in a way that shows his wish to connect with others positively, before solving problems or setting boundaries. If he is not careful to finish strong with his own boundaries, some will try to take advantage of his generosity. • He needs to be coached to ask for what he wants from his supervisors and not say "Yes" to everything. • He has an uncanny way of getting what he wants out of the parents of the most difficult students; they walk away feeling better than when they arrived at school.

FIGURE 2.1: A casting manager's talent bank chart starter.

*Visit **go.SolutionTree.com/leadership** for a free reproducible version of this figure.*

Your casting manager's role gives you a great opportunity to sit down with teachers and staff members, one to one, and ask them about themselves and what they prefer to be doing longer term at the school. Don't make any promises, but be transparent about what you are trying to do for your principal and the semiannual meetings you wish to have. Let them know that the more they work to create their talent entry on your sheet, the more their preferences will be known to the principal. Let them know that you will be adding things to this list as well that you notice, so it is best that they get as much information to you as possible.

Look for talents that they might have that fall outside of the classroom or school setting altogether. It is amazing how things cross-apply as the school or district develops new programs or support systems. I once saw a teacher use a talent for fly fishing to create a haven for a group of quiet C students whom nobody seemed to notice, as they were neither standing out nor causing trouble. He applied that same talent in offering casting lessons to cancer support groups to facilitate a sense of empowerment and control in survivorship. Might this apply to students who have been traumatized for various reasons stemming from abuse, neglect, or catastrophic circumstances, allowing you to offer a layer of help in addition to deeper, more focused, and professionally targeted support?

TIP

Every so often, strive to identify something from your background that has nothing to do with your professional training that helps you do a great job as an assistant principal. Keep a running list of these things. They might come in handy as you work with others, including teachers and staff members, in identifying their own.

A talent bank will allow you to put things like this together, possibly as you take time to think, as noted earlier in the book. At minimum, when the time comes for you, the principal, or the counselor to put together the building's master teaching schedule for the year, it will pay to have a talent bank audit over lunch with the leadership team.

Embrace and Empower Your Gatekeeper

Your gatekeepers, meaning administrative assistants or secretaries, have keen insight on what they can do for you so that you can more fully concentrate on the needs of students. Embrace and empower their gifts. Take, for instance, the distraction of, arguably, 90 percent of the mail that may still come across your desk from traditional sources via the postal service that can be thrown away. Empower your gatekeeper to do so. Don't even look at it. If it is important, there will be a follow-up message, your assistant will let you know, or it will come back to you. Trust your assistant to make that determination. You then don't have to miss a beat as you handle student issues. There are many other instances where empowered gatekeepers are worth their weight in gold.

TIP

When your assistant whom you have empowered makes a mistake, don't fret, and don't judge. Your assistant is probably doing too much for you anyway! Have an understanding that if your assistant drops the ball on anything that could get worse without immediate awareness and attention (or if it could surprise your principal), it must be reported to you as soon as possible. Stress your trust and that this is the way the system is supposed to work.

One such instance has to do with the majority of telephone calls from parents and others that come your way. Empower gatekeepers to talk with folks and discern what issues are in front of you. Have them find out what the problem is. You might find that you do not really even need to be involved in the conversation in order for the situation to be rectified. For example, sometimes parents simply need reassurance that something is being investigated or followed up on, and they want to talk directly to you. That's not a good use of your time. An effective gatekeeper can provide those assurances, take a note so that you don't forget, and probably do a better job of easing the concerns of the parent than you can. After all, gatekeepers can offer a listening ear and even concede a point or two, as they are not in the direct line of fire as you are. In other words, they don't have a dog in the hunt, and as such, unlike you, they are still perceived as the friendlies. Leverage that advantage and have your gatekeeper spend that time on the telephone.

Another instance is pep talks that have to do with disciplinary situations that are so minor that they are barely on the radar in needing attention. Sometimes, they have to do with rumors about something forthcoming, like a skip from school or a smoke out back. If gatekeepers are willing and so inclined, have them call the student to the office to offer a kind word or fire a quick shot across the bow about "What might happen if . . . ?" Some students have the best relationships in the entire school building with your gatekeepers, because often these roles are the best at offering a kind ear and a bit of sympathy before the students trudge into your office. Use this as a time-saving device. Truth be told, I have not encountered one gatekeeping secretary of typical school quality yet who has said, "That isn't my job."

The How: Strategy to Use With You

Making time for management includes both a focus on people and an efficient need to get things done, or as the saying goes, to get things off your desk. Even at your level on the organizational food chain, there will be necessary minutiae to shovel. In your own time management, know what to focus on next so that you can internally manage in a way that provides even more time for what you must focus on most. I include this strategy so you can do just that, and separate quickly the administrative wheat from the chaff so that you can be your best-managed self.

On any given day, you can designate the many things you need to do as *urgent, important, both,* or *neither*. Quick and careful designation of everything in your in-box as one of these four is a helpful tool in time management and allocation of your own personal resources in problem solving. This can be done with the help of an assistant, and over time, the both of you can be on the same page about the things that need to be addressed now, or not.

For example, if your assistant simply leaves a pile of papers on your desk as you are out and about in the school, you must come back and sort through them to see what takes priority. You want to handle the urgent things quickly but take on the things that are both urgent and important possibly even more quickly. Think about this: if you have a student throwing a temper tantrum and kicking lockers in the upstairs hallway, that is typically an urgent matter, but if students are not hurting themselves or others, it's probably not that important. However, if this same behavior is happening just before the arrival of the mayor with accompanying newspaper journalists to photograph your chemistry class that is also upstairs, then the situation becomes important as well, one that might need quicker attention, even more than that which is typically urgent. If the student with the temper tantrum is medically fragile, then that amps up both the urgency and importance as well.

Again, back to that pile of papers. Without a system, you'll first need to go through them, then you and your assistant will probably need to discuss which ones take priority, and then you will act accordingly. Time wasted. Imagine instead a bin system where you return to the office and your assistant has already divided things in your bins—*urgent, important, both,* and *neither*—to cut down considerably the amount you must scan before prioritizing. You could accomplish the same using a shared cloud-based folder system, if you are so equipped.

TIP

Having an accountability partner in your assistant is a benefit. Assistants can check with you near the end of the day for those urgent things on your desk. You don't want your urgent things piling up. Put trusted assistants in charge of your work life, and then attend to what they suggest you do.

Handle things that are *urgent and important* (*both*) and *urgent* more quickly, leave the *important* things for your closed-door desk time, and see if those *neither* items can be delegated or put off until you are at school on an occasion without students in the building. Delegation is key: for example, I would argue the school counselor might more effectively talk with a student throwing a temper tantrum than the assistant principal.

In allocating your time to things *urgent*, *important*, *both*, and *neither*, be sure you're the one in the driver's seat. Teachers may say at times, "Please do not call students down to the office during X class period, or Y instructional block. That's quality academic time that we need to protect if we're student-focused." Resist the temptation to concede. While this is a valid point on the part of the teachers—that the integrity of instruction should be a focal point that all educators ensure—from a larger perspective, urgent disciplinary matters left unattended will compound deleteriously over time. These discipline issues won't go away; in fact, they will back up, fester, and create a bottle-neck of unresolved problems, with certain students feeling they are not accountable to authority. This has negative effects on school climate and the morale of teachers, and in turn, the quality of instructional time experienced among teachers, staff, and students will be impacted. You don't and shouldn't run on anyone's standard time but your own (with the exception of the principal's, of course). The school day just doesn't allow you the luxury to satisfy everyone's pet peeves regarding when, how, and under what conditions students are brought to the office. You have an office to run, and an assistant principalship to care for. Don't get led around by others who have not walked a mile in your shoes. The key here is to be open with teachers at each year's outset—possibly each semester's—about the fact that you value their instructional time, yet you need to be in charge of your time. Share that your efficiency over time will hopefully have a trickle-down effect on the sanc-tity of their individual classrooms.

Toolkit for Tomorrow: Next Steps

These next steps provide some suggestions for how you can put the ideas in this chapter into action.

- Share openly with teachers that you believe they are the *true* instructional leaders of the building, but get your principal's permission first.

- Offer to step in to the class and teach for any teachers wishing to visit other teachers' classrooms to observe.

- Create a talent bank casting manager chart for yourself, begin meeting with teachers to hear about their preferences, and set an appointment for the end of the semester to discuss with your principal.

- Establish an *urgent, important, both,* and *neither* system with your assistant for items that come your way when you are out of the office. This can be either a bin system near your secretary's desk or a cloud-based system.

- Have a transparent conversation with your teachers about how you value their time and teaching, and because of this, you might need to pull students during instructional time for the efficiency of your entire office, and explain how it works to get students back in class as quickly and successfully as possible. Then, start making class calls.

- Complete the professional development activity on page 37 to refine your abilities to help further your school's mission on the fly by pondering your roles in leadership, management, and personal care in terms of things to do that are *urgent, important, both,* and *neither.* Figure 2.2 provides an example to get you started. This activity will help provide a framework for how you might navigate the many things that come your way, competing for your time and energy.

Role You Have	Things to Do That Are Urgent	Things to Do That Are Important	Things to Do That Are Both	Things to Do That Are Neither
Leadership (Transformational or Distributive)	1. 2. 3.	1. 2. 3.	1. 2. 3.	1. Search for new lesson plan software that will automate state-standards referencing for teachers. 2. 3.
Management	1. Calm an angry parent who is yelling profanities at your secretary. 2. 3.	1. 2. 3.	1. Put your school on lockdown when a fugitive on the run from police has been spotted on your property. 2. 3.	1. 2. 3.

FIGURE 2.2: Example of prioritizing leadership, management, and you.

continued ▶

Role You Have	Things to Do That Are Urgent	Things to Do That Are Important	Things to Do That Are Both	Things to Do That Are Neither
You (Personal Care)	1. 2. 3.	1. Ensure an appropriate amount of cardiovascular activity in a daily or weekly routine. 2. 3.	1. 2. 3.	1. 2. 3.

PLC Process   Collaboration

Plan on a Page

5 instructional Observation Points

Problem →Task →Result

Professional Development: A Deeper Dive—Making Time for Management

Instructions: For each box in the grid, write three actionable statements (starting with a verb) that are indicative of what role you have and what your priorities should be.

Role You Have *Observe*	Things to Do That Are Urgent *Teachers who* *struggle*	Things to Do That Are Important	Things to Do That Are Both	Things to Do That Are Neither
Leadership (Transformational or Distributive) *Principal need's*	1. Student/staff Safety 2. be Present in 3.	1. be present in PLC 2. Student/ faculty needs Walk Through 3. Monitor Team chat Formal Observation	1. Principal Priorities 2. respond to Teacher needs 3. feedback	1. 2. 3.
Management	1. Safety 2. be visible In hallways 3.	1. Take care of assigned 2. respons.bility respond to Emails 3.	1. be visible during passing periods 2. 3.	1. 2. 3.
You (Personal Care)	1. Brain Break 15 minutes 2. Take nothing personally 3.	1. Exercise 2. Eat healthy 3. read for enjoyment	1. Time with Wife/dogs 2. 3.	1. 2. 3.

CHAPTER 3
FOSTERING A POSITIVE SCHOOL CULTURE AND CLIMATE

I recall as an elementary student moving from the Helen Mansfield Robinson (1965a, 1965b) reading series *Ventures* (book 4) to *Vistas* (book 5). The cover art's appeal included scenery of panoramic landscapes, mountains, desert plateaus, skylines, birds flying, and far-off horizons. With my imagination, I journeyed to where the world opened up before settling into the lesson. At times, I needed tactful redirection. I recall those same feelings at age twenty-seven when moving from teacher to assistant principal. My world opened up. I took a risk; I was on a venture toward new vistas. Merriam-Webster's definition of *venture* (n.d.) is "an undertaking involving chance, risk, or danger," and *vista* (n.d.) is "a distant view through or along an avenue or opening" and "an extensive mental view (as over a stretch of time or a series of events)." Together, they aptly describe the assistant principalship, especially in what happens when one moves from a teacher into the role.

As an assistant principal, you have a unique opportunity to widen your perspective on school. In doing so, you will unearth the complexity of a learning organization that influences your future. Your contribution is needed in the danger zones, offering safe passage for those you serve toward new vantage points. Yours is a complicated place, requiring sophistication to navigate.

This chapter's goal is to broaden your view on your ventures and vistas, doing so through the lens of school culture and climate. First, let's focus on the what and the why of a positive school culture and climate, then we can get into the how: strategies to use with students, staff, and yourself.

The What and the Why

School culture refers to the way business is done, in terms of the behaviors and beliefs of the people in the organization. It is mostly influenced by the adults, as they are the long-term residents. According to Steve Gruenert and Todd Whitaker (2015, 2022), authors of *School Culture Rewired: How to Define, Assess, and Transform It* and *Leveraging the Impact of Culture and Climate: Deep, Significant, and Lasting Change in Classrooms and Schools*, school culture is the personality of the organization; it takes years to evolve, is based on values, and cannot be felt. They note that school "culture represents the unwritten mission of the school—it tells students and staff why they are there" (Gruenert & Whitaker, 2015, p. 30); it's "the way we do things around here" (p. 10). It "creates rules to define who is a member and who is not" (Gruenert & Whitaker, 2022, p. 2). School culture is what gives Mondays permission to be miserable and determines if improvement is possible. It is a big thing.

One of my favorite science projects as a student was building an ecosystem. In a large glass jar set on its side atop a wood mount, I spread dirt and planted greens from the yard. I dug a small pond and poured water in a hole bordered with rock atop a plastic liner. The best part was finding bugs and worms. My ecosystem was complete. The most interesting part of the assignment was putting a rubber glove over the mouth of the jar and securing with a rubber band. The ecosystem lived on longer than any of us would have imagined. The secret was that the parts of the ecosystem—plants, bugs, water, and so on—lived interdependently, self-sustaining.

Your school is much the same—the culture is a self-sustaining system requiring symbiotic care and feeding from each of the elements to the others within it, like my science project but on a much more complex scale. It is a system, with a whole and with parts. Unfortunately, many do not understand the complexity. As noted by experts in systems thinking school leadership, the reason many of our contemporary solutions to school problems do not work is that they are offered to school leaders as simplistic, peddled solutions that are not sufficiently holistic (Shaked & Schechter, 2020).

> **☑ TIP**
>
> As a caretaker of your ecosystem, walk the perimeter and the interior. Take a close look at signs for who does what and where. Pay attention to what people use, what locations they frequent, and what they leave behind. The latter will give you an idea of what is happening in your environment when you are not around.

Systems are big! Your school culture is hard to conceive. You don't just have the whole and the parts; you have forces working between the parts and between the parts and the whole. Pay attention to the interrelationships between system components, as well as the components themselves, as they are complementary influences (Shaked & Schechter, 2016). This is especially complicated and requires school administrators who can see the school culture's big picture, influence challenges and tasks indirectly through this understanding while factoring in several aspects of issues multidimensionally, and evaluate how things happening around them perpetuate the life of the system.

This kind of systems thinking is different than traditional, linear thinking that looks in isolation at individual parts, takes a cause-and-effect approach, and thinks there are simple solutions to technical problems (Ndaruhutse, Jones, & Riggall, 2019). It is probably why traditional, linear thinking has resulted in educational reforms that are piecemeal, incremental, reductionist, and, thus, failing (Ndaruhutse et al., 2019).

School culture exists within a social system. As such, there is always a tug between what the institution and the individual expect of each other, the push and pull between the roles we are expected to play and our personalities, and how job expectations connect, or not, with our individual needs. This is your terrain as an assistant principal, your ecosystem, your school culture over which you *can* exercise influence. Your school is in a constant state of tugging, pushing, and pulling, and you are continually brokering how to get the best possible output.

 TIP

Study the interplay between institution and individual. In terms of roles and personalities, ask yourself whether the people you talk to would do the sort of work the organization asks of them on a volunteer basis. The more you can answer yes to this question, the better the fit. If not, there might be more dissonance, which can result in problems over time.

School culture can be systemically invisible. Goleman (2013) shares how difficult it is for us to envision a school systemically: "Systems are, at first glance, invisible to the brain—we have no direct perception of any of the multitude of systems that dictate the realities of our lives" (p. 137). This can result in system blindness. Goleman (2013) says that while "a 'system' boils down to a cohesive set of lawful, regular patterns . . . as it stands, there seems to be no dedicated network or circuitry in the brain that gives us a natural inclination toward systems understanding" (p. 131).

Assistant principals must take a close look at the microsystems that exist within the larger whole of their schools. Basically, your end game is to discern indirect cues to influence the system and bring about better outcomes. Fullan's (2019) work on nuance comes to mind, as he says nuanced leaders "learn and grasp how things work, and then help themselves and others figure out how to make them work better. They help us see the trees and forest simultaneously" (p. ix). And I end with a great point of Fullan's (2019): "You have to get behind the curtain to see the play" (p. 5).

 TIP

To develop your skills in discerning nuance—as those are your leverage points—study what happens in nature, whether it is in woodland creatures or in the deep sea. Make a list of things that remind you of your students, faculty, and staff. You'll find many connections to the norms within your school and interpersonal rules of engagement.

Now that we have taken a systemic look at school culture, let's move systemically into school climate. Gruenert and Whitaker (2022) define *school climate* as group responses to particular situations or circumstances within a school, "for example, how we are supposed to feel or the mood of the group at any given moment" (p. 2). Researchers from the University of Nebraska-Lincoln and the University of Louisville have a theoretical framework for a systems view of school climate and define it as follows:

> School climate is composed of the affective and cognitive perceptions regarding social interactions, relationships, safety, values, and beliefs held by students, teachers, administrators, and staff within a school. (Rudasill, Snyder, Levinson, & Adelson, 2017, p. 46)

Assistant principals are integral to establishing and maintaining positive and optimal school climates; as researchers note, "There is suggested evidence that specific aspects of assistant principals' roles—such as coaching teachers or being visible in the classroom—or assistant principals' effectiveness could relate to student outcomes and school climate" (Goldring et al., 2021, p. 76).

Assistant principals monitor and regulate school climate as a whole-school feeling, foundational to whether teaching and learning can occur for students. Linda Darling-Hammond and Channa M. Cook-Harvey (2018a) note:

> A positive school environment is not a "frill" to be attended to after academics and discipline are taken care of. Instead, it is the primary pathway to effective learning. . . . It is important that schools provide a positive learning environment that allows students to learn social-emotional skills as well as academic content.

School climate can change on a dime. Imagine the power of a message coming over the intercom that the next day will be a snow day. Then substitute with a different message, for example that there will be a closed-campus lunch because of reports that a fistfight is planned. These could change climate either positively or negatively. Regarding the latter, Megan Tschannen-Moran and Bob Tschannen-Moran (2014) from the College of William and Mary and the Center for School Transformation, respectively, note schools have been increasingly challenged with issues of morale, which results in a personified sense that schools are in a bad mood. They point out that moods are more generalized and long-lasting than emotions, and can become habits of mind. "Some of the more common bad moods include feelings of suspicion, resentment, cynicism, resignation, and despair. Such moods influence people—what they're ready, willing, and able to accomplish" (Tschannen-Moran & Tschannen-Moran, 2014, p. 37). You can see this reflected in the news, on social media, and in person as you work with others each day. If we are not careful, we can live in a bad mood too. It is infectious. Thus, it becomes our responsibility to operate with a strategy to reduce the contagion.

Fullan (2019) got me thinking also about school climate. Remember how miners used to take canaries with them into the coal mines to gauge the quality and level of oxygen as they worked? Well, did you know that students can fulfill this role in our classrooms? They also show the first signs of distress when the environment isn't the best. Yet, unlike canaries in coal mines, when canary students begin showing signs of distress, teachers often blame the canary, not the environment—an apt metaphor for how school climate impacts our students.

As an assistant principal, you can safeguard, maintain, and enhance school climate through your own efforts. I suggest doing this in line with the National School Climate Center's (NSCC, n.d., as cited in Darling-Hammond & Cook-Harvey, 2018b) thirteen dimensions, including safety dimensions such as rules and norms, a sense of physical security, and a sense of social-emotional security. You can also influence climate through the dimensions of teaching and learning, such as support for academic learning and social and civil learning. Interpersonal relations dimensions of school climate include a respect for diversity, social support for adults and students, and the application of institutional environmental dimensions of climate, including school connectedness or engagement and physical surroundings. With your staff, you can ensure dimensions of proper leadership and the nurturing of professional relationships.

The How: Strategies to Use With Students

The following strategies—taking the temperature of school climate and developing nuanced observation—are effective ways to lay the foundation for your work with students.

Take the Temperature (of School Climate)

School climate is something you can influence and monitor as assistant principal. Because of your visibility throughout the school, you can embody school climate for others at the same time that you keep an eye on it. Take its temperature, then work to manage it.

I recommend a daily temperature check about midway through the morning and then again after lunch. It doesn't take much time. Between classes, listen to the sounds in the hallways, especially if you are behind a closed door and cannot be seen. Do a few classroom walkthroughs. Ask your front office assistants how things are going. Basically, do anything you can to quickly gauge the group's attitude, state of mind, and feelings, as school climate is an indicator of overall morale (Gruenert & Whitaker, 2015), important in understanding your social system.

TIP

Data on school climate are not just numeric; they are observational. If you observe something time and again as you walk around your building that seems to influence feeling, or if something of great magnitude upends things, both are worthy of analysis.

A final point regarding temperature taking is that once you determine the climate on any given day, you can do something about it. Look for anything getting in the way of a positive, professional tone among students and determine the culprit. What you want to do is to look for the things that, if not urgently attended to, could result in people making bad decisions and getting in trouble. Then, spend some effort to correct if appropriate.

TIP

If school climate takes a dive, be a good steward, not a rescuer. If there is a legitimate reason for sadness or grief in the student body, don't try to artificially reverse that. Use authenticity as your guide.

You can always do preventive climate maintenance. This might include ensuring you have clear expectations for behavior and consequences for misbehavior and that you gauge your efforts in terms of fairness and equity through data analysis (Austin, O'Malley, & Izu, 2011). What could be your data? They could include the number of office referrals, the number of tardies or absences, the number of students wishing to leave school early, and so on.

An example might be an overall downer of a mood because of a big loss at a sectional competition over the weekend. Get your team captains and athletic director to make an announcement after lunch thanking the students for their support and the coaches for all they have done, with a rallying cry for next year. Or perhaps you have a family whose house burned down. Why not set up a place in the cafeteria during lunch for the signing of a large well-wishes card and a donation station? Coming together to help provides positive energy. You might have some tension in the air with rumors that students are going to demonstrate because of an unfair or unjust situation. Meet with key communicators in the student body, listen to their concerns, assure them that you wish to help, and remind them clearly of the parameters through which demonstration would be appropriate and boundaries beyond which demonstration would result in consequences. Be proactive.

The point here is that you should not remain passive regarding school climate. Especially if there is hostility in the air, address it transparently. Don't avoid taking action. Take the temperature, figure out what's going on, and then work to do what you can about it. Remember the bigger picture and your responsibility to it.

Develop Nuanced Observation

In every classroom, cafeteria, and commons area, groups of people form. We have in-groups, out-groups, cliques, and crews. *We*s and *they*s. Yet, *I*s are everywhere: individuals searching for a place of dignity among others. Just like there is a tug between institutions and individuals and the roles expected of people, the same exists between groups and the individuals within them. Studying these disconnects helps you develop a nuanced ability to see your school with a wide-angle lens. You can almost predict the forces at work that will influence behavior, even before the behaviors occur. I suggest in order to gauge how your social system is doing, pay particular attention and study the behaviors of individuals while they are in the group versus when they are on their own. It is all a part of your school's culture.

TIP

When you see a student not with a group that student typically frequents, one of a handful of things might be going on. First, of course, it could be nothing. Or, the group might be ostracizing the student, or the student might be struggling with someone in the group. Keep an eye on things.

In every group, norms exist that create expectations for membership. These norms define how members of the group behave, what they are supposed to believe, and, even more deeply, what they value. Those with more influence within the group serve as living ideals of group identity, and observing their interactions will help you predict what might be coming your way. Look at the groups' daily membership. Look for disconnects. Who is not with the group who usually is? Differences here could signal a conflict or something else negative. What about typical group interactions? Are they normal (and hopefully positive), or is there any disproportion to who is the butt of jokes and recipient of sarcasm? I have seen it happen because of dating and relationship decisions (where students enter in to relationships with friends' former significant others, and others feel they must align accordingly). Sometimes, a group may decide as one that the behavior of certain members has become extreme. I recall one instance that had to do with substance abuse, and the person who was no longer with peers was in dire need of an intervention, not the ostracism and distancing this person was receiving. Particularly with younger students, I have found that when students withdraw from peers, the problem might not lie with the people or situations that the students avoid; it might be something outside of school creating consternation, worry, or self-isolation.

Don't just look on the surface. Watch what happens when the group disperses and moves to class. Discern the nuances. How do the members behave when they become individuals once again and walk down the hall? Don't discount your intuition when looking to understand your ecosystem; don't write the little things off as happenstances or side effects of something obvious but perhaps inconsequential. Goleman (2013) notes that what we see as side effects in systems are misnamed; they are instead effects *of* the system. Thinking that a system has side effects is flawed understanding; all happens for a reason.

In viewing group and individual dynamics, zoom in, pan out, and scan elements both micro and macro. Look group to group as well. I like Goleman's (2013) description of how an "emotional aperture, the ability to perceive such subtle cues in a group, operates a bit like a camera. We can zoom in to focus on one person's feelings, or zoom out to take in the collective" (p. 239). And pay attention to trends over time, those that escape the immediacy of the moment. Don't miss invisible things that influence the school environment over time, yet are ever-present:

> We are finely tuned to a rustling in the leaves that may signal a stalking tiger. But we have no perceptual awareness that can sense the thinning of the atmosphere's ozone layer, nor the carcinogens in the particulates we breathe on a smoggy day. Both can eventually be fatal, but our brain has no direct radar for these threats. (Goleman, 2013, p. 143)

It behooves assistant principals to spend time in effortful, nuanced observation, when supervision allows. Stand around with a purpose. Don't just look at what your students are doing; look at what they're not doing. Think about things from your standpoint, but also theirs. How are they seeing the world, right now, through their eyes? What influences might exist for their behavior and what could these say about others? Contextual cues are our gifts; they signal what is visible in front of us as well as what is invisible yet still adjacent. If we ask ourselves, "What might this mean?" a healthy curiosity will serve us well in environmental prevention through observational acuity.

The How: Strategies to Use With Staff

The following strategies—connecting the dots in school culture and seeing a new why in resistance—are effective ways to lay the foundation for your work with staff.

Connect the Dots in School Culture

Make efforts to know your school culture. This is not something you can immediately influence because it is much larger than one person, or even groups of people. Yet you can plant seeds to move culture over time and take stock in the meantime, an important aspect of intelligence gathering that will help your principal and the administrative team make decisions about what to focus on long term.

Connecting the dots of school culture allows for you to understand context. Why do staff behave the way they do? The type and strength of school culture will influence which adults will send which students to your office, and under what conditions. The school's culture will offer your colleagues the *dos* and *don'ts* of referral and how their peers reinforce or sanction those actions. School culture provides expected roles for people to portray, such as the anti-administration lounge lizards, the teachers with the big stick, or the big egos that fill any room they're in.

TIP

Don't try to move the wall of school culture. Moving the wall doesn't make sense. It is going to be there for a while, so learn to landscape around it and build doorways through it.

School culture has rituals, such as where certain staff members drink coffee in the morning or where they have their lunch and with whom at what table. It has ceremony, such as expected events held perennially that determine what the school honors and what it does not. Again, a school's culture is its way of doing business. Don't try to change it quickly; it would be like trying to speed up a glacier. It's naïve for school administrators to profess that they will change both climate and culture in the same breath. Rather, you can gauge whether your role makes sense within your school's culture in terms of how you are doing with it because it will affect the quality of your professional life.

Assistant principals connect the dots of school culture so that they can be instrumental to their principals in improving their schools. They do so by working over a period of time to mitigate and reduce the influence of or, better yet, eliminate elements of culture that are working against student learning. The key in your influence over school culture as an assistant principal is to make the most out of choreography so that the school's norms become those that your principal wishes to see; this can occur both directly through rules and policy implementation and indirectly through relationships and influence.

These changes to school culture don't happen overnight. Gruenert and Whitaker (2015) suggest things that can be done to improve a culture, such as asking teachers why they like snow days, celebrating Mondays instead of Fridays ("TGIM"), praising risk taking, asking folks to describe the elephant in the room, and encouraging the development of a subculture of your most effective staff. Even with these strategies that seem intriguing and might be fun, changing school culture is like chipping away at a mountain with a Swiss Army knife. Your role is to understand your school's culture better than anyone else as a systems thinking expert. Probably best to get started.

See a New Why in Resistance to Change

We have heard for many years about different strategies of handling resistance when working to make school a better place. John Kotter (2012), author of *Leading Change*, proposes a process that includes establishing urgency, putting together a guiding coalition, developing vision and strategy, communicating a change vision, empowering employees, generating short-term wins, consolidating gains, and anchoring new approaches into the school culture. This approach is logical and linear and builds on the positive energy and capacity in people to move forward and get desired results. Fullan (2020), author of *Leading in a Culture of Change*, offers his own conceptual model of change, more recently including his own notions of "nuance" in understanding change. What I like best about Fullan's model is a focus on "relationships, relationships, relationships" in making sense of it all and bringing people together. A focus on relationships couldn't be more critical.

As an assistant principal, you'll likely be asked by your principal to lead change initiatives and to do so within an existing school culture that has its own ideas about whether or not to move forward and how things get done. That culture is made up of people: your colleagues on staff at the school in which you work. I suggest that as an extension of what the experts I've discussed tell us about moving organizations forward, a must is to see a new why in resistance and to do so by focusing on people.

I was first inspired in this by J. Stewart Black and Hal B. Gregersen's (2002) book, *Leading Strategic Change: Breaking Through the Brain Barrier*, and later by Black's (2014) *It Starts With One: Changing Individuals Changes Organizations*, which presents a cycle of change and explains that folks in organizations do, for the most part, the right things and do them well. Over time, the right thing no longer works, yet people still do it well because it has become part of the routine or even a favorite thing—except it's now the wrong thing to be doing. In order to do the next right thing, we need to do it poorly at first—to go through a learning curve—before doing the new right thing well. And who would want to come to work and do things poorly in front of colleagues from whom they hope to garner respect?

Consider the use of technology in teaching. For years, technology complemented what we were doing as teachers, as face-to-face instruction was, by and large, the right thing to do. We would never think to replace direct teacher instruction with something over a computer. After all, nothing could replace in-class instruction with real, live teachers, correct? Even the notions of flipped instruction were seen as ancillary, yet admittedly innovative—such as recording the direct instruction and having students watch the video prior to class, then using class time to collaboratively reinforce skills that were a byproduct of the knowledge included in the video.

The notion of traditional instruction without a technological component was, for a long time, very much the right thing. Then, tragically, we experienced a world-changing pandemic that rendered traditional instruction, in many cases, impossible. Face-to-face time together was at a premium. Staunch adherence to face-to-face instruction is no longer the right thing; it is the *wrong* thing when infection is spreading and concerns for safety are heightened. The new right thing is, thus, to expand our repertoire technologically, and learn to teach online when necessary. This includes flipped instruction, as in some cases getting all students into class consistently is a rarity, so it behooves teachers to standardize their delivery through a flipped video model. That way, they can focus on who is able to be with them on a daily basis to reinforce things as students are able to attend. Using Black and Gregersen's (2002) cycle, it's a reality that embracing a new way of teaching technologically means some of us might do it poorly at first before doing it well. It's a natural implementation dip en route to mastering the new right thing.

Let's take another example: full inclusion of students who are in special education programs. For years, we had been educating these students outside the general education classroom with a

combination of resource-room academic support and categorical programming in pull-out scenarios. Then, we heard that a free and appropriate education in the least restrictive environment
required us to educate students with special education needs to the extent possible with their peers
in general education. For a while, we did this to a larger degree for certain parts of the school day
(known as *mainstreaming*), but full inclusion, when appropriate, was eventually the expectation.
Thus, we found out that the old right thing (separate educational experiences) was now the new
wrong thing, and the new right thing (a more inclusive education) was something that, at first, we
were not very adept at.

And some teachers resisted these efforts.

It was with my involvement in the special education process that I experienced my a-ha moment
with respect to change and resistance. It is not that people want to work against us; it is that they
don't want their own professional reputations and competencies to work against themselves. In the
case of the inclusion example, some folks resisted not because they didn't want what's best for students but because they honestly worried about the students' willingness or abilities to take part in
this new process, and many more worried about how they would be perceived doing something
they didn't feel professionally equipped to do (as they noted, they were not trained as special educators). Black (2014) reinforces that while change is hard, expensive, and time consuming, it is best
accomplished with a direct focus on the people who simply are letting their own barriers get in the
way of themselves. It is a matter of helping them move beyond their denial that change is necessary
and their temptation to do more of what they know as they try new things. Black (2014) shares
that sometimes even a change penalty exists—that is, successful implementation of what we are
being asked to do may dip for a time as we move forward with expectations. Temporarily, we may
not completely fulfill our roles or succeed at our jobs. In the inclusion example, the change penalty
was that students in special education didn't do as well academically as the adults got things figured
out. Yet with anticipation, aspiration, and commitment, the eventual payoffs are worth moving
forward with new things.

Thus, if you allow yourself to see a new why in resistance, and remind yourself and your principal that what you have are good folks who simply need a way to safely do new things that are
difficult, you'll be in position to uplift and influence school culture simultaneously. In order to do
so, commit to the following. When you see or hear of resistance to something important to the
school, don't talk to the staff in general about the resistance. Instead, ask someone you trust to identify a few of the quietly resistant folks who are respected and connected. Then, visit these colleagues
individually and ask if they would be willing to provide you guidance. Share what you hope to do
and why it is important to you, and give them permission to offer some constructive criticism. Let
them know you have broad shoulders—that you can take some criticism. They will then probably
offer concerns in terms of negative effects on students, which may be good points yet are probably
not entirely why they are resistant.

Then, ask them a different question: "What could be a reason that some of the staff members
might be resistant that has to do with their own professional discomfort, in addition to concerns
about risks for students?" Ask them to envision newer staff members, those who are early in their
careers, or, let's say, those less confident. You're much more apt to get a glimmer of what they, themselves, are worried about, though they may not say it as such. It is safer for them to talk about others.
Ask them if they would be willing to gather a small team they trust and discuss some possible ways

to design a work-around to the staff concerns. See if you can convince them that a new approach might be good for students, given the points they made. This positions them alongside you in the driver's seat of how many, and under what conditions, changes are to come. They now feel less like recipients and more like co-constructors, which assuages their own concerns.

The How: Strategy to Use With You

In working to become familiar with your school's culture, you must understand how your leadership identity influences the staff with whom you work and what gets done. This is most typically the result of a balancing act between tasks needing to get done and relationships with people. Deft balance is the key, and it's one way to move school culture toward a positive place where it needs to be. The strategy I call becoming a daily pathfinder will help you do just that.

If you wish to influence school culture positively, you can do so through leadership style and behavior. It is through a daily strategy of leadership focus and identity that authors Todd Whitaker, Sam Miller, and Ryan Donlan (2018) describe in *The Secret Solution: How One Principal Discovered the Path to Success*. It has to do with a leader's focus on and attentiveness to accountability and climate (Whitaker et al., 2018). Figure 3.1 describes four leadership roles: leaders with (1) a low focus on both accountability and climate as *hibernators* (hiding in their offices), (2) a high focus on accountability and low focus on climate as *thumbs* (putting their thumbs down on people), (3) a low focus on accountability and high focus on climate as *glad-handers* (all smiles, little follow-through), and (4) a high focus on both accountability and climate as *pathfinders* (en route to success).

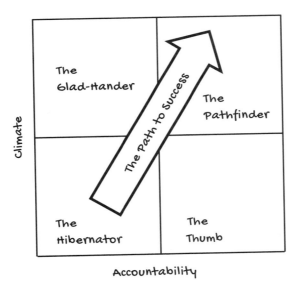

Source: © 2018 by Todd Whitaker, Sam Miller, and Ryan Donlan. Illustration by Eric Cleveland and Ryan Donlan. Used with permission.

FIGURE 3.1: The secret solution grid.

Your strategy is to become a daily pathfinder, and I'll tell you why. Leaders who are hibernators have negative effects on staff, including a lack of reinforcement and connection for those who are superstars. With hibernators in charge, teachers who are mediocre look for leadership in all the wrong places, and those who are more negative become powerful and fill a leadership void

(Whitaker et al., 2018). As a leader, you'll feel indecisive, afraid, and powerless to influence the school culture, and you'll have the unintended consequences of negative people gaining power and the good people losing confidence (Whitaker et al., 2018). Hibernators certainly cannot influence school culture positively.

If you're a glad-hander, you'll have negative effects on staff as well, including the superstars being frustrated with unresolved problems and not feeling valued for their teaching excellence because all are treated the same. Underperforming staff will love it and will become entitled with very little work done, and negative people will continue to place more and more demands on you, almost like spoiled children (Whitaker et al., 2018). While you may feel good for a while with this approach, you'll get taken advantage of because whatever you do will not be enough, and over time, less and less work gets done, and you lose respect (Whitaker et al., 2018). Glad-handers certainly cannot influence school culture positively.

If you're a thumb, you'll have negative effects in that your superstars will feel restricted and stop taking risks; they will shut their doors to stay out of the fire. Your underperforming staff will align with those more negative for protection from you, and your most negative people will build membership and will lie in the weeds, ready to strike (Whitaker et al., 2018). While you may feel empowered at first, you'll see people gravitating away from you, and you'll end up alone. You'll lose support for any good ideas that you have over time because people are fearful of you, and your best people may wish to transfer out of your school (Whitaker et al., 2018). Thumbs certainly cannot influence school culture positively.

As a pathfinder, you have both high levels of climate and accountability to empower your superstars, who have unlimited energy and are willing to take risks and work with others. Underperforming staff will act more like superstars under your pathfinding leadership, and negative people will have their power and influence reduced, some of it through your expectations of accountability. You will find that high levels of climate mindfulness and a focus on accountability provide you much satisfaction and prepare you to take on challenge. You will not be the only source of positive morale and school culture movement; this positive driving force will come from everywhere.

Toolkit for Tomorrow: Next Steps

These next steps provide some suggestions for how you can put the ideas in this chapter into action.

- From the list in figure 3.2, examine various areas in your school that have both institutional expectations and individual preferences of teachers and staff. These can solidify school culture positively or negatively. First, jot down your institution's expectations in the key areas listed, as compared to the individual preferences of staff. These might be similar or different. The farther apart they are, the less in touch leadership might be to the school culture's preferred way of doing business. Work with one or two key staff members to gather ideas on how you might align expectations and preferences more closely and offer ideas of your own. I have provided space for you to offer four additional examples specific to your school. This way, you can begin right away to identify what school culture does not support and see if there is a remedy that can bring your institution and individuals together. I provided some example text in the curriculum development row to give you an idea of how to get started.

Focus Area for Systems Analysis	Institutional or Administrative Expectations	Individual Preferences of Staff	How Similar or Different Are They?	Ideas of Your Own to Bridge Any Gaps
Professional Dress and Appearance				
Curriculum Development	The school expects all teachers in any given content area or grade level are involved in curriculum development, and that curriculum activity is site based.	Some staff members feel that time spent in committee work on behalf of curriculum improvement detracts from their planning time for effective instruction. Many wish that curricular work would go to others who are interested in this sort of work. They will then run with whatever they receive.	While these two perspectives seem different on the surface, in reality they share a common theme: teachers in the classroom are the best determiners of what students need in day-to-day instruction, so teaching expectations should not come down upon them from above.	One possibility is a curricular steering committee comprising one teacher or staff member from each content area or grade level to gather input on how teachers prefer to be involved in curriculum development work. Members can ascertain whether they have a coalition of the willing in each area who would readily assume the heavier lifting in terms of unpacking curricular standards and putting together aligned curriculum maps for others' review. Everyone involved in teaching would ratify. Those not directly involved in curriculum could work in smaller teams on other issues of instruction and assessment; thus, everyone plays to their strengths. Also, make a space on each committee for those who wish to participate individually or asynchronously. In other words, not everyone prefers to do things in a group. Allow for some tasks to be fulfilled by individuals on their own time and by themselves.
Lesson Design and Planning				
Student Supervision				

continued ▶

FIGURE 3.2: Institutional expectations and individual preferences of staff.

Focus Area for Systems Analysis	Institutional or Administrative Expectations	Individual Preferences of Staff	How Similar or Different Are They?	Ideas of Your Own to Bridge Any Gaps
Professional Development and Training				
Involvement in Electives, Advisory, or Extracurricular Activities				
Committee Assignments				
School Improvement				

*Visit **go.SolutionTree.com/leadership** for a free reproducible version of this figure.*

- Do the same things with roles expected by the institution and personalities of staff members in figure 3.3. This time, discuss any incongruencies with your principal and inquire as to whether they will let you make proposals on how to bring these together. Often, this has to do with the master schedule or supervisory duties. Once again, I provide sample text in one row to illustrate.

Roles Within the Institution	Personality Expected Within This Role	Personalities of Staff Appointed	How Similar or Different Are They?	Ideas of Your Own
Front Office Receptionist				
School Counselor				
Lunchroom or Hallway Monitor	The ideal person for this role is someone curious about students and who genuinely likes social settings and informal conversations; however, it should also be someone students respect and do not want to disappoint and who has a mind for detail and nuanced observation. It should be someone who, while friendly, inspires respect rather than friendship.	At times, those who are more dogmatic and officious are appointed to these positions— seemingly those who will wield any small amount of authority given to them at the drop of a hat; someone who always seems to choose to act (fire, aim, ready), rather than use a ready-aim-fire approach.	These two could not be more different in surface behaviors and the resultant effectiveness of doing the role. Over time, the second of the two (personalities of staff often appointed) can work against the school, as students spend time engaging in energy that creates conflict for entertainment purposes.	Hire for the underlying dispositional traits, as these are harder to train. Thus, look for non-negotiable curiosity, patience, and a genuine like for students where they are developmentally. Other job-specific skills, such as navigating social settings, developing nuanced observation, and making decisions that others respect, rather than trying to be liked, can be taught more readily if positive dispositional traits already exist.
School Custodian				
Cafeteria Server				

FIGURE 3.3: Institutional roles and personalities assigned.

continued ▶

Roles Within the Institution	Personality Expected Within This Role	Personalities of Staff Appointed	How Similar or Different Are They?	Ideas of Your Own
Child Advocate or Parental Liaison				
School Resource Officer				
Assistant Principal				

*Visit **go.SolutionTree.com/leadership** for a free reproducible version of this figure.*

- Practice your ability to be like the aperture of a camera during student commons or cafeteria supervision. Strive to find one disconnect per day and figure out what it means. This will develop your repertoire of context-savvy skills and nuance.

- Gather a small team of affectively inclined teachers, staff, and students who are willing to help you take the temperature of school climate each week, and provide a communication space or electronic forum where you can share thoughts, concerns, and ideas. Ensure face-to-face chats as well.

- Complete the professional development activity on page 56 to widen your perspective on school culture. In it, I have assigned playful names to various archetypes I have often encountered in my experience. See figure 3.4 for an example of how you might approach the activity with one archetype.

Name of School Archetype	Archetype Description	What do you think their role in school culture provides to them personally (their creature comforts)?	What are the effects on school climate when they are left to act as they do naturally, to satisfy their own personal needs yet not consider the school's?	Why might they be behaving like this? Could it be factors outside of school?	How might you invite them to feel like heroes so that they can work to improve both themselves and school culture?
M. J. McNasty	Those who belong to this archetype often still believe in sparing no rods in behavior management; usually found in leadership or teachers or staff members with supervisory roles.	This role in school culture provides feelings of mission commitment, righteousness, and a belief that one is saving others from themselves, by harkening back to traditional values long forgotten.	This archetype plays a fire and brimstone despot who rules with an iron fist and inflicts brutality on those who oppose. The effects on school climate are negative overall, as students and others associating will develop an anti-adult perspective, thinking school officials are out to get them, to catch them doing things wrong, rather than providing opportunities for them and seeing the good in their efforts. This archetype can cause students and others to see authority figures not as allies but as entities to outflank.	It's possible that this archetype acts this way to satisfy a need for recognition of meaningful work and conviction that may be lacking.	Involve them in conversation when they are around. Take the initiative to approach them and ask their perspective on something that does not involve your wanting permission from them to do something. In other words, provide a safe place where they can share their opinion without having the burden of making a decision one way or the other. Show interest in them as dispensers of knowledge, and commend them on their commitment to the school and willingness to provide good guidance. Mention to them that their input helps.

FIGURE 3.4: Characters and creature comforts—Sample archetype.

Professional Development: A Deeper Dive—Fostering a Positive School Culture and Climate

Instructions: This professional development activity will help widen your perspective on school culture. Take time on this activity, have a bit of fun, and refer back to the chapter as needed for information and strategies to gain thoughtful insight on how you might turn the creature comforts of the people in your school who reinforce their eccentricities in a negative way into learning opportunities that will leverage their best selves. You can only accomplish this by developing a wide perspective on what makes school school and the people within it.

Listed in the following activity are archetypes of school employees you might find inhabiting any school culture across the United States or beyond. The cheesy, made-up names offer insight into who the people fitting these archetypes really are. I have provided short archetype descriptions for each. When you work with so many different people day after day, you may start to notice patterns: idiosyncrasies in the way people behave, what they believe, and how they fulfill their professional roles. As assistant principals, if we can consider the underlying influences and reasons for their behavior, we can positively influence the way they bring their professional selves to each work day. It starts by trying to delve inside their heads psychologically, and brainstorm things we might say and do, to help them out. There are several blank rows at the end for you to include archetypes you have noticed in your own experience.

Name of School Archetype	Archetype Description	What do you think their role in school culture provides to them personally (their creature comforts)?	What are the effects on school climate when they are left to act as they do naturally, to satisfy their own personal needs yet not consider the school's?	Why might they be behaving like this? Could it be factors outside of school?	How might you invite them to feel like heroes so that they can work to improve both themselves and school culture?
M. J. McNasty	Those who belong to this archetype often still believe in sparing no rods in behavior management; usually found in leadership or teachers or staff members with supervisory roles.				

Gabby Gossip — Members of this archetype tend to be overinvolved with student groups, act as social butterflies, and are prone to gossip, often with a mild lack of self-awareness.	**Clark Tie-rod** — Members of this archetype are often crusty veteran teachers who are anti-administration and proud of it.	**Melba Fang** — These are often hyper-judgmental with a foul morning disposition that gets better by day's end. They tend to be found in the front office or at the negative end of the teacher or staff lounge.

Name of School Archetype	Archetype Description	What do you think their role in school culture provides to them personally (their creature comforts)?	What are the effects on school climate when they are left to act as they do naturally, to satisfy their own personal needs yet not consider the school's?	Why might they be behaving like this? Could it be factors outside of school?	How might you invite them to feel like heroes so that they can work both to improve themselves and school culture?
Stephen Stratos	Members of this archetype tend to be introverted and often invisible by choice, often staring out the window while their students work in their classrooms. They are often found to be artistic.				
Julie Jumpstart	People in this archetype are generally eager new teachers assigned to way too many committees and coaching or extracurricular obligations.				

This archetype includes people who are known for giving out hugs, know all the families, and spend most of the day on the telephone and social media. They are usually found in supporting roles.		
Penny Pleasant		

CHAPTER 4
DEVELOPING RELATIONSHIPS

I recall from my first few years of teaching a wonderful school counselor, Mr. "Smo," as students called him. To the staff, he was Mark Smolinski, consummate gentleman and student advocate, but they called him Smo as well. Smo had great relationships with everyone. No one ever had a negative thing to say about Mr. Smo; there was this effervescent affability about him and true, genuine warmth. I learned that Mr. Smo once played with the American Football League's World Champion New York Jets. He retired from football to take a coaching position in a high school, and I found him serving admirably still when I started my career. Upon my arrival, Mr. Smo was living another dream as an educator; he prioritized positive relationships with adults and students alike, he was a never-ending source of support for me, and he was a student-centered champion.

When students were kicked out of their classes or when a rift between students and teachers was hard to mend, I invited Mr. Smo and our other counselors to send them to me. I extended an open invitation to use my room as a time-out room as needed, but I more often than not ended up adopting students for the duration of the term. In order to accommodate the number, I moved in extra desks and purchased couches and bean bags from resale shops. Everywhere there was a nook and a cranny, there was a student. I think the record number was forty-two in one class at one time.

The strangest thing was that while students were tossed from other classes for behavioral disruptions, academic insubordination, and a refusal to do much of what my colleagues wanted, I didn't have a problem with them. My classes provided these students something that did the trick, every time. It was relationships. Like I learned in watching Mr. Smo, each student, each day, needed a positive relationship experience. When I moved from my teacher's role into the assistant principalship in that same school, Mr. Smo continued to model positive relationships as he encouraged me in my new role. The leadership team started a school-within-a-school alternative education program, where I took a page out of Smo's playbook yet again. With a focus on relationships that I saw embraced and modeled by Mark Smolinski, all things move forward. I see it to this day.

In this chapter, the focus is on building those relationships. First, we'll get into the what and the why of this essential aspect of the assistant principalship, and then we'll move to the how: strategies to use with students, staff, and yourself.

The What and the Why

Assistant principals work to leverage outcomes of student success through a terrain that at times seems to offer more land mines than lifelines. And as with any trek, it is better traveled when you have good relationships with those walking alongside you. The American Educational Research Association (AERA) published a meta-analysis involving ninety-nine research studies on students from preschools to high schools in the United States, Canada, Europe, Asia, Australia, and Africa, in which the authors find an association between positive teacher-student relationships and positive student engagement and achievement as well as a negative association with negative relationships (Roorda, Koomen, Spilt, & Oort, 2011). The researchers' analysis found, as well, that relationships are as important or even more influential the older the students get (Roorda et al., 2011).

All the things accomplished in school move through relationships. In a special issue of *New Directions for Youth Development* on teacher-student relationships, authors Beth Bernstein-Yamashiro and Gil G. Noam (2013) note a growing body of research and a host of findings on the power of relationships, including the fact that a lack of connection to caring adults leads to "student alienation, failure, and disaffection from school and finally dropout" (p. 18). Bernstein-Yamashiro and Noam (2013) also note "relationships tend to create a personal investment that motivates students to perform well academically" (p. 33), and "for students, a teacher's personality, a teacher-student relationship, and the learning process appear to be integrally intertwined" (p. 35).

Darling-Hammond and Cook-Harvey (2018b), in a report for the Learning Policy Institute, note key lessons on relationships from the sciences and learning development research and conclude, "Human relationships are the essential ingredient that catalyzes healthy development and learning" (p. 5). Further, responsive relationships during school years "can buffer the potentially negative effects of even serious adversity" (Darling-Hammond & Cook-Harvey, 2018b, p. 5). In schools, building positive relationships starts with trust. Fullan (2019) notes how trust starts: "You have to invest in trust before people have earned it. Trust is a verb before it becomes a state" (pp. 84–85). Trust is the foundation for good relationships, and students will work harder if they trust we're in their court and we have their backs. Adults are much the same.

As an assistant principal, you serve as the matchmaker for positive relationships. Your matchmaking involves not only selecting the best people to work together for a particular outcome but evaluating to what extent they will stay positive in interacting while in that relationship until the task gets done. This could be more formal, such as who serves on a school project or working group, or more informal, such as students needing to walk a certain hallway each day to get to their lockers when they have had difficulties with others nearby, such as other students or teachers or staff. All of these need to be accomplished through positive and sometimes difficult relationships with others, and that's all in the natural course of a school day.

Developing relationships in schools involves a conscientious effort to foster connectedness between adults and students, students and students, and adults and adults. We are not just in the business of helping students develop positive relationships with others; it is equally important for us to work on relationships ourselves as adults and to model appropriate collegiality to students. Students learn as much about navigating life and people while in school as they do academics. I recall observing teachers who were experts in their content but struggled with positive disposition not only with school administration but with colleagues. At times, I would see an engaging and charismatic performance in the classroom, yet what also caught my attention was how the students were behaving. A few were behaving with eerily similar disposition to how their teachers acted. If their teachers were toxic rather than relational—in other words, if they act arrogant or condescending, go against leadership, and discredit others who are trying to make a difference (Gruenert & Whitaker, 2022)—then students tended to mirror this behavior with their own younger peers. It manifested in how they formed in-groups and out-groups, and they seemed to care more about themselves than others around them.

What is interesting is that I have seen the opposite in students who are in the classes of those who are more authentic and relational as a rule; rather than trying to blame, indoctrinate, and sell their forms of obstinacy as toxic teachers tend to (Gruenert & Whitaker, 2022), they instead work to collaborate with other adults in the school and make the school a more positive place overall. In short, students practice to be adults by watching the adults around them. They learn the behavior that teachers model just as they learn content and academic skills, which can have a positive impact on relationships when teachers are good role models.

Schools are also charged with developing skills in students that depend to a large degree on relationships. I am thinking here of 21st century skills, which are continually cited as important by countless partnerships, organizations, and agencies, such as those noted in the Asia Society Global Cities Education Network and RAND Corporation's *Measuring 21st Century Competencies: Guidance for Educators* (Soland, Hamilton, & Stecher, 2013) and Gallup and Northwest Evaluation Association's (NWEA, 2018) *Assessing Soft Skills: Are We Preparing Students for Successful Futures? A Perceptions Study of Parents, Teachers, and School Administrators*. While the exact skills articulated vary among groups, many include the ability to establish and maintain positive relationships with others, such as communication, collaboration, cross-cultural interaction, effective listening, working well with others, self-management, collaboration, critical thinking, making connections, and adaptability. It's tempting to relegate to the back seat an intentional focus on relationship development in school, as relationships are not assessed on standardized tests, but it is our obligation to ensure that students develop them. "Students' interpersonal skills, including their abilities to interact positively with peers and adults, to resolve conflicts, and to work in teams, all contribute to effective learning and lifelong behavior" (Darling-Hammond & Cook-Harvey, 2018b, p. 7). Assistant principals can ensure this focus.

Developing relationships in schools involves creating opportunities for people to overcome the difficulties of academic workload. Often there is a gap between the daunting nature of the demands placed on us and our capacity in terms of the ability or strength to successfully address those demands. Bridging this divide are the energies that we can muster through our self-concept, self-esteem, and self-efficacy. How we believe others to perceive us is foundational to these attributes. When students feel like they matter, in other words, they will have robust self-concept, self-esteem, and self-efficacy. And through positive relationships, educators can help them feel this way.

School administrator Shelly Wilfong's pioneering work on mattering in education provides something important to think about regarding relationships. Wilfong (2021) defines mattering as the feeling we are significant and would be missed if we were gone. One of Wilfong's (2021) discoveries in mattering is the notion of community, something that creates energy and belonging within your preferred group. Another is authenticity, which has to do with the degree to which we feel comfortable being ourselves when we are around others; both would be impossible without positive relationships. Thinking about when we are asked to do difficult things—like school—in full view of others, doesn't it make sense that if we had a supportive community and were our authentic selves, our jobs would be easier? Of course they would. How often do you have students who come to you feeling that they just don't matter? And when you look into the reasons why, you find invariably it has much more to do with the people they were interacting with (staff and other students) than with what teachers are asking them to do (academic tasks)? Relationships are interfering with their ability to get the tasks done; it usually has little to do with the tasks themselves. Shelly Wilfong and Ryan Donlan (2021) likewise find mattering to be strongly correlated with collective teacher efficacy, which, as I have already noted, has the most powerful effect size among strategies that influence student learning (Donohoo et al., 2018).

Ensuring positive relationships in schools involves trusted adults who are willing make a positive difference in the life of each student. Darling-Hammond and Cook-Harvey (2018b) note supportive, responsive relationships with adults during students' formative years provide for healthy development and learning. They share that cognitive scientists at MIT have found that conversations between students and adults have a more pronounced impact on students' brain physiology than the sheer amount of information provided to them. One trusted adult with unconditional positive regard has implications for a student's school and life success. Beyond cognitive development, relationships offer a protective factor to students experiencing adversity. Research has shown that a "stable relationship with at least one committed adult" (Darling-Hammond & Cook-Harvey, 2018b, p. 5) can buffer students from even more serious adversity because of the consistency of emotional security provided by empathy, modeling, perceiving needs, and responding accordingly.

You will find that one of the most valuable arrows in your quiver is the adults who make coming to school worthwhile for students. Even if they are just making school barely tolerable, the same reasoning applies: students trust them. With all the money and resources infused into preK–12 education to help students who struggle—whether that's programs, practices, or people—nothing is more valuable to you in terms of intervention, support, and saving students than adults who are students' lifelines. For this to work well, you must prioritize your relationships with these adults to the same degree they are prioritizing their relationships with the students. The adults acting as lifelines need to feel they matter as well, and this works when you prioritize relationships with them.

This brings up the notion that relationships are critical and the question of why assistant principals must focus on them before most else. Developing relationships in schools is important because it impacts student achievement. According to a National Institute of Justice report of research findings, schools with positive and communal climates have better academic achievement and social-emotional health, and they display lower levels of student absenteeism as well as positive effects on teacher morale, efficacy, and retention (Payne, 2018). Darling-Hammond and Cook-Harvey (2018b) note, "Positive relationships, including trust in the teacher, and positive emotions, such as interest and excitement, open up the mind to learning" (p. 7).

The importance of positive relationships in schools is supported by brain research, particularly that which notes the importance of the limbic system on learner readiness, learning, emotional regulation, and cognition (Fathima, Sasikumar, & Panimalar Roja, 2012). When human beings perceive the world around them, they use their senses—sight, hearing, taste, touch, and smell. The organs associated with the senses take in information and send neurochemical impulses to the brain. These neurochemical messages first go through what is known as the limbic system, a part of your brain that acts like a gatekeeper (Fathima et al., 2012), and the limbic system sorts the incoming impulses as safe or not. If the limbic system identifies the information as nonthreatening, it allows it to travel freely to the cerebral cortex, where higher-level thought takes place. However, if the incoming stimuli register as a threat, the limbic system sends the impulses to your brain stem, where one of two things happens—fight or flight. In other words, when the limbic system is overloaded with stressful stimuli (like stress or fear from bad relationships), it is unable to effectively process other stimuli that it might otherwise send to the cerebral cortex, like logic, informational discernment, or the ability to reason effectively. In short, students cannot learn effectively while their brains are overloaded by harmful stimuli.

Kimberley Holmes (2019) from the University of Calgary writes in her article "Neuroscience, Mindfulness and Holistic Wellness Reflections on Interconnectivity in Teaching and Learning":

> We need to bring the brain out of a flight or fight response in the limbic system and into the higher levels of empathy, compassion, and creativity within the hemispheres of the neocortex. We can do this by creating safe and caring learning communities. (pp. 450–451)

Holmes (2019) adds that when learners are experiencing stress, they are unable to engage in higher-level thinking because they are trapped in their own basic survival skills. It's simple: bad relationships are stressful, produce threatening incoming stimuli, and engage the automatically acting part of our brain—meaning that students fight us or flee from us. Good relationships provide safety and comfort that allow incoming stimuli to make it into the thinking parts of our brain.

The How: Strategies to Use With Students

The following strategies—learning what's on the outside; speaking the language of personality; and using reciprocation, commitment and consistency, and scarcity for positive influence—are effective ways to build positive relationships and lay the foundation for your work with students.

Learn What's on the Outside

Outside school, students are involved in activities influenced by the beliefs, values, and assumptions of those whom they respect. These may or may not reinforce what you are trying to teach inside of school. Knowing what students experience outside of school hours in their family structures, work, and leisure provides a wealth of information into what might help motivate them positively in school, both academically and behaviorally. If you work to know what your students do in their spare time and what interests they have, you will have something powerful at your disposal in your interactions with them. In most situations, a bit of small talk before getting down to business helps ease the transition onto delicate ground.

The first thing you can do is study your student information sheets on family structures, the occupations of parents or caregivers, and any siblings or extended relatives students live with. If you are not currently asking these questions on your form and if it's appropriate under your laws, consider doing so. Start with those students who are the frequent flyers to your office and work to know their personal lives. Then, branch out to others. Further, acknowledging that you know something about your students and their families shows that you have a healthy respect for them as people and that you believe they matter.

In office visits, start by sharing what you know or ask a question: "Hey, I hear you're doing well in your racing; how'd you do in the time trials this weekend?" or "I hear you're now working for my friend, Sarah, at the pet store. How are things going?" or "I'm impressed; your dad's letting you drive the wrecker nowadays? That's pretty cool." The first thing you'll notice is that their eyes will light up because you've noticed something about them that's positive. Enlist your assistant to gather intel, and keep a note in your computer or on file for each student you learn about. This way, you won't have to recall it from memory; just quickly read it on the screen, prior to calling them into your office.

One reason why you want to learn what students do outside school hours is because those people who are involved in their hobbies, interests, jobs, and so on often have deep credibility with your students in terms of influencing their beliefs and opinions. For example, you might have a student whom you have seen in your office more than once. But if you know where he works and who his manager is, and find something positive to say about her if he respects her, you can show him he has a network of adults in his life who, while they may have differing perspectives on things, have one thing in common: an interest in his success.

Offer patronage in as many family-owned businesses as you can. Chart out from the student information sheets the businesses you need to frequent in the course of what you need to accomplish personally, then try your best to link with those that employ your students and their family members. Remember parents' names, and if you see these folks when visiting, please extend a hand and a kind word about their children. You'll also want to mention these interactions casually when seeing students, something like, "Hey, it was nice to see your dad last Saturday at the dealership."

You'll want to indirectly influence your own reputation when in those businesses. Be the one who is ever courteous and engages fellow customers with small talk, be helpful, offer a good tip for services, and be a return customer. Over time, you'll develop a favorable reputation among coworkers of your students' parents and even your students themselves. This helps students and families who may only know you in the capacity of an authority figure or disciplinarian see you in a different light, and it authenticates the positivity you have at work if you're noticed as such.

Finally, being seen outside of your superordinate role and seeking guidance and advice from the families of students with whom you work offers a respectful reciprocity. It shows that you can learn from others, are curious about their expertise, and are thankful that they have taken the time to help you in their domains.

Speak the Language of Personality

Part of being human in a community with others is that personalities don't always gel with others. This happens to all of us, and for some, it gets in the way of effective relationships, both personally and professionally. Some, in fact, struggle to such a degree with social interactions that while it's not intentional on their part, they just rub others the wrong way. You have probably experienced this in the meetings you have at school. Whether they go long in what they are saying or seem wishy-washy far more than definitive, some of those you work with simply are not speaking your language. Some seem curt; others use *but* way too often and by doing so negate what others are saying, and some will react quickly to what is being said, even before thinking about it. They do not intend to be on a different page, and it is not their fault. It is just they seem unaware of how they are being perceived and don't know how best to connect with those around them.

Assistant principals have a superpower at their disposal to address this issue: the art of adaptive communication. Communicating adaptively involves learning about how people's personalities are put together—understanding first, before being understood—then learning to speak the language of personality so that you will not be off-putting as you work to be of service to others. Each and every person you work with has a preferred perceptual structure to receive incoming communication, and knowing *how* to deliver information with influence is a gift that you can develop and leverage. It involves focusing on your *process* of communication over and above your *content*.

Psychologist and communication expert Taibi Kahler began the development of a model of personality and communication while doing a Purdue University doctoral internship at a local psychiatric hospital in 1969. The Process Communication Model (PCM; Kahler, 2008) has influenced how people worldwide interact at work and in business, government, and education, as well as in their personal lives. It is, according to Kahler, "the science of communication . . . the GPS of relationships . . . [and] . . . the MRI of personality structure" (Regier, 2020, p. viii).

Research, theory, and practical applications of Kahler's (2008) model hold that people experience the world in six unique ways: through (1) thoughts, (2) opinions, (3) emotions, (4) actions, (5) reactions, and (6) inactions. While everyone has all six, one or two predominate in each person (different for different people) and serve as the default ways of perceiving (Kahler, 2008). In applying this model to assistant principals and students, I draw from the work of Gerard Collignon (2017); Gerard Collignon and Pascal Legrand (2016); Gerard Collignon, Pascal Legrand, and John Parr (2010); Michael Gilbert (2020); Gilbert and Donlan (2016); Kahler (2008); Judith Pauley, Dianne Bradley, and Joseph Pauley (2002); and Regier (2020).

As an assistant principal, within seconds of beginning an interaction, you can distinguish the perceptual frame through which students are viewing things at that moment and can connect with them by using that same frame that exists inside you. How you connect with them may not be with your favorite or default frame, and thus, using it may take some practice. Where interactions often break down is when you get into a groove of using only the frame that is comfortable for you to use, and come at things from a different perceptual frame than the student is using to converse with you.

Here is a breakdown of how these six frames might look in students.

1. Some students prefer the perception of *thoughts* with which to view experiences (Gilbert, 2020; Gilbert & Donlan, 2016; Kahler, 2008; Pauley et al., 2002). Those strongly preferring this perception search for facts, and try to identify, sort, and categorize stimuli (Collignon, 2017; Kahler, 2008; Regier, 2020). Data help them make decisions because

they are deft with analyses. Often, to navigate conversations, problem solving, and circumstance, they employ logic as an option for moving forward (Gilbert, 2020; Gilbert & Donlan, 2016; Kahler, 2008; Pauley et al., 2002).

2. Some students utilize their *opinions* to view experiences (Gilbert, 2020; Gilbert & Donlan, 2016; Kahler, 2008; Pauley et al., 2002). Those strongly preferring this perception evaluate closely whether or not they can trust the person or situation in front of them (Collignon, 2017; Kahler, 2008). They use a moral and ethical barometer to see if circumstances align with their belief systems. Often, to navigate conversations and problem solving, students employ their values as a way to offer perspective (Gilbert, 2020; Gilbert & Donlan, 2016; Kahler, 2008; Pauley et al., 2002).

3. Some students use *emotions* when handling experiences that come their way (Gilbert, 2020; Gilbert & Donlan, 2016; Kahler, 2008; Pauley et al., 2002). Those strongly preferring this perception are concerned first with the feelings of those around them, and how they are feeling themselves (Collignon, 2017; Kahler, 2008). Empathy and sympathy come naturally for these students, and they are natural caregivers. Often, they use compassion to get through their experiences (Gilbert, 2020; Gilbert & Donlan, 2016; Kahler, 2008; Pauley et al., 2002).

4. Some students use *actions* when dealing with the hands they're dealt (Gilbert, 2020; Gilbert & Donlan, 2016; Kahler, 2008; Pauley et al., 2002). Those strongly preferring this perception view things by experiencing them (Collignon, 2017; Kahler, 2008). They get things done. Often, to get what they want, they adapt and take the initiative (Gilbert, 2020; Gilbert & Donlan, 2016; Kahler, 2008; Pauley et al., 2002).

5. Some students *react* first when stuff happens (Gilbert, 2020; Gilbert & Donlan, 2016; Kahler, 2008; Pauley et al., 2002). Those strongly preferring this perception either like what's going on, or they don't (Collignon, 2017; Kahler, 2008). These students love to have fun. They can bring creativity to the group if there aren't too many rules to follow— and sometimes when there are. Often, to get through the day, these students use humor (Gilbert, 2020; Gilbert & Donlan, 2016; Kahler, 2008; Pauley et al., 2002).

6. Some students move more into themselves and use *inaction* as their main perception (Gilbert, 2020; Gilbert & Donlan, 2016; Kahler, 2008; Pauley et al., 2002). Those strongly preferring this perception are still acting, but on the inside rather than the outside (Collignon, 2017; Kahler, 2008). These students prefer to reflect about what is going on, to synthesize what's in their mind's eye. They need solitude to do so. Imagination is what they use to handle what is expected of them (Gilbert, 2020; Gilbert & Donlan, 2016; Kahler, 2008; Pauley et al., 2002).

To succeed in interacting with students, you must communicate first by using the filter through which they view the world (Gilbert, 2020; Gilbert & Donlan, 2016; Kahler, 2008; Pauley et al., 2002). That way, they can receive you in the best way possible. You would not want a communication barrier to take place even before the heart of the conversation starts. To gauge where students are coming from, first try to identify whether they using logic, values, compassion, initiative, humor, or imagination (Gilbert, 2020; Gilbert & Donlan, 2016; Kahler, 2008; Pauley et al., 2002). Given this, ask yourself, "Do they seem strongest in thoughts, opinions, emotions, actions, reactions, or inactions?" You'll then be in a productive zone with them, communicating in a way that minimizes barriers and maximizes pathways.

TIP

When working with students and their parents, use a technique I call "getting to the nod." It is an attempt to get reinforcement from parents through the use of their perceptual frame. Start by noting that you are mindful of the parent's expectations of you. Share ideas that you and the parent might agree on in the perceptual frame you perceived works best for them. Keep your eyes mostly on the student, with respectful glances to the parent. Talk *to* the student and parent, not *about* the student *to* the parent. If you do this well, you'll see parents nodding along with you, and once they get to the nod, it becomes *you and them versus the problem*, not *you versus them*. Your ideas will be reinforced.

Fullan (2019) shares, "All good things (or bad for that matter) happen within processes" (p. 54). I agree. Kahler's (2008) model of personality and communication is based on *process* and shows us how to interact in a way that uses the process of communication to move content forward. This notion distills Kahler's rich theories into a four-part strategy: (1) ask, (2) tell, (3) play, and (4) care (Regier, 2020). Once again drawing from the work of Collignon (2017), Collignon and Legrand (2016), Collignon and colleagues (2010), Gilbert (2020), Gilbert and Donlan (2016), Kahler (2008), Pauley and colleagues (2002), and Regier (2020), I present how this strategy can work for assistant principals working with students.

1. Students who predominate in thoughts or opinions prefer to be *asked* about things and to do things (Gilbert, 2020; Gilbert & Donlan, 2016; Kahler, 2008; Pauley et al., 2002). Asking rather telling them to do something produces a more favorable response. Speaking the language of personality means asking those who tend toward the thought and opinion frames what they think, what options might be available, and what they would suggest (Collignon, 2017; Collignon & Legrand, 2016; Collignon et al., 2010; Kahler, 2008; Regier, 2020). You might ask, "What are some options here?" For those tending toward the opinion frame, ask them their perspective, what they believe would be fair, or what they would recommend, such as "What do you believe should be our next steps?" It's critical to keep the conversation moving forward productively by soliciting their thoughts and opinions along the way so that they can leverage their logic and values toward solutions.

2. Students who predominate in actions and inactions prefer you to *tell* them what do rather than ask (Gilbert, 2020; Gilbert & Donlan, 2016; Kahler, 2008; Pauley et al., 2002). Those who predominate in actions just want to know what needs to be done, so they can get right on it. Speaking the language of personality means students tending toward inactions often have difficulty initiating action themselves, so they benefit from direction (Collignon, 2017; Collignon & Legrand, 2016; Collignon et al., 2010; Kahler, 2008; Regier, 2020). With both, you can say some variation of "Tell me about _____." They will respond well to this, with their initiative and imagination respectively.

3. Students who predominate in reactions don't connect as much to being asked or told; rather, they just want to have a bit of fun along the way (Gilbert, 2020; Gilbert & Donlan, 2016; Kahler, 2008; Pauley et al., 2002). Speaking the language of personality, in short, allows you to connect with them as they want *play*, or react with playful interaction (Collignon, 2017; Collignon & Legrand, 2016; Collignon et al., 2010; Kahler, 2008;

Regier, 2020). With a high five or "Hey, dude," you'll be well on your way to productive conversation. Nonverbal cues are critical, as you want to appear jovial, with a sparkle in your eyes and an enthusiastic expression. They will react and give it back to you, with creativity in spades.

4. Students who predominate in emotions need *care* when communicating (Gilbert, 2020; Gilbert & Donlan, 2016; Kahler, 2008; Pauley et al., 2002). Speaking the language of personality will allow you to connect with them, as they want a nurturing, comforting tone with a warm expression (Collignon, 2017; Collignon & Legrand, 2016; Collignon et al., 2010; Kahler, 2008; Regier, 2020). Affect is everything with those coming from emotions. Rest assured, they will respond with compassion as well, which can be helpful to you as an assistant principal looking to solve problems for others.

A summary of the frames and strategies to interact with each (Kahler, 2008; Regier, 2020) appears in table 4.1.

TABLE 4.1: Speaking the Language of Personality

Perceptual Frame	Character Strengths or Talents to Deploy	What They Prize or Value	Tips for Assistant Principals in Conversation
Thoughts	Responsible, logical, and organized	Data and information	*Ask* questions that are factual and provide options to them.
Opinions	Dedicated, conscientious, and observant	Loyalty and commitment	*Ask* questions that draw out what's important to them.
Emotions	Compassionate, sensitive, and warm	Family and friendship	Use a nurturing tone and let them know they are appreciated and you *care* about them.
Actions	Persuasive, adaptable, and charming	Spontaneity and creativity	*Tell* them what you want them to do and make them a deal.
Reactions	Spontaneous, creative, and playful	Self-sufficiency and adaptability	Use an animated, lively tone, *play* around, and use humor.
Inactions	Imaginative, reflective, and calm	Privacy and their own space	*Tell* them what to do one thing at a time (start with a verb), and give them time and space to follow through.

Source: Kahler, 2008; Regier, 2020.

Use the Techniques of Reciprocation, Commitment and Consistency, and Scarcity for Positive Influence

You have the potential to influence others. This involves not only what you say and do in person-to-person conversation but also how you position yourself and that which you can control in your environment to invite those around you to buy in to what you say and try out what you suggest. This strategy is inspired by the work of Robert B. Cialdini (2021), whose book *Influence, New and Expanded: The Psychology of Persuasion*, shares six powerful techniques of influence used widely by professionals to get clients and customers to do what they want them to do. Cialdini (2021) calls these techniques *social jujitsu*. While in some cases, these techniques can be used nefariously, I'm suggesting you use them benevolently to help students; while they are manipulative to a degree, they are used toward good ends.

Cialdini's (2021) techniques include social proof, liking, authority, reciprocation, commitment and consistency, and scarcity. Here I focus on three of these techniques; you can intentionally weave them into your professional life so that when you ask students to do something for you that may be difficult, they will make a concerted attempt if for no other reason than out of an unconscious obligation. The ones I'll not address are social proof, liking, and authority because it's obvious that students will find something acceptable if their peers find it acceptable or if they like the person asking them, and mostly they follow authority as well. The other three—(1) reciprocation, (2) commitment and consistency, and (3) scarcity—are covered here.

The rule of reciprocation says that when someone else provides or does something for us, we try to repay in kind. What's fascinating is that we have a certain degree of indebtedness to those who have provided us something with or without our conscious knowledge. Cialdini (2021) makes a point that it is so ingrained in us that a synonym for *thank you* in the English language is *much obliged*. Assistant principals can work each day to use the rule of reciprocation for good results. Little things really do matter. Have a cup in your office full of extra stylistic pens that you collect at conferences, and offer them to students. Keep a candy dish handy with treats that students can grab if they stop by. I've found that fancy candy canes tend to be a big draw during the holiday season. One day per week consistently, bring a dozen baked cookies or snacks to the office, and share them with the students who stop by for attendance or behavioral infractions. Another idea is to brew fine coffee or tea, and offer disposable cups that students can fill and take back to class. Provide these when you're on commons-area duty as well. The key here is to continually make deposits in your relationships with students who might visit you on their not-so-good days. Students' sense of obligation in turn can be very helpful for you, but of course never take advantage of this in an unfair or harmful way.

Commitment and consistency is another aspect of influence and has to do with a fairly strong and, some might say, obsessive desire to remain consistent with what we have already done. This is especially true if we go on record and make a commitment to something (Cialdini, 2021). Once we take that stand, we tend to behave fairly consistently with the stand we have taken. This is particularly influential when someone makes a small commitment; the chances are that the person will make a much bigger commitment at another time to the same person.

Have you had the opportunity to request such as an assistant principal? Take, for instance, a conversation regarding attendance in class. One request might be innocuous, such as asking a student to make a commitment to receiving no tardies for the rest of the week. What about asking a student in another sense to go for at least the remainder of the day without saying something that will anger teachers? Where this factor of influence becomes particularly powerful is when folks commit to things in writing (Cialdini, 2021). The power of the principle magnifies, and as an assistant principal, you can easily ask for someone's brief statement that you can pull out later and celebrate with them. Writing it down is powerful, and subconsciously, they are much more apt to follow through because of consistency and commitment. You can reach a trifecta by asking for commitment in full view of others, if students are willing, which has unbelievable power.

Cialdini's (2021) scarcity principle notes that the opportunities we have seem more valuable to us when they are limited. It is amazing how powerfully motivating it is for people to think they are about to lose something they have. Cialdini (2021) also shares that something else is going on psychologically when scarcity is upon us: we lose freedoms when opportunities become less available. In short, we have fewer options to choose from once something valuable that is in limited supply is off the table.

Scarcity provides you great power in influence if you're willing to use it. It's a bit more sleight-of-hand, and some may find discomfort in it, because it is akin to a bluff while playing cards. If you are offering some options to students, whether in discipline, attendance, conflict resolution, or other conversations you are having while trying to redirect their behavior or holding them accountable, you provide an offer and allow students a bit of time to think about it. Then let them know that the offer is limited in terms of its availability. The point is that your option is scarce, and scarcity influences behavior. It is a valuable card to play.

I suggest using a combination of intentional and ongoing reciprocity, consistency and commitment, and scarcity as communication tools to influence students and colleagues. Cialdini (2021) notes, regarding principles such as these, that they have an "ability to produce a distinct kind of automatic, mindless compliance from people: a willingness to say yes without thinking first" (p. xvii); that is why they have both power and risk inherent in them. Thus, it makes their use by the good folks such as yourself even more important, as you will use them when naturally appropriate toward good and desirable ends. Cialdini (2021) shares, "The use of these levers by practitioners is not necessarily exploitative. It only becomes so when the lever is not a natural feature of the situation but is fabricated by the practitioner" (p. 446). Assistant principals have neither the need nor the inclination to fabricate, and they have others' best interests at heart when the situation naturally calls for an influential nudge in the right direction.

The How: Strategies to Use With Staff

The following strategies—meeting, then moving, and fostering interaction safety—are effective ways to lay the foundation for your work with staff.

Meet, Then Move

Inductive outcomes—those that materialize positively over time and are not rushed—work well to solve problems. Fullan (2019) says, "It's best to be right at the end of a meeting, not necessarily at the beginning of the meeting" (p. 16). Very true! He notes the need to find an entry point into a conversation, and work from there toward an amicable end. This is important for you because often staff with whom you're interacting have a much different view of things going into the conversation than you do. Resist the lure of hyper-efficiency. Don't think too hard about the long list of things on your desk and your need to check off the current conversation you are having. Doing so will cause you to move before you meet, and this is not optimal for addressing issues. You need to *meet* before you *move*, and moving is best done inductively.

The notion of meet, then move comes from the notion of meeting people where they are, a critical consideration for counselors and interventionists. Regier (2016) notes a similar strategy for helpers and clients that he learned from a mentor and supervisor early in his career. It is one in which "the helper joins the client, seeking to understand their frame of reference, validate their worldview, and affirm their experience. Together, then, the two move on a journey" (Regier, 2016, p. 134). Regier (2016) applies his signature "match and move" technique to productive problem solving. For assistant principals, the notion is much the same, with you as the service provider and the person you're working with as your client.

To meet, then move, simply be open to staff members' emotions when beginning a conversation; just listen. Meeting and moving is all about their feelings, their story, their worldview, and their dignity. You want to affirm all of it. They will know if you are. Goleman's (2013) work on social-emotional intelligence informs our strategy. Meeting involves the notion of emotional empathy: "we join the other person in feeling along with him or her; our bodies resonate in whatever key of joy or sorrow that person may be going through" (Goleman, 2013, p. 98). Moving is all about empathic concern, "leading us to care about them; mobilizing us to help if need be" (Goleman, 2013, p. 98).

Notice what your colleagues are saying and how they are saying it; strive to act as a supportive and nonjudgmental reflection of their emotions. Ensure you listen to what they say and how they say it. Look at their nonverbal cues. While doing so, conceive in your mind something you know about the other person that means something to them. You may or may not find a meaningful way to work it into the conversation. That's OK; just be aware. Once they share what is on their mind, offer a respectful pause. Then, when you respond, meet them by affirming first the emotions they have and the information they have shared. Paraphrase what you heard, and let them know you are doing so because you care to understand. Don't lead the conversation with policy, position, or presumption; instead affirm their perspective and demonstrate to them that it is you and them versus the problem. Nonverbal cues on your part are key in showing them that problem resolution is a team sport. Nod your head. Give them an affirming look. Say back to them what they say to you; this ensures they know you are listening and are interested. Through paraphrasing, accept openly any corrections they wish to suggest so you ensure you get it right. Then, invite them to move forward with you toward a resolution.

TIP

When confronted with a colleague who is upset, lead with your ears and your heart, not with your mouth and your head. Your mouth and head can always catch up later if needed. Staff members who are emotional often need to feel and hear things before analyzing them.

Foster Interaction Safety

It is ironic that in some cases in schools, the behaviors in students that raise the ire of staff members are the exact same behaviors that adults exhibit in monthly staff meetings. You see this with doing other things during meeting time, such as grading papers while the principal is talking, having sidebar conversations that distract from the main meeting message, and, probably most troubling, not treating each other with respect. In some cases, a few big personalities dominate the discussion, and if these are negative, they can derail what you're working for collectively as a school. Sometimes staff members are hesitant to speak up because others scoff at their ideas or belittle them with rolling eyes, furtive sneers or laughter, or even outright rebuke. In short, there is a need in our profession for interaction safety in relationships, and there's no better point person to foster this than the assistant principal. You're key in this role because you can model it indirectly and through strategic topical discussions rather than asking your principal to address the behaviors directly.

Here's how it works. Authors Frederick A. Miller and Judith H. Katz (2018), in *Safe Enough to Soar: Accelerating Trust, Inclusion, and Collaboration in the Workplace*, note organizations are only as successful as the interactions of the people within. They note interaction safety "accelerates building the trust so vital for inclusion and collaboration in one-to-one interactions, among teams, across departments, and throughout an organization" (Miller & Katz, 2018, p. 5). Teams with interaction safety are governed by assumptions or norms such as team members intentionally using skills to add value, the best solutions weigh all perspectives, ideas should be built on instead of torn down, and more can be achieved together than alone (Miller & Katz, 2018). With interaction safety, people feel as if they can share ideas without risk or being judged negatively, they're more inclined to embrace different viewpoints, and they are comfortable sharing that they do not have all the answers. They disagree agreeably (Miller & Katz, 2018).

Your job is to foster interaction safety in your organization, moving beyond islands of safety to safety as a way of life. I suggest you do this indirectly rather than advertise on a billboard what you are trying to accomplish. After all, it may be that little or no safe interaction exists in your school presently, and it will take some strategy, vulnerability, finesse, and resolve to bring it about. The experts share that the following indicators mean you have a ways to go: poking holes in ideas; a lot of *yes, but*s; criticizing more than thinking critically; a rush to show one is the smartest in the room; and walking on eggshells (Miller & Katz, 2018).

Here's what I suggest. Get permission from your principal for a fifteen- or twenty-minute discussion on a topic of your choice in each of your regularly held staff meetings. Let the principal know that you wish to facilitate using a technique you read about in this book. Make it more an exploratory discussion than one in which you plan to solve a problem, as this will allow you to get various points of view without the hazard of power plays if folks have selfish interests in the particular outcome. For example, don't try for a solution on who is going to get next year's student teachers assigned to them; rather, focus on how preservice teaching candidates in the future might receive both variety of experiences and continuity of placement with students while in the building.

First, share clearly with the group that your goal is to support the idea's energy rather than the idea's priority. Let group members know that you too will offer things in your head that have not spent much time getting refined, and request that they be kind in holding their criticisms. Encourage everyone to have your back and do the same for them. This offers vulnerability on your part to model what you wish others to use while brainstorming. Be honest that your goal is conversation safety; admit that there is a lot of wisdom in the room that can be at times intimidating for you, and possibly for others, even if that's not intended. The key is to frontload your hope for a safe experience in these conversations.

Let the group know that your goal is to replace the word *but* with the word *and* in these conversations, and ask for members' help in doing so. Also, with a wry eye and a smile, let them know that the word *however* is not welcome either; as Regier and King (2013) remind us, *however* is simply "*but* in a tuxedo" (p. 85). Use intentional pauses where you say, "Let's take a moment to reflect on what's been offered thus far, before continuing the conversation," and choreograph moments that allow everyone to listen to what's been said rather than wait for the next opportunity to jump in with an idea of their own. In fact, say directly that this is why you are doing it so that the energy of brainstorming doesn't upturn the ratio of two ears for every one mouth in the room. Humor helps when offering tactful requests and reminders.

If people self-deprecate and say that theirs was a not-so-good idea, commend them for their willingness to toss it out anyway. Don't offer false praise; rather, say their idea was necessary to keep creative juices flowing. Reinforce that the goal of idea energy is more important than idea priority. If you experience a feeling that you are not safe in the interaction for whatever reason, model what Miller and Katz (2018) suggest by leaning into that discomfort, disclosing it to the group, and letting the group know again you wish to feel safe in the interaction. If you sense that there were some awkward moments during your idea session, follow up individually with those you trust or those involved and ask them how things went. Get ideas on what you might do differently in facilitation the next time around.

Finally, ensure your technique includes solicitation of a balance of input from veteran staff, new staff, introverts, extroverts, and so on. Practice some transitions for introverts that include comments like:

> *We've had some great conversation, and I'm also going to be asking some of you who have been doing more of the sharing on the inside of your heads, rather than with the group thus far. I'm going to beg in advance your permission to ask some of you what's on your mind, in just a few minutes. I'd love to hear from you, and you are welcome to pass if you wish.*

After a few more people share out, call on some of your quieter folks or those more hesitant to share because of a perceived status differential. You'll be pleased at what you hear.

To ensure your idea sessions are productive as well as safe, follow up with a more formal, smaller, and representative group to do the work of taking these ideas and prioritizing them for future decision making. A good rule of thumb is to pilot an approach stemming from these sessions during the next semester, and if your pilot works well and receives positive feedback, expand into a new way of doing business the semester after that. This is a good pace that keeps things credible, productive, advancing, and, of course, safe.

The How: Strategy to Use With You

As you focus on developing positive relationships with students and staff, you'll find over time that when you work to bring out the best in others in terms of their dispositions, motivation, and performance, the way you come across yourself provides a ceiling for their capabilities. You can only invite others to act positively and pro-socially when you are there yourself. Thus, it becomes necessary for you to develop almost a clairvoyant awareness of your own relationship dynamic so that you can maintain a positive position that invites others to be the same. And when you move from an optimal state of being your best self toward something else, you must work quickly to recalibrate so that you are at your best once again—that's the strategy I'll discuss here.

Conversations with others are most effective when we have positive conceptions of both ourselves and those with whom we are conversing. With historical backgrounds in the foundational theories of transactional analysis, this idea comes our way via the book *I'm OK, You're OK* by Thomas A. Harris (2004). Discussions of life position undergird later work in adaptive communication (Collignon, 2017; Kahler, 2008; Regier, 2020), which terms the notion +/+.

Less optimal positions include those in which one of the people in the conversation moves away from a +/+ perspective and has a negative view of either the self (feelings of unworthiness for self, thus −/+) or of others (projecting that unworthiness on the other, thus +/−). This is when conversation breakdown can occur. Thus, recalibrating your position stems from an awareness of when you find yourself moving away from a +/+ perspective and from an ability to intentionally move yourself back into a +/+ frame of mind. It starts when you can identify what is happening when you're moving out of +/+. Building on the theories of Kahler (2008) and the leadership writing of Regier (2020), when you notice one of the following six mental or behavioral cues taking place, you are moving from +/+ toward either +/− or −/+ and know you must recalibrate.

1. You have an urge to show others you can think perfectly and often share too much detail in what you say with parenthetical statements. The latter can be a killer for those having to listen to you, and often their eyes glaze over. You then make more effort in overexplanation, and they tune out.

2. You have an urge to focus on what's wrong in a situation rather than what is right with it, and share too much detail in parenthetical questions. Others then think you are devaluing or disrespecting them and build up a wall against what you are saying.

3. You focus too much on trying to keep the peace in a situation rather than on addressing the issue with critical conversation. Often, you dance pensively around a delicate issue, do not get to the heart of it, and leave things half-solved. Problems then recur or get worse.

4. You struggle with thinking clearly and wish others would just solve the problem for you. You are perceived by others as lacking the responsibility or capability for solving the problem.

5. You say or think that others should tough things out or suck it up. This can be accompanied by a feeling that others deserve whatever predicament they're in, so they can just deal with it.

6. You pull away from others and even separate mentally from your own feelings or thoughts. Thus, you do not follow through with any problem solving that has begun.

If you identify any of these in your own behavior, the key is to step back, assess what is going on, spend time collecting yourself, ask for help if necessary, and then circle back once recalibrated. Remember, value both yourself and the person with whom you are having the conversation as worthy of an individual perspective, and remain the bigger person if you must.

TIP

Visualization helps you recalibrate by recalling a prior conversation you had when you were not in +/+, then imagining you were a fly on the wall watching yourself in a conversational redo. What would +/+ look like this time around? What would you say differently? What would you do differently?

You can be proactive in recalibrating. Embrace the fact that positive relationships are never a given; they are works in progress, and they can take more effort than negative relationships. Be sure to visualize success in the interaction. Imagine others bringing either a +/− (where they are pointing fingers at you) or −/+ (where they are getting down on themselves). Imagine your choice to avoid their lure of drama. Don't be a rescuer looking for a victim to save, a victim looking for a persecutor, or a persecutor looking for a victim (Karpman, 2014; Regier, 2016; Regier & King, 2013). During an interaction, thank them for sharing, and paraphrase what they have just said to show you heard them, then say something like, "I would like also to explore [insert what you wish to explore together as allies]. I'm happy to work to solve this. May we schedule some time? I'm free later this afternoon or tomorrow." This gives a bit of a cool-off period and time to recalibrate.

TIP

Assistants can be helpful when angry people storm into your office. They can say, "[Assistant principal], I know you'll want to spend some time with [angry person], but I have [person X] on your calendar in the next ten minutes. May I schedule your conversation with [angry person] for a little bit later in the day so you can spend at least half an hour together?"

Don't be too hard on yourself when you move outside +/+. Someone invariably will push your buttons, and you'll probably end with something less than a win-win. Assistant principals have hundreds of chances for redos each day, as when you stay +/+ more and more, the neural grooves you build provide you the strength to do it more and more over time. If you can remain out of this dance of drama and above the fray, you'll avoid a lot of trouble.

Toolkit for Tomorrow: Next Steps

These next steps provide some suggestions for how you can put the ideas in this chapter into action.

- If you find yourself struggling in conversation with others, share with them that you are trying to envision the two of you beside each other with the same goal ahead, and ask if they are willing to give it a try with you.

- Ensure every conversation in your office is an opportunity to build capacity. Start the conversation by showing folks how much you care. This can be as simple as asking them how they are doing or noticing something about them recently that deserves a compliment. Then, share with them what you know and what you wish to accomplish. End the conversation in a way that preserves their dignity and increases agency.

- Do not sit across your desk from parents visiting your office; instead, sit next to them and position yourself at a forty-five-degree angle to them when having a discussion. As author and leadership development specialist Todd Whitaker (2014) says, "Sidle up."

- Connect more intentionally with each student with the perception in which they view the world; begin asking, telling, caring, and playing intentionally to see the response you get.

- Complete the professional development activity on page 79 to help reinforce communicating adaptively. You will think about various individuals you work with and come up with strategies for communicating with those with whom you have difficulty. This will offer you a candid glimpse into something you'll need to put some effort into.

Professional Development: A Deeper Dive—Developing Relationships

Instructions: Use the information from this chapter to first identify the filter through which the following individuals view the world (thoughts, opinions, emotions, actions, reactions, or inactions), brainstorm some things to say to connect with the filter, and then rate the level of comfort you have in viewing things from their perspective (low, medium, or high). Next, list how best they might be approached, by either asking, telling, caring, or playing.

Role	With what filter does this person view the world? (Thoughts, opinions, emotions, actions, reactions, or inactions)	What specific things can you say to connect with this filter?	How comfortable are you with communicating through this filter? (Low, medium, or high) What might you do to build your own capacity to access this filter for interaction?	How best can you approach this person? (Ask, tell, play, or care)
School principal				
Guidance counselor				
School custodian				
School secretary				

Role	With what filter does this person view the world? (Thoughts, opinions, emotions, actions, reactions, or inactions)	What specific things can you say to connect with this filter?	How comfortable are you with communicating through this filter? (Low, medium, or high) What might you do to build your own capacity to access this filter for interaction?	How best can you approach this person? (Ask, tell, play, or care)
Teacher with whom you have difficulty communicating				
Student with whom you have difficulty communicating				
Parent with whom you have difficulty communicating				
Someone else with whom you have difficulty communicating				

CHAPTER 5
PROTECTING AND PROMOTING PRIORITIES AND PEOPLE

Each day, parents send to you their most precious resource. They trust you to protect their kids amidst myriad influences affecting growth and development. Schools and parents make a pact: parents forego caretaking for the better part of each weekday, and their children will return home safely and better off educationally and developmentally. As with any promise, no matter how well intentioned, things can go awry. Standing between that pact and a broken promise is you.

You are your school's sentry of safety and vanguard of security. You have keen awareness of what people can accomplish on their best days and what they're prone to do on their worst. You must discern who is having a bad day, even when they're not advertising it, and provide help. Basically, your actions must serve to protect and promote the priorities of your school and the people within it.

This chapter offers a look at the heart of your role, which starts by framing your daily approach to handling situations and what you employ strategically for positive outcomes. It shows the what and why of where you spend your time, as well as how, by offering strategies to use with students, staff, and yourself.

The What and the Why

Yours is a high-velocity position from the moment you arrive each day. Anything that has happened to your students from the time they left school the day prior to the time of their arrival on the current day can influence how things go for them and for you. Good assistant principals deftly handle most things thrown at them. Better assistant principals establish a proactive game plan that frames their daily approach in both thought and behavior, which helps them head off problems before they start. Deft framing is like a GPS, keeping you in the right space to approach situations and represent yourself; framing ensures you are making the most of your role.

An ideal way to envision a viable approach to framing comes from the work of Lee G. Bolman and Terrence E. Deal (2017) in *Reframing Organizations: Artistry, Choice, and Leadership*. Based on twenty-five years of research and observation, Bolman and Deal (2017) call on leadership to operate simultaneously through four frames. Those frames look like this for assistant principals.

1. **Structural frame:** The titular authority you have and how you manage under the rules of school

2. **Symbolic frame:** What you project in terms of image

3. **Political frame:** How you work with groups and constituencies and maintain your school's reputation

4. **Human relations frame:** How you connect with people

Bolman and Deal's (2017) frames anchor you nicely, as they provide a four-point guidance system on how you operate. They keep your bases covered and ensure you stay on track. Another way to think about them is a four-paned window through which you can look to ensure you are acting comprehensively.

For example, let us say you encounter a situation where you learn that a small group of students is smoking—possibly marijuana—while on lunch. Your structural frame would be the standards to which you use your managerial authority to enforce school policy and local laws. Your symbolic frame would project your image of reasoned temperament, along with disappointment and seriousness regarding how drugs adversely impact safety. You might reach out personally, through your political frame, to homeowners nearby who may have witnessed the event to assuage their concerns; the goal would be responsiveness and a positive reputation for your school. Finally, your human relations frame would ensure all are accorded dignity during the ordeal and help you connect empathetically to the students in question. One goal of framing appropriately is so that you can "keep the main thing *the main thing*—and that main thing is student success," as my superintendent used to say (J. Jeffrey, personal communication, September 3, 1996).

Protecting your priorities and people has you asking yourself the question, "What do I do each day that inspires students to dream?" While this might be a tough question to answer, it is critical to explore. Some students simply do not have anyone at home who inspires them to do anything; in fact, they may have family or others in their lives who cast doubt on their potential. Some have it even worse than that. These students need you to keep your main thing as their main thing. Others are fortunate to have mentors, heroes, and parents who love them. For those, there is always room for another advocate, champion, and dream whisperer.

Something I have learned about students is the fact that whether they admit it or not, they wish to be known. Students want us to know and respect them as individuals. They want us to accept them for who they are and what they represent. They want to be able to be themselves during some pretty challenging years of their lives, and they want others to allow them to discover themselves if they aren't quite there yet. More so, they want to know they matter—that they will be missed if they're not around and that they mean something to others (Wilfong, 2021). The strategies I offer in this section allow you to connect with students and keep their main thing as your main thing.

The How: Strategies to Use With Students

The following strategies—"playing catch" each morning, being a moment maker, and playing the name game—are effective ways to focus on priorities and to lay the foundation for your work with students.

"Play Catch" Each Morning

I recall an old U.S. Army television commercial stating that soldiers in the U.S. Army did more before 9:00 a.m. than most people did all day. "Playing catch" each morning allows you to focus on relationships to build strengths within your students, and just like in the Army, all before 9:00 a.m. It has to do with your own interpersonal responses to students. The idea here is to stand at the school entrance to greet students as they arrive. Coffee or another beverage is optional, but no matter what, bring a smile. Playing catch really refers to the notion that you want to have students share something with you on arrival to school each day so that you can gauge how things are going not only individually with each student but overall with school climate and the day ahead.

The next step in playing catch is to have a team on hand if any red alerts hit your radar. Have a few folks on the inside of the school who are at the ready if you detect something is not going well with a student's day. It could simply be a matter of a student needing a kind ear, or it could be something that requires greater intervention. A few key staff members who assist you inconspicuously by serving as interventionists to help ensure the day starts off safe and sound are well placed if you see something afoot. People serving in these roles might include school volunteers, paraprofessionals, school counselors, school social workers, or your office staff members. Teacher volunteers are also great, especially those who have an interest in future leadership roles and wish for some hands-on experience working with students in this capacity. In order to prioritize these interventions and ensure that volunteers are on continual standby, consider your interventions as a key and natural part of any given school day, coexisting with and complementing other roles each of you have.

For example, you might see a student avert his gaze while on his way in with a group of friends. If this student is typically gregarious and greets you with a high five or smile, the change in behavior—while maybe nothing—might be something. Of course you don't want to make a mountain out of a molehill or call for a red alert unless one is really needed. In this case, you would quietly whisper in the ear of your office receptionist, who might make quiet outreach to an interventionist standing by. That person could then casually walk by the student's locker or classroom and offer the same friendly greeting you did at the door, take a reading of the situation, and then decide if the student would benefit from a conversation.

Another example might be a student who makes a quick comment that things could be crazy today; perhaps she also shares some information pertaining to some conflict or drama outside of school that happened over the weekend. In this case, you might offer the same whisper to your office assistant, who might make two calls this time—one to a school social worker who could casually find one of the reported people in conflict, and another to a teacher volunteer who might look up the other. Both can hold casual conversations individually, sharing nonchalantly but candidly that they heard from another staff member there was a bit of concern over the weekend. In each case, they would ask whether it's all good in terms of how the students will conduct themselves in school or if they would like some time and space to navigate the situation before it begins to bother them even more. In all cases, your trained interventionists would help them work the problem. School adults should always stick to the story that they heard it from other adults, not from fellow students. Now, students might not believe this, and that's OK; the operative point is that students know that it is safe to report things to adults without their confidence violated, and that your adult interventionists care enough to follow up discreetly and quickly.

TIP

When playing catch at the entrance to school each day, ensure you offer a smile, nod, and wave to those dropping off students at school. It takes effort for parents, guardians, and loved ones to move through the hustle and bustle and get their kids to your doorstep on time; affirm their efforts.

Over time, it will reassure both parents and students that you are not only eagerly awaiting their arrival at the front entrance but also are quick to mobilize support if the school day is not off to a good start. Your vantage point is also key in that you can watch what happens with family members in the car as the students deboard. It provides keen insight into family dynamics or anything that might have happened last evening or on the way to school that can get in the way of a positive school experience that day.

Be a Moment Maker

Your connections with others are high-impact opportunities that deserve strategic framing. You're not moving about a school just to get from point A to point B; connections along the way, and the moments that comprise them, are just as important, if not more so. Typically, when people approach you, they have something on their mind they wish to discuss. It could be something nagging at them and preventing them from thinking about anything else. As well, when you approach students, your title has a tendency to put them on high alert, especially if they have done something shortsighted and think you have just found out about it. Your interactions with students are a few of the hundreds you'll experience in a given day, yet their time spent with you might be the only thing they remember at the end of the day. It is a big deal; don't minimize the moment.

This brings up an important point—those in conversation with you need your full attention and devotion, especially given that in the back of your mind there are undoubtedly ten or more situations awaiting you in your office when you return, and probably more you haven't uncovered. Think about it this way: when you walk away to deal with what is next, you'll be thinking about the *what's next*, and the other person will still be hanging on every word you said, taking it far beyond the bell at the end of the day. Thus, it is critical you envision yourself as a moment maker.

I recall watching the television show *American Idol* for many years when Simon Cowell was one of the judges. Cowell was known as one with incredibly high standards and a frank style that would lend itself to some direct feedback indeed. False praise was just not Cowell's modus operandi. So when a truly incredible performance captivated the audience, judges, and home viewers alike, Cowell would predictably utter the phrase to the contestant, "You just had *a moment*." In doing so, Cowell was serving as a moment maker for those contestants because he invited them to own their potency and savor success.

You can do the same as an assistant principal, not necessarily by just copying Cowell's phrasing, although at times, that may be appropriate. Rather, be truly *in the moment* with the person to whom you're talking, and show unwavering interest in what that person is saying or doing. Further, when talking with people, you can show you're in the moment by noticing something about them that is special, unique, and outlying. Let them know it. The key is to be all in with the people you are sharing a chat with or receiving information from, taking time to absorb and digest what they are saying because what you say next has few do-overs. Ensure you do not telegraph that you are thinking about your next meeting, and hopefully you'll not be in your next meeting's headspace until the conversation is done. Be a moment maker.

TIP

Environments create moments. In commons areas, design intentional spaces for conversation. Do this by adding comfortable chairs for students to sit in duos, trios, or small groups. Flank them with plants and small tables for drinks and their supplies, so that they can work on laptops and devices. Use these areas yourself. When someone wishes to speak with you, invite them to sit down and talk. You'll still be able to supervise the commons area from your vantage point and will probably be more in tune with what they say.

Play the Name Game

For many years, I worked with students who came to our school after having difficulty at other schools. I learned quickly that students who feel disenfranchised haven't felt, in their school experiences, that educators know much about them. I tried to undo this. One of the strategies that helped was the name game. I played it two times per year. Here's how it goes.

When new groups of students arrive at your school, divide their student orientation sessions into groups of about twenty-five or thirty if you can; this works for groups of up to fifty. You'll want a good-sized group such as this as you'll be breaking them down into smaller groups. The goal is not to have students learn about rules and regulations; rather, it is to build community. As students arrive, the public address system is playing music—typically something upbeat. Welcome students as they arrive with a wireless microphone; have a small group of faculty and staff to greet them. Give students five or six name badges with adhesive backs. Ask them to put their first names with bold marker on the front of all of them. Then they put one badge on themselves and drop the rest into a big bucket or box.

Arrange chairs in one large circle—all twenty-five or thirty and up to fifty. Add some chairs for the teachers and staff, who intersperse themselves among the students. As the students move in to their seats, act as host, chatting with them as they arrive. Have nearby your co-host—someone on faculty or staff who is into team building and is an extrovert (or who can fake it). When all students and staff are seated and the circle is full, turn things over to your co-host (both of you should have a microphone). Move to the outside of the circle and wander around the circle while your co-host gets things started from the inside.

At this point, you'll want to fade out the introductory music to signal that your program is about to begin. Your co-host then welcomes everyone, shares a bit about the school, and lets them know what a positive experience the school year will be. No school rules are mentioned. Your co-host will then pass the microphone to teachers and staff to introduce themselves. After this, your co-host announces it is time for a grounding and greeting activity. Some students will predictably groan, and that's OK. This is when you get out the other name badges.

Have faculty and staff randomly pull five name badges for each student and provide them to students sitting around the circle. Each student has around five randomly named badges. Let the students know that the next time they hear music played—in other words, at your musical signal— they are to find those with the names of the badges they are holding, and stick the badge on them. It can be on the arm, shoulder, back of the head, back, leg—anywhere that is appropriate, of course. After about five to seven minutes, you'll notice that most students are having a great time. Introverts may need help from staff. Once most names are affixed, ask everyone to go back to their seats in the large circle. This is where the first part of the name game ends, but the fun is just beginning. Thank them for being good sports and for their cooperation. Tell them you had a lot of fun learning some of their names and finding friendly faces. It's now time for some group work as part of your orien-tation. What they don't know is that you'll still be focusing on their names during the next activity while their minds will be on something else.

Break students into groups of five to seven to form smaller circles facilitated by a teacher or staff member. These discussions involve whatever content you wish. It could be talking about worst fears and best outcomes or discussing the question, What do you need from your school? One group member from each of the smaller group circles will record responses on a flip chart. Then the group reports its responses to everyone else from time to time, facilitated by your co-host.

While these small-group discussions are going on, you move among the groups, circling on the outside, making eye contact, and offering positive affirmations, yet in actuality you are doing some-thing else entirely: *learning names*! Names are everywhere. You can look across a small circle and see them on student foreheads, you can look down and see a name on a student's back. Each student has five name badges randomly placed—with some furtive effort, you can start learning names. This activity continues for a while until the small-group activity goals are met and also until you are more comfortable yourself with student names.

Now, all this can end here. You can go about your business and simply begin using student names more effectively, as you take a break and ready the day for what is to happen next. Yet if you want to challenge yourself in plain view of others and have the risk orientation, you certainly can extend yourself and prove to students how important their names are to you. This is a bold strategy that I used for many years, and I only suggest this if you really don't mind the level of difficulty and pres-sure it provides. Having said that, it *is* powerful, if you have the stomach and memory for it. Here's what we did, two times each year.

After calling students and staff to bring their chairs back into a big circle, the co-host asks students to remove name badges. Your co-host then asks you as the school administrator for your wallet. The co-host pulls out a random bill from your wallet (with your prior permission, of course)— sometimes a one-dollar bill; other times, a twenty-dollar bill. The co-host promises the students that if you cannot go around the entire circle, shake hands or fist bump, and greet each of the students by their first names, they will get the bill, and the co-host will just keep pulling bills from your wallet until you're all the way around the circle. Jaws will drop.

TIP

Be intentional in the name game. Start with the student whose name you've had the most difficulty remembering. Pretend you are starting randomly. This way, you get that person's name out of the way first—*sigh of relief*—and the student feels like the most important person in the room.

The point here is that through the name game, students know they matter enough for us to know them as individuals and to expend that effort. The power of a name is a connection worth making and keeps the main thing as the main thing, with priorities and people.

The How: Strategies to Use With Staff

The following strategies—having regard for regard and valuing the personal in the professional—are effective ways to lay the foundation for your work with staff.

Have Regard for Regard

What we see when we look into the eyes of staff is directly proportional to the relationship we are going to have with them. If we see them as prone to mediocrity, tunnel vision, or noncompliance, we will look for things to curb, curtail, and circumvent. If we see them as prone to teaching excellence, engagement, and enthusiasm, we will look for ways we can celebrate their energy. Assistant principals benefit greatly from *having regard for regard*, meaning keeping the main thing—student achievement—as the main thing by having unconditional positive regard for those with whom we work.

TIP

Two affirmations help in offering unconditional positive regard: (1) forgive in advance and (2) baby steps. Thinking to yourself *forgive in advance* when you see someone coming toward you who is about to be hostile helps put you in a good place. Over time, if the person becomes only marginally tolerable, keep in mind *baby steps*; at least things are moving in the right direction.

Noted humanist psychologist Carl Rogers (1957) made unconditional positive regard a staple of his work and terms of client-therapist relationships. He shares that it involves an unwavering acceptance of people and support of them, no matter how they are behaving or what they are saying. He notes the importance of client-centered therapy (Rogers, 1989), which also has educational applications, as I have found and will note in this book. If you judge unconditional positive regard as important and an integral part of your perspective, you will find opportunities to embrace the diversity and uniqueness of those with whom you collaborate. I believe that if we see colleagues positively and imagine they have a dream or ask them to share it, we will see them as people experiencing the best version of themselves. I hope you want your staff to see themselves in the best possible way at least once each day. Projecting unconditional positive regard on them might bring about just that.

Value the Personal in the Professional

Staff members arrive to school each day to do important work for the school and those within. They bring with them myriad professional skills and talents and have hundreds of conversations critical to student success and the next pedagogical discovery. Yet, behind the polished visage is a real person who is anything but uniform and, we might also say, anything but polished. We all bear burdens. We all carry hope, interests, personal dreams, and love for those on the outside. These all serve as a filter through which we direct professional productivity and agency.

In short, we are all very personal beings operating as professionals, and the more we find that we can take care of both, the more successful we are. It is impossible to shut down your personal life when walking into the school building. Administrators who do not understand this will not invite peak performance in staff. We are simply older versions of our student selves when we had an inability to separate our lives outside from the inside. While we may conceal it better, as adults, it still resides as a duality.

Valuing the personal in the professional means to have compassion and tolerance for when the personal bumps up against the professional—give a bit of space and even lend a hand. It could be that a staff member caring for an ailing parent may need to take a phone call during class. If you feel this is not optimal, help design a workaround for your staff member, such as someone taking the class for a few minutes, rather than making teachers feel like they must act subversively. School administrators would do well to provide individual accommodations to staff members regarding arrival and dismissal times because of their own childcare limitations. I realize this is more the principal's call, with potential collective bargaining agreement limitations. Still, it is something important to people, and it's real. People need *equitable*, not necessarily *equal*, treatment.

Valuing the personal in the professional means to remember things that people say to you in passing. Know your staff members' spouses' names; remember them and use them in future conversation. Recall the names of children or favorite family activities. If you have to keep a list in your cloud-based filing system, do so. Glance at these lists before walking down the hall to meet people. Be kind in asking about that summer vacation. Recall someone's favorite dessert or hobby. Bring a smile to colleagues' faces because you remembered something about them that they would have never thought. This is important stuff in the big picture of the people business we're in.

Note you spend at least forty hours per week at school, probably more than the waking hours you might spend at home. So, doesn't it make sense to create an environment where people can be themselves, know that they have others to help them when they need it, and feel that they are appreciated for being there? Of course it does. You'll find that over time, your principal will be thankful that you have a finger on the pulse of school staff, and it will help them with better leadership decision making as well if you have someone's rest of the story. You might find valuing the personal in the professional fosters better staff morale, trust, and mutual respect, and it won't go unnoticed that these things result in better staff retention.

The How: Strategy to Use With You

Protecting priorities and people is the way you provide yourself a true north in determining why you went into this profession in the first place and the legacy you might leave. With good modeling, others may follow your lead and take steps to protect priorities and people from their own vantage points, which I would hope are contributory. Inarguably, one of your own priorities is to ensure that teaching takes place in an environment conducive for learning to happen. The strategy in this section, starting your days with SODA, offers a way to examine your priorities.

SODA is an acronym I developed that stands for *safety, order, discipline*, and *attendance*. It's like a recipe that relates to how you sort out what's urgent, important, both, or neither. A good recipe helps with most everything. Recipes involve a sequence of necessary ingredients, certain conditions under which to implement those ingredients, and indicators of whether or not you were successful in your attempt.

By starting each day with SODA, you'll have a game plan for efficiency and effectiveness. Attend to each part of the acronym in order. Each component depends upon the one preceding. Order doesn't happen without safety; discipline does not happen without safety and order. Regarding attendance, some students might be apprehensive in attending if you do not tend to safety, order, and discipline under your watch. Other students admittedly attend school no matter what, and because of how they behave, they are much of the reason you must focus on the first three ingredients. Thus, this is your method each morning to establish your daily coordinates, and with a bit of intentionality, SODA can move you ahead smartly.

After you greet students at the front entrance, supervise the commons, and wish them well on their way to class, walk the building, and pay attention to what's going on around you through the lens of safety. What happened this morning? What were students talking about? Are there any concerns or issues that could boil over if not addressed? Did the students seem extra squirrely or disorderly and resist heading to class? If so, why? Are they upset about the way something was handled that could manifest in a lack of safety or order later in the day?

Ask your assistant if any news concerning safety and order has spilled into the office. *S* and *O* are covered. Once you've considered them, turn to *D* and ask yourself, "Are there some pressing disciplinary issues that need to be handled sooner rather than later?" Often, a quick conversation with a few students is all that is necessary to help them understand their situations are a priority. A quick touchpoint with discipline and a few well-placed assurances may head off any preemptive behavior on their part.

Finally, with the *D* of discipline taken care of, is there anything you can do with *A*, attendance, to ensure little issues don't become bigger issues? With safety, order, and discipline duly handled, you can then turn your attention to a handful of students nearing their limit on unexcused absences and prioritize a bit of work with your attendance secretary to ensure they are in class. You might make quick contact with parents or guardians. This morning check of attendance helps keep work off your desk later and prevents students from becoming their own worst enemies. Quick attendance attention might be a stroll through the building or a walk around the grounds, just to ensure that all students who left for school are no longer in the hallways, parking lots, or streets nearby.

TIP

For attendance efficiency and minor infraction follow-up, send notes to students shortly before they leave for the day, inviting them to meet you in the office area at a certain time the next morning, after your touchpoint with SODA. Your focus is to move through infractions efficiently and minimize student time out of class.

Toolkit for Tomorrow: Next Steps

These next steps provide some suggestions for how you can put the ideas in this chapter into action.

- If you have a spouse or partner with whom you like to share, find a moment-making example each day to share in the evening over dinner or drinks. It helps to put the heavy lifting of the day into perspective if you end it focused on one difference you have helped to make.

- Ask your teachers to provide the name of at least one quiet student who seems to blend in and does an average job. This may help you in your quest to search and connect with students each day, as you can strategically place yourself outside of a classroom where these students are exiting.

- Complete the professional development activity and worksheet on page 91 to practice prioritizing all the tasks that you encounter daily as an assistant principal.

Professional Development: A Deeper Dive—Protecting and Promoting Priorities and People

Instructions: First, read the following scenarios. Then answer the questions to practice prioritizing the wide variety of events that may await you in your assistant principal in-box on any given day.

SCENARIOS

These scenarios represent the kinds of situations you might encounter when you arrive at school in the morning. You might not face all of these on one day, though it could happen on a particularly busy day.

- *A local reporter is sitting in your office, hoping to interview you about a hotel party that was raided last evening. Your football starting line and three members of your National Honor Society were in attendance.*

- *A student is awaiting you in a side office, as he has arrived at school realizing that he has his shotgun in his truck. He was up at the crack of dawn, hunting so that his mom (who is on public assistance) could make bird stew for dinner. Your state has recently enacted a mandatory expulsion provision for firearms brought to school, subject to four exceptions under state statute.*

- *The school custodian wants five minutes of your time to discuss an ongoing problem he is having trouble staying on top of: evening bathroom facilities at middle school athletic events.*

- *You find a note from the band director, who is incensed that a nostalgic jukebox has been installed in the student cafeteria to play songs during lunch. Students love the new jukebox (actually, the "old" jukebox), as they have never seen anything like it. The note reads, "Some of these songs we are hearing every day played 100 times have profanity! Please SEE ME!"*

- *Three sophomore students want you to visit the cafeteria where they are working and see the "Stop, Drop, and Roll" posters they made for the elementary students.*

- *You have a disciplinary report for three students (varsity football players) who beat up another male student last Friday, just after school and prior to suiting up for the football game. The student who was beaten had been behaving very disrespectfully to others in the building, making derogatory remarks and even violating personal space. He was a student who relocated from another locale to live with his grandparents in your town, as he had been in quite a bit of trouble where he came from. The football players mentioned to your secretary last Friday that they just didn't like their friends treated like that. The athletic director was planning to let the students play football. Your principal wants a report by lunchtime on what you plan to do, noting that some in your community would consider what the football players did "community service."*

- *Local law enforcement is bringing a K9 unit to your school at 9:15 a.m. to conduct a surprise sniff of the lockers and commons areas of the school. Their arrival is a secret, yet you hear that their handlers stopped at the local pastry shop to get coffee. Students walking by on their way to school learned of the dogs' planned visit when they saw a big "K9 Unit" on the truck and alerted their friends.*

- *You receive a list of students who need to see you this morning for reasons having to do with discipline or attendance:*

    + *Anne—Excessive tardies*

    + *Edwin—Told teacher to "F off"*

    + *Lynnette—Skipped third class period*

+ *Carrie—Getting bullied*

+ *Bronson—Cyberbullying another student*

+ *Scotty—Violation of technology policy (downloading crude content)*

+ *Robert—Forging hall pass signatures*

+ *Connelly—Skipping fourth class period*

+ *William—Says someone is going to beat him up sometime today*

+ *Rich—Defacing school property*

+ *Katherine—Reported to have drugs on her, selling frequently at lunch*

+ *Liza—Under the influence of drugs in class, reportedly bought them before school*

+ *Michael—Reportedly poured sugar in a teacher's car's gas tank last evening*

+ *Jasper—Could have a knife longer than what is allowed by state statute in his pocket*

+ *Aaron—Refused to do his work for his teacher*

+ *Of the preceding student referrals:*

    » *Which situations are urgent?*

    » *Which situations are important?*

    » *Which situations are urgent and important?*

    » *Which situations are neither urgent nor important?*

- *A group of senior citizens is going to be eating brunch in your hospitality program dining room adjacent to the cafeteria, and you are expected to give a speech of about five minutes. This speech is happening soon, and you have done nothing yet to prepare.*

- *Many teachers are absent on this particular day, and it does not appear that the substitute teachers are reading their lesson plans, which state that they are supposed to be out in the halls before school and during passing times.*

- *The principal wants you stop by her office this morning to chat about the upcoming leadership retreat.*

- *You are facing an agreement with your teacher's union regarding deadlines for classroom observations, and two five-minute walkthroughs are scheduled for this morning.*

- *Your choir teacher wants to have five minutes of your time to discuss the fundraiser planned for the upcoming holiday.*

- *Your administrative assistant, who is your trusted number two and the "mirror" that you need to see yourself in from time to time, wants ten or fifteen minutes of your time. She notes that she may have some information that will help you today.*

- *A parent is in your office. She is in tears. It involves her son's desire to drop out of school, as his frustration has reached a tipping point. She is hoping you can help talk him down and is willing to bring him in from the car if you have a bit of time.*

- *You have a web filter on school email. At 10:15 a.m. you get a notification that the filter caught an email addressed to a teacher who is out ill. The message from a girl to the teacher is a cry for help saying that suicide is a possibility. The girl's mother has prior run-ins with school administration and has made it clear she does not want you or the "know-nothing counselor" talking to her daughter.*

page 2 of 4

QUESTIONS TO ANSWER FOR EACH SCENARIO

I encourage you to make multiple copies of this worksheet and work through the scenarios one by one. While handling these types of situations in actuality, a worksheet might in fact slow you down rather than help you; however, these scenarios and the worksheet can allow you to practice the thinking, analysis, and prioritization skills you'll need to employ for each.

This would make a great team learning activity, where you might take scenarios separately and strategize what the worksheet should include, in terms of your notes and thoughts. Just like in actual situations, decisions do not happen in a vacuum. Be a good talent scout, look around you and gather a trusted team, and challenge yourself with this in-box activity.

Scenario:

Classification of Event (circle one):

Urgent   Important

Urgent and important   Neither urgent nor important

What do you do? Choose options that make sense from the following list, and make notes about your plan of action.

Connect with others for more information:

Consult an expert source:

Coordinate a team response:

Move on it individually:

Act:

Pause:

Delegate:

Ignore:

What else do you do?

Unknowns or unintended potential consequences:

What were you thinking?

Source: © 2017 by Ryan Donlan, David Hoffert, and David Robertson. Adapted with permission.

CHAPTER 6
LEVERAGING FIRM AND FAIR DISCIPLINE

School discipline, done well, is a both–and obligation, rather than an either–or. What I mean is that our best systems of school discipline are both firm and fair, not simply one or the other. When you don't have both, what do you have? School discipline that is fair without being firm runs the risk of providing no deterrence for future misbehavior. Such is the case with systems of discipline that are rehabilitative but overly restorative and only mildly punitive. Any of us who has worked in schools can attest, anecdotally, that when discipline is too light and touchy-feely, student behavior can run amok and may even create unsafe situations. Yet the converse can be harmful as well. School discipline that is firm without being fair does well for deterrence yet does little for rehabilitation.

Take, for example, school policies that are overly prescriptive regarding what could be defined as a weapon. Perhaps you recall seeing news stories about students getting expelled for bringing a knife to school to cut up treats to be shared with the class or that was used only for whittling. One important takeaway here from these stories is that strict adherence to rules about weapons—or anything that is defined as dangerous in school—taken without adequate analysis of context or common sense can end up causing more harm than good. Shortsighted and unflinching decisions can have you working against your own community standards rather than in support of them. Families will lose confidence in you as one who understands what developing children and teenagers are all about.

When discipline is both firm and fair, it is educational, rehabilitative, deterring, restorative, and, over time, positive in terms of students' growth and development. This chapter presents information on what assistant principals must focus on and learn regarding discipline—at the very least, why it is important—and techniques to use with students, staff, and yourself.

The What and the Why

As an assistant principal, you deal with a range of issues, such as skipping infractions, bad decisions off or on campus, rumor mongering, student conflict, substance abuse, vandalism, hostile behavior toward staff, class disruption, theft, academic dishonesty, and many others. There should be little doubt who is in charge. Your obligation is to get to the truth of any situation quickly, and thus allow all involved to be their best selves restoratively, not their worst selves by covering things up. Keep in mind that often when students are in your office, there are handfuls of others hoping these students' behavior will improve. Firm and fair consequences today will help with better decisions tomorrow, either through learning or deterrence. In chapter 7 (page 115), I will discuss how these circumstances can give rise to teachable moments that you can use to students' advantage; for now, let's focus on the immediate needs of the situation.

Because your actions as an assistant principal are likely to overlap at some point or another with students' rights under the law, it pays to be conversant in the policies of your country; state, province, or territory; and city. In this section, I will go into some detail about laws in the United States that may pertain to the assistant principalship. I strongly recommend that whatever country you work in, you familiarize yourself with these laws as necessary. In the United States, student discipline comes with the obligation to protect student due process, both substantively and procedurally. "The Due Process Clause of the Fourteenth Amendment prohibits the states from depriving any person of life, liberty, or property without due process of law" (Roth, D'Agostino, & Brown, 2010, p. 191). When states make education public, it then becomes a property interest when all children have the right to attend (Alexander & Alexander, 2012, 2019). As well, as public schools are funded and regulated by the state, they have a lawful obligation to provide due process, in line with the expectations inherent in the Fourteenth Amendment. Substantively, this means that in the case of considering student discipline, schools should provide notice of action, and levy consequences that fit the infractions—the punishment should fit the crime, as the saying goes (Schimmel, Stellman, Collon, & Fischer, 2015). Procedurally, due process in student discipline requires your policies or practice prescribe that the school needs to do certain things, such as protecting student privacy, contacting parents of minor students, and following time lines on decisions (Schimmel et al., 2015). Parental contact is often a challenge in disciplinary circumstances and can vary with expectation, with procedures often informed by nuances of in loco parentis, case law, or the specifics enacted in each state and subsequent procedures expected from local school districts. It is with these ideas in mind that I present some key areas for your disciplinary learning and consideration.

Schools' jurisdiction over student expression has its limits; no school can completely constrict what students do and how they behave. Assistant principals will often encounter situations in discipline that invoke laws regarding student freedom of expression. A landmark case regarding student freedom of expression was *Tinker v. Des Moines Independent Community School District* (1969), in which students were wearing black arm bands to share their views on the Vietnam War. The Supreme Court ruled that people at school do not "shed their constitutional rights to freedom of speech or expression at the schoolhouse gate" (as cited in Schimmel et al., 2015, p. 162) and said school officials cannot prohibit a particular opinion "to avoid the discomfort and unpleasantness that always accompany an unpopular viewpoint" (Schimmel et al., 2015, p. 163). Further, the Supreme Court states that students are not simply "closed-circuit recipients of only that which the State chooses to communicate. They may not be confined to the expression of those sentiments that are officially approved" (Alexander & Alexander, 2012, p. 338).

As an assistant principal, you can limit students' freedom of expression when it is found to "materially or substantially" interfere with the school or disrupt those within it; when there is significant evidence of a "reasonable likelihood of substantial disorder"; or when you have a legitimate educational interest in doing so (Schimmel et al., 2015, p. 164). This includes offensive speech and cyberbullying over the internet; speech promoting drug use; true threats to individuals or the school; lewd and indecent speech; certain public displays of affection; hate speech that could cause fights or threaten, intimidate, or cause substantial disruption; or messaging on clothing that "collides with the rights of other students to be secure and to be left alone" (Schimmel et al., 2015, p. 172). But if you say, "You can't wear that T-shirt, just because I don't like it," you'll not be supported by a court.

TIP

If you find that you do not have a right to ask students not to wear a particular garment, it is always an option to let them know that you do not have that right, but ask, as a favor, if they would be willing not to wear it again, *for you*.

Knowing the laws on student searches and seizures is also important. You can conduct reasonable searches and seizures on school property for items that may be contraband and not in the school's best interest. You don't need probable cause; you do need an analysis of the reasonableness of the search or reasonable suspicion (Alexander & Alexander, 2012, 2018, 2019; Roth et al., 2010). Areas deemed the school's include lockers, parking lots, classrooms, and buses traveling to and from school. Per the court's ruling in *New Jersey v. T. L. O.* (1985), you can search "when there are reasonable grounds for suspecting that the search will turn up evidence that the student has violated or is violating either the law or the rules of the school" (Schimmel et al., 2015, p. 263). The reasonable suspicion standard states you can search "according to the dictates of reason and common sense" (*New Jersey v. T. L. O.*, 1985). Reasonableness is when your action to search is justified at the outset and if the scope of the search was reasonable for a specific rule thought to be violated. In other words, don't go looking for a stolen bike in a student's wallet.

School searches considered reasonable are to be grounded in individualized suspicion (Roth et al., 2010); are typically limited to personal items, pockets, bookbags, lockers, and other such items; and, in most cases, do not involve strip searches or other highly intrusive searches (Alexander & Alexander, 2012, 2019), which would require arguably a much higher standard. If students bring laptops or personal devices to school, those items can be searched with reasonable suspicion (Schimmel et al., 2015). Lockers are in most cases considered school property, and students with access can be held responsible for what they store within through *controlled possession*—when students have control over a space to which they have access.

Typically, you have the right to question and interrogate students, as you are in your role in loco parentis, and thus in the place of a parent. Even for those over the age of eighteen, you can stipulate that if they choose to attend your school, then they are subject to questioning and interrogation of school authorities when warranted. If you believe with reasonable confidence that students have information that will help you maintain the safety, order, and discipline of your school and students, you have a right to a conversation. Key in all of this is to remember that while questioning and interrogation must occur in order to keep things safe, there remains the fact that you will need to have a relationship with the student and family once the discomforting circumstance is over. In other words, if you are overzealous in securing today's confession and bulldoze or berate the student in question, you'll have a short-term win, but you will have to live with a negative relationship thereafter.

You will find that when the rubber hits the road, you've got to make decisions that decide students' fate based on certain standards of evidence. We often hear about proof beyond a reasonable doubt when watching courtroom dramas on television in terms of the standards of conviction, or taking action. This is not the standard of evidence we use as assistant principals. In reality, when considering such issues in school, we do not need proof beyond a reasonable doubt. Rather, we need a preponderance of evidence, and I have always used the rule that if a wise and loving parent would act on the evidence, you should act similarly. This brings both opportunity and risk. The opportunity is that you can take action on more things to keep the school a safe place to be. The risk in this is that with a lower standard of evidence, you are increasing the probability of making a mistake, and students' lives could be affected. All this said, others are counting on you to act.

TIP

Ensure as best you can that you have a rock-solid handbook. Student handbooks are critical in keeping a school safe and orderly. They must cover every possible situation you can conceive of, either point by point or under a general umbrella of definition. The most effective handbooks are authoritative and autocratic in substance but not style. To the reader, they should not sound authoritarian. When they present consequences for actions, these should be preceded with the rationale that the intent is to keep a safe and orderly school for everyone where the best teaching and learning can take place. For currency, have an open handbook revision folder for every situation you find yourself in that does not have language to support what you wish to do. Fill these gaps each semester with new language to your advantage. Keep homing in toward enhanced safety all the time.

In short, prioritize your learning about school discipline and leveraging the law. Take time to read. Pore over your law materials topic by topic. As such, gather and keep each and every informational legal resource disseminated at trainings and conferences; create your own legal library by dating and filing these so that you can gauge currency at a glance. Purchase a nationally recognized law book. One can't go wrong with education law experts Kern Alexander and M. David Alexander's (2019) ninth edition of *American Public School Law*, or Alexander and Alexander's (2018) *Law of Schools, Students, and Teachers in a Nutshell*, or various encyclopedias for school law as quick references. The internet, of course, offers a wealth of information that's well worth your time to read and reference. Nonprofit organizations often have websites that contain a wealth of these types of materials. The American Bar Association, for example, has a division for public education (www.americanbar.org/groups/public_education) with general materials on the law for teachers, the public, and legal professionals. The National Education Association has a legal resource library (www.nea.org/legal-guidance) available from its general counsel. The Student Press Law Center (https://splc.org) has provided resources and publications for many years that are of high quality.

Get anything authored state-specific to your location. State departments of education make legal resources available on their websites as well, especially pertaining to state laws and administrative codes they are asked to interpret. While checking through these resources, don't assume that something that is legal in one state or province is legal in yours, including what I have presented in this chapter. Double check all content here with the laws of your locale. Do the same with your local board policy and administrative regulations. Avail yourself to any resources or contacts available through state administrator associations that often publish monthly briefs written by partnering school attorneys.

Work with your principal to have a firm understanding of when you should contact a school attorney. Get on the same page. Strive for a relationship where you and your principal can call your school attorney directly, within reason. The more you know about the law, the more often you'll make better and safer decisions for your students, your school, and yourself. Prioritize learning the law as a key strategy for your success.

Student discipline is also so very important because of the weight it entails. In handling student discipline, keep in mind you're dealing with someone's most precious resource, no matter how they are acting, what they are doing, or whom they are affecting. Next, understand you are dealing with families who may have different expectations, beliefs, values, and assumptions about how their children should conduct themselves. In school discipline, you're dealing with the law, which in many cases has potential consequences if you mess things up. You also have an obligation to protect the very students you are disciplining, which means protection from you if you become overzealous.

The How: Strategies to Use With Students

The following strategies—leaving nary a stone unturned, working from the fringe forward, and designing doorways of dignity—are effective ways to lay the foundation for your work with students.

Leave Nary a Stone Unturned

Often, when situations move full speed ahead, you do not have much time to act. There are only so many minutes in the day. You have the obligation to address all of the discomforts in each situation before the people involved do anything more counterproductive than they have done so far. Situations of conflict are complicated. Lots of he-said, she-saids—you hear the typical adversarial one side versus the other, when the truth is somewhere in between. Getting to the truth involves leaving nary a stone unturned. After all, deciding with a preponderance of evidence is what you must do, and you have a good chance to decide wrong if you fail to gather all the facts.

Your role is to control as many variables as you can, including what people share, where and when they share it, who stays in class while you investigate, who stays sequestered with you or your colleagues, who goes home, and under which circumstances students forego the use of their phones or devices during any given investigation. The latter is increasingly difficult, I realize! Try to have students providing evidence leave their devices with your assistant for a short period of time until you get enough witness accounts on paper.

TIP

Have a soundproof box on your desk with a hinged top where you can ask students to deposit their devices safely while you have a conversation. This way, they won't text, and you won't be recorded.

In any investigation you undertake, you will want to get witness accounts committed to paper, signed, and dated as quickly as you can. Do this with speed and finesse—with students in all corners of your office suites feverishly writing (quite possibly spinning half-truths, and that's OK)—as you will not have time for more than a glance at what they state until after the flurry is complete. Leaving no stone unturned means spending time with the students to get verbal testimony, both before and after they commit it to paper. Your ears will guide your immediate next steps. This is where your fact-gathering efficiency and deft intuition come together, as both what students say and how they say it will identify new stones you must unearth. It is important to share with students that if they or anyone they know is involved with something that violated school rules, the faster you all can get to a fair and just resolution, the more they might be involved in deciding the outcome.

TIP

Leave no stone unturned by using social media to screen threats or potential hostility to your school, staff, and students. Your increased efficacy with technology will help ensure a safer school environment, as you can read the tea leaves, as the saying goes, and better understand what is taking place.

You will also have to contend with a traffic pattern that emerges in terms of student communication of what is going on in your office, because every student leaving your general area during your investigation will have the story of the office visit to share with others. You might choose to allow certain students whom you can trust to be confidential leave your office. With others, you can also plant information you wish to dispense without them realizing. Use select information to help protect students from each other while you are getting to the bottom of things. Always say that you derived your information from adults, and never say who they were. This leaves students guessing, and provides your student informants the cover they need. To recall an earlier example, if you hear that two students had a conflict over the weekend and you are worried the conflict might spill over into school time, then have a side conversation with those students separately, ensuring as always that you say you heard about the scenario from staff, rather than from other students. If you say you heard it from students, and certain students were seen meeting with you that morning, those students may be unfairly cast in the reporting light, and they could face repercussions. Sticking to the adult source works for you even if students know you may not be entirely forthcoming because it serves the larger goal of encouraging them to trust you with their own information. Should they ever feel compelled to report something and worry what other students would think of them, they will remember this and know that when you follow up, you'll do so with their confidence in mind and not break story along the way.

An important thing I have learned in situations of student conflict and potential violence is that you cannot undercommunicate that you have things under control. If students feel the situation is unsafe, you'll have a problem. Students must have a sense that you will protect them satisfactorily so that they don't need to take a situation into their own hands. If you sense that they do not have this trust, you might need to remove them from school temporarily until you can get things sorted out. If you sense they will stay calm, ensure you apprise them of your efforts and time lines. Heaven forbid a student being bullied steps in front of the bully and punches him in the nose—a preventive strike that could have been avoided with better attentiveness from you and no stones unturned.

At the end of the day or when you have some breathing room, study the different written affidavits almost as if you were a qualitative researcher looking for patterns and themes. Look for the contradictions as well as the commonalities. Connect enough dots to know where to circle back the next morning and press for a more realistic view of what took place. You need to have enough dots to connect to leave no stone unturned to make the right call. Just how to go about moving through those involved is the subject of the next strategy.

TIP

Ensure that you make good use of your school video surveillance system if you have one. Become an expert at navigating its features to make inquiries into things that happen. Work the camera in late afternoons or evenings after the students leave. Message to students that your camera system exonerates as many students as it convicts, which will probably be true over time.

Sometimes, you will find that the information you receive leads you to believe that someone is in possession of something that shouldn't be at school. In this case, you'll want to conduct a search of the individual's personal items, including pockets. This involves discretion. Searches and seizures should be smartly conducted in private so that students are not exposed to unwarranted embarrassment, stigma, or shame. We're not talking strip searches, of course—but in any personal item search, you may uncover things the student is not comfortable sharing with the public. As an assistant principal, you must be cognizant of and sensitive to the students' embarrassment when you find personal items, as well as mindful of those belonging to a different gender than yourself. The goal is to keep the school safe and respect students' dignity at the same time.

It pays to have a same-gendered person search personal items whenever possible or, at minimum, to have a same-gendered and appropriately qualified and confidential same-gendered witness to any searches that might take place. For trans students, keep in mind how they identify, and strive to involve an adult the student trusts. This is also true for nonbinary students. If you have any nonbinary members of your staff, resist the urge to recruit them to help with sensitive matters like this simply because of their gender identity. Keep in mind that just because someone identifies as nonbinary (or, indeed, as any nondominant identity), it does not mean they wish to represent all others who do as well, so take great care when putting your team together. In fact, I would suggest that unless people unilaterally volunteer for such roles because they feel compelled to serve in that capacity, do not recruit based on your employees' gender identification.

At times, in leaving nary a stone unturned, you'll need to contact law enforcement. Never hesitate to have law enforcement with you to handle a situation if there is a possibility of adverse impacts to safety. That said, if there are none, do not use law enforcement as an arm of your authority or with convenience, because it's a double-edged sword. As an assistant principal, you don't have as much authority if you have a police officer alongside you. The police have different and higher rules of engagement.

TIP

For strange vehicles on campus, defer to law enforcement before approaching them. Just call the police. It is not worth the potential danger of your approach, and to be frank, those in the vehicle might not like you asking them to leave and may take it out on the school building after hours. They don't typically think like this if the police ask them to leave; they're just glad they didn't get arrested.

If you involve law enforcement too quickly, you might have to operate under a probable cause standard rather than move forward with reasonable suspicion. When someone's safety is not jeopardized, it may be better to investigate, search, and then turn whatever you find over to the police. Note one hazard is that in some cases, you might find something that is, in certain contexts, illegal for you to possess as well; this involves certain types of pornography or loaded weapons. Keep your hands off these items or materials at all costs and secure a perimeter so that others cannot see, touch, or approach them. However, if a small amount of contraband is unsecure in an area where students may be present or continued presence of the object would be distracting or unsafe to the school environment (such as classroom, hallway, vehicle in some cases, or locker), the best way to create this perimeter is to secure it appropriately with administrative witnesses on hand and transport the contraband to the school's office for secure storage until the arrival of police.

Work From the Fringe Forward

Investigations are ethically relative, rather than morally absolute. Because some situations are ripe for unsafety if they do not get resolved quickly, you may have to use an occasional bluff or influence strategy to worm out some of the facts and details. The more precarious a situation is, the more latitude I feel you have to work deftly from the fringe forward while questioning and interrogating.

TIP

Do not sit between the students and your doorway while questioning them. While you do not want them to leave, you do not want to block them from doing so either. The more emotional students might bulldoze past you. Others could say afterward that you trapped them in your office. Rather, have a firm, actionable school policy that offers stiff disciplinary consequences if students leave your office without your permission during an investigation. Consider that there is also a psychological component here—wherein students who feel trapped might resist, but just the feeling of having an out, or some space, creates a more amenable environment where they might be more likely to choose to cooperate.

Situations in which groups of students are involved in misbehavior, such as theft, vandalism, bullying, community embarrassment, and so on, typically have a few main actors who do the majority of the deed and a fringe group with varying levels of culpability. The fringe typically has some students who will have more to lose if they get in trouble than others, such as athletes or members of the National Honor Society at the secondary level and, at all levels, students whose parents will discipline them even more sternly at home. Those with probation officers also fit the bill. Some students are less afraid of consequences and can stay the course of any story; others cave quickly by nature. You'll have a wide variety of students at arm's length in any given investigation.

Before you start, isolate and sequester those who are reported to be the main antagonists, so to speak, and let them sweat for a bit without their electronic communications devices while you begin working the rest—from the fringe forward. Keep the main perpetrators within eyeshot for careful supervision.

TIP

Have your assistant sit within earshot of students who will be called into your office as part of an investigation. Assistants can work nearby unobtrusively and report to you anything they might hear via text or message. You can be reading these messages, even if at your desk talking to another student, though you'll need to be nonchalant with your multitasking.

Begin with the fringe, with the few students who definitely have a firsthand account of what went on and possibly participated to a small degree but weren't the main perpetrators. These are the students who may have a vested interest in minimizing their own consequences. The bigger the worriers, the better, especially those who have something to lose, like extracurricular participation or a violation from their probation officer.

TIP

If students are eighteen years of age or older and wish their parents not be informed of their circumstances, have them sign an age of majority document, which states that, in this case and in the future, their parents can't come to their rescue and that, as an adult, they are 100 percent responsible. In many states, you can simultaneously inform parents that students are signing these papers, in some cases retroactively. It is miraculous how many students, at this point, wish to quickly retract their signatures and thus involve their parents. As always, check your laws.

Keep in mind that the clock is ticking; you can only hold the main perpetrators for so long, so keep things moving. Get what you know out of the students on the fringe, and keep them separate from each other. Direct them to write things down and sign and date the document for you. Ensure their devices are with you or your assistant unless they must have them for some reason (parent has a medical condition, for example). Those on the fringe who will maintain confidence or those with whom you plant information you wish they share can go back to class. If they advertise what you are investigating to others, there is typically more of an upside in deterrence if you have already gathered all the relevant people for questioning.

TIP

Use a recursive style in your investigatory conversations with students. If they think you don't know it all and are not figuring it out, that's the point. Give them the impression that you might be back to talk with them again later; keep them guessing. Let them know that everyone could be on the hook until you have this all figured out.

Then, it is on to the main perpetrators. They'll have no idea how many conversations you have had, and they'll have no idea of the evidence against them at this point. This is when you share what you want them to know that you know and that they have been implicated. Let them know there is one of two ways they can handle things: (1) as part of the solution restoratively or (2) as part of the problem. A common technique that I find successful is to say something like:

The way I see it is that you are a great kid going about your day, and something happened to lure you in that, with 20-20 hindsight, you probably would have avoided. This is how I see things, and here is what will happen if we can wrap this up soon. I hope it is not the other way around, where I have to take a lot of time and effort, then find out what I'm going to find out anyway.

TIP

In a fast-paced investigation, take a few moments to curate your staff confidants—those who will report to you discreetly what the students are saying to them. These folks have student-centered respect, so they'll need to know you really have the students' best interests at heart. If you curate their involvement, they will trust you over time and will provide you some of the best intelligence that can help students.

At that point, it is often best to excuse yourself for around ten minutes, returning with a pencil and piece of paper for another conversation. You'll get some hard-nosed students who will stay defiant and dishonest through consequences and beyond, but for the most part, the fringe and the pauses and the sweating work. Another strategy is to send the main actors home overnight, or for the weekend, to think about things and bring them back with their parents in the next day or so. It is important to remember that when working from the fringe forward, you maintain always that any information you receive, you got from a staff member and not a student. Do not divulge that a student provided you information directly. Over time, students might know you are not being completely forthcoming regarding who provided you information, but what they will know is that you will never break their confidence if they are the ones to share information with you about another student or their school.

TIP

Stories will change the minute students leave your office and return to their classroom to discuss. Often, students will wish to come back to change their story. Allow them to do so in writing, and keep what they wrote previously. Ensure that you date and time-stamp all submitted affidavits. The changes in the narrative can be as informative as the initial narratives and help you discern what went on. Students who falsify may be held accountable, but you should have compassion if they were intimidated. Hold responsible those who put the pressure on them.

Design Doorways of Dignity

Your feedback loop as you use discipline as a teachable moment relies on those who work with you trusting that you have their best interest at heart. Whether they appreciate what you are doing or not, it is critical to start from a place where they at least know you are not out to get them. This is no matter how they behave, by the way. One strategy that I always kept in mind to build this trust over time was to be mindful of the entrances and exits from the assistant principal's office, that is, the doorways.

A trip to the assistant principal's office can be eerily reminiscent of *The Green Mile*, a walk down death row toward one's eventual execution, as depicted in a 1999 drama film based on Stephen King's novel of the same name. From that call over the classroom loudspeaker and resultant "Oooohhhh" from classmates, a student's trip to the assistant principal's office can be anything but enjoyable right from the outset. Assistant principals must always keep this in mind when students arrive and when they are dismissed. When students arrive, their defense mechanisms might be on alert. It is often nice to have your assistant greet them warmly, saying that the assistant principal appreciates that they have taken the time to come, it will be just a few minutes, and they should be able to head back to class soon. Offering a cup of water from the water cooler can help ease the tension and nerves a bit. I call this creating doorways of dignity. Doing these things with an awareness of how stressful the visit is for the student makes a difference.

Your greeting is key, especially if others are watching. Don't overdo it; don't underdo it. You don't want to say, "Hi so-and-so, I really appreciate you coming down because I need your help in solving a problem." That might make the student look like one who is a stooge or "narc." You don't want to say, "Get in here!" as this is off-putting. Something like, "I appreciate your taking the time, so-and-so, and it's good to see you. Please, come in," is probably more appropriate.

At this point, if your business is confidential, I hope you will have the benefit of a soundproofed office. Particularly important is that the doorway to your office is not in a direct line of view from the waiting area if this can be arranged. If there are windows, such as with a conference room setup, and if folks can see inside from the outside, sit in a collaborative fashion so if viewed by the outside, you look like colleagues in the office having professional dialogue. In other words, don't lean over your desk pointing a finger. While discussing, minimize if–then statements, as these invite combat.

When the student says something to which you disagree or have a counter-opinion, use the word *and* much more often than *but* to expand on what students say. You don't want to negate their viewpoints. When they share something more emotional, it helps every once in a while to say, "Give me a second," and think more deeply about what they have said before responding. You might tighten your lip thoughtfully and exhale gently while pondering. Actor Tom Selleck, who portrayed police commissioner Frank Reagan on the television show *Blue Bloods*, exemplifies this technique. Often, it pays dividends to delve deeper into why students did what they did. If you have a choice-consequences model of discipline, be sure to ask the students why they did what they did before levying consequences. You might find it was a response to something your staff is not doing so well or an attempt to avoid embarrassment or angst because of wanting to project a certain image to their friends.

When designing doorways of dignity, keep in mind the exit from your office. Your goal is to end the meeting, no matter how it goes emotionally, with everyone's head held high. Again, dignity is key. You want this to be *you and me versus the issue*. To do so, think who has which dogs in this hunt. What are the students' constituencies here? What could happen after the student's exit to cause collateral damage? Then, think of an exit strategy that will get this student out of the office and back to class with as much dignity and confidentiality intact as possible. If you have a side door or back door to your office suite that does not go back across the student waiting room, that is ideal. If you can have someone walk the student back down the hallway, such as a guidance counselor or someone who will not raise the eyebrows of fellow students, that is great too. It also is critical to maintain the dignity of those who are getting suspended. Allow for a quiet exit, and if consequences are pending, follow up over the telephone or via video call. This can avoid making the situation worse.

TIP

Strive to meet with suspended students as they return to school. Avoid a "Now you better . . ." approach; rather, just say, "Glad you're back," and leave it at that. Even if they are dismissive or still angry, the meeting saves avoidance as you both work your day.

If the student exiting your office must walk again past friends or peers in the waiting room, allow them to do so in a way that will preserve the reputation they have built. Your assistant can help here by offering a warm salutation and will probably get one in kind. As their destination and visit were, again, often perceived as the execution room at the end of *The Green Mile*, you'll want to do whatever you can to make it not so, in your own way. Doorways of dignity are the key, and you want your stakeholders to be aware that you are making an effort toward these ends.

TIP

If you do not have a discreet exit from your office to an adjacent hallway outside the view of the visitors in the waiting room, spend a few seconds prepping your student for the walk past others. While they might scoff at you for broaching, let them know it is to offer them respect in the eyes of others. Whether they want to hear it or not, how they come across to others as they exit is for *them*, not for you. And let them know it.

In designing doorways of dignity, leave one open for yourself. Don't have a game face as you appear from all the discipline in your office while heading back to supervising the halls. Students need your consistent, positive, and warm disposition, and most were not a part of the last incident you just handled. Don't vicariously make them a part of it. Take a deep breath and put on a fresh face before you exit your office. Maintaining dignity for yourself and those around you necessitates that you always keep student-to-student relationships in mind first and foremost when you move through each day. What students say among themselves after you walk away is an area where things can go well or not. There's so much that you cannot do to avoid negative relations that you have to be constantly vigilant about how students will treat each other, depending on what you do or represent to and around them.

The How: Strategies to Use With Staff

The following strategies—focusing on factors that prevent and empowering staff to save and adopt students—are effective ways to lay the foundation for your work with staff.

Focus on Factors That Prevent

Focusing on factors that prevent reminds me of two mentors who stood side by side with me through the thick and thin of school discipline: my school attorneys. One of the first I learned from provided the springboard for my legal savvy. He was an incredible in-the-trenches school attorney, open to litigation and never worried about sparring. I imagine that as a child, he was competitive and dared you to take the first shot at whatever he wished to play. The last school attorney I worked with refined and extended my legal savvy. He was incredible as well, more an architect, wishing not to litigate if it could be avoided, yet certainly ready if needed. Much of his playbook was designed to prevent, to head off little issues before they became big problems. I imagine he was more of the peacemaker as a child, one who tried for team cohesion.

I encourage assistant principals working with their staff to consider here the playbook of the latter attorney with whom I worked: a preventive approach to school discipline. Sure, as assistant principals, we can remedy most all that comes through our door, but imagine the possibilities if you can outflank that typical trip to the office. Teachers are powerful in determining the amount of traffic to your office by heading it off in the first place, through three things that are better than most others at reducing student misbehavior: (1) interest, (2) engagement, and (3) success. I'm telling you they work just about every time to keep problems to a minimum and head off the little issues before they become big problems. Here's why.

Students who are *interested* in their teachers and their teaching are living inside of their best and most well-adjusted selves. There is safety and comfort in what they are doing, so they are operating not out of their brain stem but rather at the peak of their cognitive capacity. Because teachers are providing this experience to them, they are unlikely to disrupt it. They have a vested interest in continuing their positive feelings, and they may lose track of time.

Students who are *engaged* are expending energy in something productive. Contrary to popular thought, people don't really have the capacity to multitask as well as we think (Junco, 2012). It takes energy to engage, even poorly, and students who are involved with their teachers and classmates naturally stay those courses rather than choose others. They are not thinking about what they can do differently to pass the time, because with engagement, time has already passed.

Students who are being *successful* are doing so in full view of others. They are living exactly how they intentionally wish to manufacture each day—avoiding any sort of embarrassment in front of their friends. Students are not thinking about what they can do differently to pass the time because any disruption might be riskier than what they are successfully doing in full view of peers.

Interest, engagement, and success are a winning combination. A strategy you can use is to reinforce this continuously with teachers in terms of things that they cannot afford to discount. Be a broken record in the most respectful of ways. Let teachers know these elements of a student-centered classroom culture are performance-enhancing supplements to their lesson design. Share with them that you depend on them as necessary ingredients of keeping students out of trouble. Let them know that, as they often remind you, students do better in their classes with consistent attendance. Understand that academic demands placed upon teachers require that students learn tested subjects, whether or not they feel inclined to do so. There are really two routes to take: (1) without interest, engagement, and success or (2) with these forms of involvement.

Beyond reinforcement, be sure you offer to deliver a lesson of your own to their students, intentionally planning for those elements of interest, engagement, and success. In short, bring your own game! Invite teachers to watch you and critique. Be a good sport. If the content area that certain teachers cover is too far out of your reach, get a willing teacher partner in your own content area, and invite other teachers to watch. Strategies are strategies, and they can apply across contexts. This is important in that if you are willing to do this in front of your own peers—the adults—you then can build the trust and credibility to offer to be their own partner in clinical supervision, where you provide feedback to them on their efforts. In this, you would sit in on their lesson with a two-column sheet as shown in figure 6.1 and jot down elements of the lesson that sparked your interest, engagement, and success, and offer suggestions of other things they might try.

Things That Worked for You	Other Things to Try
Strategies for Interest:	Strategies for Interest:
Strategies for Engagement:	Strategies for Engagement:
Strategies for Student Success:	Strategies for Student Success:

FIGURE 6.1: Elements of interest, engagement, and success in lessons observed.

*Visit **go.SolutionTree.com/leadership** for a free reproducible version of this figure.*

Above all, be candid in your whole-school staff meetings that the more students are down in your office for disciplinary reasons from classroom misbehavior, the less they will be learning and the more the cycle of frustration will continue. It is actually better for teachers to pull back on the gas pedal with content covered, at times, to ensure that activities interest, engage, and allow students to succeed along the way. It's better to have 100 percent immersion in coverage of 80 percent of the planned content than far less immersion in 100 percent of the covered content, as the latter will yield low retention. Students moving forward with experiences of interest, engagement, and success will have more positive perspectives of themselves and their abilities to do well in school. As such, they can dial down their defense mechanisms and dial up a more positive disposition.

Empower Staff to Save and Adopt

Most students have teachers in your school whom they do not want to disappoint. And might I say that, in some cases, they have only one. Especially with the frequent flyers to your office, if you took a straw poll in the teachers' lounge, you would find a majority of teachers would *not* give those students a thumbs-up. Yet, there's typically someone either inside the lounge, or down the hall avoiding the lounge, who would say something positive. That's who you want to empower.

Involve teachers in your disciplinary processes, especially when things seem to be getting to the point that suspension or longer-term removal from school is a possibility. You will need to get the student's and a parent's or guardian's permission to do so, as sometimes what they are doing is a part of a school record that needs to be protected in terms of its confidentiality. Upon getting permission for you to involve a trusted teacher, ask the student to bring the teacher along to the office at a convenient time. This is when you sit down and discuss as a team. It is going to be *you and the student versus the problem*. The problem you're going to tackle is whatever is getting in the way of your student's success.

In short, what you say to the student in full view of the teacher is that the situation has now gotten to the point where you alone cannot prevent the student's removal from school. Only in combination with the teacher and the student will you get special dispensation to handle this another way. Ask whether the teacher would be willing to "adopt" the student during the school day; this practice allows teachers to provide these students a place where they can go if they feel they are about to make a bad decision. Then, assure the student you will talk to the other teachers about this avenue for redress. The agreement, however, will be that the student continues working on assignments for the teacher's classroom and will see that teacher later for a discussion about any missed work.

Basically, this is the *save*. You provide a safe spot, where a teacher is empowered to adopt and receive the student upon request; thereafter the teacher provides a respite so that the situation does not escalate. The notion of adopting can go even further. If you find that the student's school schedule needs to be amended to provide balance for a positive school day, you can provide a larger percentage of the time with the teacher who sees the good in this student. Empowering, saving, and adopting takes great effort on the part of the teacher, so if policy allows, ensure you provide this teacher a disproportionate strength of voice in discussing this student's needs, strengths, and capabilities in any formal, decision-making meetings. In short, allow teachers fulfilling this role to advocate and embrace their voice and expertise as you would a fellow administrator. It is critical that you reinforce to students that they are still in school because, as a team, you all care, but they have a certain teacher with faith in them. And that is a very special thing.

The How: Strategy to Use With You

Leveraging firm and fair school discipline is not for the faint of heart. It involves direct involvement with situations that are by their very design tenuous, time consuming, and fraught with distress. Your actions have real consequences, and people are not always happy with what you do and how you do it. Depending on the circumstance, what you do could be overturned on appeal after you have invested much energy and even, at times, your own professional reputation—and, if you're honest, your ego—in the outcome. Worse yet, if you violate someone's rights, you and the school could be in legal trouble. The next strategy for you encourages you to know what can come back to haunt you; I call it minding your backside.

Assistant principals must have eyes in the back of their head, a situational awareness that offers some flashing yellow lights to ensure that they don't get themselves or their schools in trouble when doing the good work of school discipline. This strategy starts with being mindful that most of what those in the United States deal with has implications with the Family Educational Rights and Privacy Act (FERPA), while those in other countries may want to keep in mind their own national or provincial privacy laws, such as the European Union's General Data Protection Regulation or Ontario, Canada's, Freedom of Information and Protection of Privacy Act. FERPA in particular includes the stipulation that when an educational record is made, such as the filing of a disciplinary referral or a note in the school management software, this information is private and not to be disclosed to others without the express permission of the student's parent or guardian. The exception to this would be other school officials with a right to know, such as the guidance counselor or any teachers involved.

First, know that all you say and do can be seen and recorded. Supervise your commons areas as if you work in an aquarium. In other words, you can watch everyone and see all that they do, but the glass works both ways; they can see you just as clearly. What you say and what you do can be discerned, with clarity, and shared publicly. When caucusing with others on staff during your supervisory assignments, understand that even from a distance students can read your lips or hear what you are discussing. This is where privacy violations get risky, for sure, if you are sharing situations that you are dealing with in the office. Thus, the strategy of minding your backside depends on self-control. Self-control also means withstanding a desire to be overly democratic or creative with your disciplinary processes. Don't give away your control of the disciplinary process for the same reason—student privacy. Even with good intentions, be careful of student involvement in disciplinary alternatives, such as student court, restorative justice decision models, and so on, as they can also violate student privacy expectations without some careful protections embedded, as well as parental permissions. This doesn't mean you can't use them; just be careful.

Beyond self-control, you need self-preservation. This has to do with how you navigate your duties as a school official and responsibilities as a citizen civilian. Undoubtedly, you'll run across items that are against the law as you do your job. How you handle these situations, such as possession of contraband while awaiting law enforcement, is something you need to be very careful with. You can protect yourself by keeping eyes on the contraband until it can be sealed, and lock it in a securely stored location while awaiting the arrival of law enforcement. This is called chain of custody. Also critical is that if you begin searching a student's electronic device for information, you must keenly understand the laws of your state, as well as your local board policy and administrative regulations. Don't go headlong into moving through the student's electronic files and apps, only to run across child pornography and then to possibly be in possession of it *yourself* at that moment. I would suggest letting law enforcement conduct searches such as this or ask the parents of students to pull up information on their children's devices if they are willing (and many might not be).

Finally, minding your backside includes self-commitment. There are key trip wires to look out for in terms of student discipline, and I'll share some things you must commit to memory. These items refer to students with disabilities. Students with handicapping conditions—students in special education and, in the United States, Section 504 classification—have a different set of rules than those in the general education program. Please apply these examples to whatever degree of certainty they might have in your context. This is a tough sell for general education parents whose children are facing expulsion for the same offenses committed by students with handicaps who are not. For students with disabilities, commit to the following.

- Prior to any disciplinary decisions, check your student's grades and attendance to see if you can discern any patterns that could be a result of the student's current placement and accommodations that teachers are not providing. If the individualized education program (IEP) has not been followed to a T, you could have a problem.

- For each student experiencing behavioral difficulties, there is the possibility that you haven't done your job in terms of placement. Provide for this student's success in terms of schedule, colleagues working with this student, or other supports.

- Learn what limits your school has on removing students from their educational placement for a period of time cumulative over a given year. Always check students' files to see the number of days they have been suspended outside of school, especially if there is more than one assistant principal in the building.

- Understand what a manifestation of disorder hearing is and what it entails. A manifestation of disorder hearing is a meeting in which a group of people knowledgeable about the student who is considered for discipline reviews the student's records and educational program to determine whether any inappropriate behavior is related to the student's disability (Alexander & Alexander, 2019). In short, ensure you have one of these hearings before implementing a longer-term suspension for a student with a disability. Learn the questions that must be asked at these hearings. Ensure all people required by law are present. Understand what happens next by law if the student or family disagrees with the school.

- If you find yourself out of compliance with any special education or student disability paperwork, time lines, services, and so on, even if it's the prior school's fault at its inception, immediately contact your district officials who supervise those programs and work toward immediate rectification. The longer you wait, the more you might be on the hook for compensatory educational options, which can be costly and right out of your bottom line.

Toolkit for Tomorrow: Next Steps

These next steps provide some suggestions for how you can put the ideas in this chapter into action.

- Order a copy of a current law book and schedule some professional reading time in an environment conducive to reading heavy material and thinking deeply about its applications to circumstances in your school. I often found that a higher-end bar or coffee shop with a fireplace made for good evening or Sunday afternoon reading.

- Take each of the legal topics presented in this chapter and do some research pertaining to your state and local allowances. Do the same with your local board policy, as you always want to act within those parameters and the guiding administrative regulations.

- Develop alternatives to out-of-school suspension that are academic, restorative, supervised by your best staff, and enhancements to community and climate. These could include an in-school restriction in a focused, supportive setting; community service contributions to local businesses or organizations; school service opportunities such as tutoring or participating in recreational activities with younger struggling students; or involvement of the students and their parents, guardians, or loved ones in creating solutions to resolve the problem at hand.

- Use a thumbs-up strategy to connect with students after they are involved with a disciplinary incident in your office or a suspension from school. To do so, when you see students in this situation approaching you, offer them a thumbs-up gesture with an accentuated nod and a supportive look. If they respond with a nod or similar gesture, you know that all is now good. If not, you know that there's some work to do; you can circle back to tend to the relationship, which needs some further nurturing and effort (P. Marshall, personal communication, July 13, 2021).

- Complete the professional development activity on page 113 about developing a strategy to address students who struggle with attendance.

Professional Development: A Deeper Dive—Leveraging Firm and Fair Discipline

Instructions: In this professional development activity, you'll develop a strategy to address students who struggle with attendance. These students may be elementary students who have truancy, or they could be middle school or high school students who are either truant or skipping school. The activity provides three options as prompts and then a short story in order to get you thinking. After this, you are encouraged to design a plan for your particular school context, and know that you only need to select one context of the three if that is all that applies.

ELEMENTARY SCENARIO

You have five families with high rates of truancy. Each family has between two and four children, and when one is absent, the siblings typically are as well. Even on days when they are in school, they arrive late and are often ill kempt and unfed. The parents have a history of moving from school to school once the local family courts become involved.

MIDDLE SCHOOL SCENARIO

Your school typically has around 85 to 90 percent attendance of the student body on any given day. A number of your students come from migrant families, and during certain times of the year, you find that these students are helping with family work and have attendance patterns that interfere with passing grades. Local courts have taken notice yet are not proactive in taking action, unless the students are causing mischief. You have about twenty students who skip school often and are seen around town. Some are involved with the law, but not all.

HIGH SCHOOL SCENARIO

Your school has 95 to 98 percent attendance rates, and a small number of students who skip frequently. They profess that they do not care about their grades. The model in place has been a choice–consequence model with progressive consequences for each subsequent offense: from after-school detention to Saturday school, moving to one-day, three-day, five-day, and ten-day suspensions thereafter. Often, students are being suspended for skipping, a system you inherited and one that finds favor with staff. They say with *those students* not around, they can concentrate on those who wish to learn.

STORY ACTIVITY

Now please read the following story to see if you can find any parallels between the potential lesson embedded in the story and how you might approach your selected scenario when addressing your issue of school attendance.

Three friends were walking along a river one day when they spotted some turbulence in the water. Two people waded in and, alarmed, discovered a drowning child. They pulled the little boy up on the bank but then saw more turbulence. This time it was a little girl flailing and fighting for her life. They pulled her out too—then realized their buddy was missing. They called out and eventually he walked back.

"Where were you?" one man said, exasperated. "We needed your help and you wandered away!"

"I know," the friend responded, "but somebody needed to find out who was throwing the children in the river to start with." (Books, 2011, p. 47)

Design a Plan

Again, using the information from one or more of the scenarios—elementary, middle school, and high school—as well as the story's theme to guide your thinking, use the following template to design a plan of action for how you will address the attendance challenges thrust on your desk as an assistant principal. Be sure to detail what you will do, whom you will involve, what resources you will apply, over what time you expect results, and why you believe it will work. Be sure to incorporate a way to assess how your plan is working.

Scenario (elementary, middle school, or high school)	What will you do?	Whom will you involve?	What resources will you apply?	Over what time do you expect results?	Why will your approach work?	How will you assess your plan?

Reference

Books, S. (2011). *What we don't talk about when we talk about "the achievement gap."* In R. Ahlquist, P. Gorski, & T. Montano (Eds.), *Assault on kids: How hyper-accountability, corporatization, deficit ideologies, and Ruby Payne are destroying our schools* (pp. 35–50). *New York: Peter Lang.*

CHAPTER 7
CAPITALIZING ON TEACHABLE MOMENTS

I recall, early in my tenure as an assistant principal, taking some heat from veteran teachers for spending so much time with students in my office. One colleague said, "You're not their teacher; just fix them, and send them back to class." Others wanted to determine what the result of the office visit was if they were the one issuing the student referral. I tactfully differed with them and settled into a few beliefs that informed my practice: first, my role, if not my title, was still as a teacher, and when students came to my office, there was something going on behaviorally, emotionally, or interpersonally that lent itself to a teachable moment. Next, when teachers sent students from their classes, they had (or should have) exhausted their best efforts working with these students and thus had abrogated an opportunity to determine the outcome. For the most part, folks understood and supported me.

This chapter offers a permission slip to take advantage of these moments; in fact, it encourages assistant principals to capitalize on teachable moments. I suggest that your office is your classroom, and you should be encouraged to fashion it environmentally so that you can differentiate your instruction. This might, for example, include seating arrangements that involve traditional one-to-one conversations, dyads for students solving problems together, or consensus-building activities for small groups. Décor can inspire and marry the messages you share with students and should reflect your desire to teach how to navigate life. You might even provide a space for student work and things they gift to you. Do students see something of themselves in your space like they do in their best teachers' classrooms?

With all this said, I'll also show you the what and why of recognizing and capitalizing on teachable moments. Then I'll discuss how you can go beyond the environment—to teach—with strategies for students, staff, and yourself.

The What and the Why

How can you be a teaching assistant principal? The answer is, quite simply, through just about everything you do. This is especially helpful if you're new to the role, as you may still feel very much a teacher, and for those in the assistant principalship for some time, it might offer a healthy way to press the reset button or extend your expertise. Your role is to teach continually, and in teaching, to know well what strategies work best to help students visiting your office. A confident adult presence is necessary. Students pay particular attention to you. You serve as a pillar of safety and security; everyone around you is taking cues from how you present yourself. In doing so as an assistant principal, you can provide for students in your office—your classroom.

An assistant principal's curriculum is very much like a teacher's; it has standards that guide instruction and serve as your goals. Goals include positive relationships, prioritization, and efficiency, and they help keep the main thing as the main thing. Assistant principals teach students and adults to leverage conflict as a catalyst for natural, positive energy. This influences life in and out of classrooms. In classrooms, teachers influence climate. You can do so for the entire school.

What, figuratively, is your classroom practice as an assistant principal? It involves just about everything you do each day and everywhere you go. Teachable moments will occur time and time again with those with whom you work. One particularly important teachable moment, for example, is when you are helping others move from conflict toward consensus. I want to differentiate my focus here from that on discipline in chapter 6 (page 95). School discipline is restorative because harm is caused, rules are broken, or better choices apparently need to be made, and thus the assistant principal imparts consequences at times to redirect behavior. This chapter, which also includes a focus on conflict, comes at it from a different perspective. The conflict I am talking about here is not inherently wrong, it does not necessarily need a restorative prescription, and it doesn't necessarily involve clear aggressors and aggrieved. It's much more complex—and thus something more human. We often think of conflict as something where incompatible perspectives are clashing, and through a figurative or literal battle, someone will emerge as the winner and loser of material gain, emotional satisfaction, or perceived reputation. It is no wonder that with this definition, schools spend countless hours and resources trying to manage conflict and, by their own definition of managing conflict, minimize or eliminate conflict. But conflict can lead to valuable opportunities for growth. This misunderstanding demands a teachable moment, for students and adults alike, and it rests on a premise, an ingrained view of what conflict is, that is unworkable at its best and arguably inaccurate by definition.

Conflict specialist Regier (2016), in his book *Conflict Without Casualties: A Field Guide for Leading With Compassionate Accountability*, teaches us, "Conflict is energy. Conflict is unavoidable. The only real question is: what will you do with the energy created by conflict? How *will* you spend it?" (p. 14). Conflict also provides assistant principals with opportunities to find creative and innovative ways to teach others the skills of problem solving where those involved grow from a new and deepened understanding of how others see the world and approach solutions. This is a key component to be taught and reinforced.

You can teach those with whom you work that effectively navigating conflict takes time. It involves people having thorough and sometimes lengthy conversations. All have a voice. Hopefully, the conclusion boils down to a shared awareness that we all can live with the outcome—that is, acceptance of the results, what is positive about them and what is negative. With divergent groups, this is sometimes all we can hope for to move beyond conflict; even getting to where we all can live with something takes much time.

Capitalizing on teachable moments is important not just because the windows to capture these opportunities are fleeting. It is important because the learning that teachable moments inspire and generate is also necessary for the long haul—college, careers, and life. If you are to be effective in your teaching, you must be as much about the journey in helping people with the challenges they have as about the destination. You will always be immersed in the energy of struggle and interpersonal growth, and if you project yourself as vulnerable in this journey as well, you will have authenticity and build trust with those who choose to confide in you.

Don't hold yourself up to the expectation that you will become so effective at using teachable moments you will get any less busy with them. The fact that situations come at you like waves on a shore is not an indication your efforts have not worked; rather it shows that life is happening for people who are growing, maturing, and learning from circumstance. Enjoy what you have and your efficacy. You will benefit over time from a sense of satisfaction that your approach, style, and perspective are a fit and make a difference. Folks will know you are close by and willing to help.

The How: Strategies to Use With Students

The following strategies—teaching for tenacity, sharing ownership in the lesson, and facilitating effective conflict resolution—are effective ways to lay the foundation for your work with students.

Teach for Tenacity

Assistant principals must teach students to succeed with tenacity. This is critical because one reason they are in your office is likely that they have not developed either academic tenacity, interpersonal tenacity, emotional tenacity, or otherwise. Carol S. Dweck, Gregory M. Walton, and Geoffrey L. Cohen (2014) inform us that academic tenacity involves students belonging academically and socially, seeing school as relevant to them, working hard and deferring immediate gratification, staying on course despite intellectual or social difficulties, seeking challenge, and remaining engaged over the long term. As an assistant principal, you must teach students how to develop academic tenacity as a foundational tenet. Academic tenacity is present when students work both hard and smart, moving beyond short-term concerns and challenges toward long-term, higher goals (Dweck et al., 2014). Many of the things assistant principals do to promote success in themselves are the same as those that promote academic tenacity in students, so modeling and sharing are key.

Tenacity in students includes how they organize themselves, solve problems with others, get along with their teachers even when they are not playing nice, make good decisions even when bad ones seem more enticing in the short term, stay in school and don't leave when they're stressed, do difficult things such as academics in front of their friends they are trying to impress, and stay the course even when they want to give up.

Tenacity involves self-efficacy, students' beliefs about whether they have control over whether they succeed and fail, rather than being destined or programmed one way or the other. As defined in the NEOS (2014) self-efficacy instrument, students with self-efficacy stay motivated, trust, bounce back quickly, accept failures, stay focused, ask for help, solve problems, understand strengths and weaknesses, and finish what they start.

TIP

In inviting self-efficacy, take great care in what you say to students. Choose your words wisely. Ensure you say things that pertain to their effort and hard work rather than natural ability or happenstance. You might say "Way to go!" or "Good effort!" rather than "You're great at this stuff!" Also suggested would be "Go get 'em!" if sending them off for the big test in class, rather than "Good luck!"

Teaching students about tenacity is important for you because no matter what you do in the moment or in crisis for students and families, the end game is a student's ability to succeed in school and in life. Tenacity is the crux: the ability to take in new information, digest it, retain it, and apply it to something productively. Tenacity serves as the bedrock for lifelong learning. Our best assistant principals teach tenacity through capitalizing on teachable moments. There is a method to their madness, in other words; their offices are about more than simply infractions and consequences.

Share Ownership in the Lesson

I learned long ago that one of the more transparent discussions faculty and staff can have about their teaching is when they seriously consider the possibility that when students don't learn, it's the fault of the educators teaching them. It is a sweeping generalization for ownership responsibility, mind you, and fully embracing the notion is not the point. The point is having the courage to examine the possibility that you might be responsible for something not working well and to have the conversation about that possibility openly.

Similarly, I would say the same for our best assistant principals who think like teachers in terms of where they point the finger when students, families, and others under their watch are not learning. Do they blame those who are supposed to get it when they teach? Do assistant principals review what they had hoped would be the intended outcome and say, "Well, if they can't do what I suggested, it's on them!"? Certainly, our best would not say this. They would probably instead look at how they capitalized on teachable moments and delivered their lessons to students in their office and think of a creative way to retool, revisit, and reteach. That's sharing ownership with the results. That's teaching.

One of the most important aspects of shared ownership is that you do not keep your level of responsibility and feelings toward such a secret. This is best shared during your lesson—during modeling and guided practice—while working with students. You might say, "Hey, you and I have a vested interest in this outcome. I certainly hope it works, and if it doesn't, we'll be having a conversation about how we both need to try again," or "I'm giving you my best shot in what you say to Mrs. so-and-so when you return to class so that you get off on the right foot. If it doesn't work, don't blow a gasket; instead, get through the class period, and come back to me. I'll take 49 percent of the responsibility for anything that doesn't go how we want things to go, OK?"

TIP

If teachers get upset with you for prepping students to return to class by suggesting they *do* certain things or *say* certain things, don't get defensive; rather, ask them why they are upset. Be curious. You'll notice in some cases, it all boils down to insecurity. Invite them to offer an idea on what these students can do next instead of what you suggested. Seek their answers rather than guess again for them.

Model as well how the strategies of life and of restoration and interpersonal relationships are a work in progress for all of us—and that getting along with others and working to build positive relationships with people from whom we differ is not easy. You do not want students to think you have all the answers. Take responsibility for the advice you share, embrace next steps together, let them know this ahead of their efforts, and share ownership in the result. One of the best parts about this is that doing so necessitates that you make time for follow-up in which you can dissect what took place, strategize anew if things went awry, and celebrate success if all went well.

Facilitate Effective Conflict Resolution

Teaching appropriate skills in conflict resolution is necessary because unresolved issues can often cause emotional, social, or physical difficulties for students in school. Assistant principals must take the lead to ensure they address these situations proactively, even though it takes a bit of time and effort. You should not avoid conflict and assume it will go away; rather, embrace it and leverage its energy into a teachable moment. Doing so over time with students, faculty, and staff will help make effective conflict resolution and the dialogues that go along with it part of the fabric of your school. In short, a system of structured conflict resolution—taught, used, and reinforced—will help people disagree agreeably. The following is one process that could serve as a foundation on which to build, adapted from a system designed by Bob Chadwick (2012) of Consensus Associates in Terrebonne, Oregon. It is not the only system available, but it is one you can teach, use, and reinforce with students and staff alike. This is what it involves.

When students are in conflict, murmurs typically abound. This is when, ideally, a well-meaning student or adult in the school will whisper in your ear that something is up. At the news, you try as best you can to clear about a half hour on your calendar for a conversation. First, talk discreetly with both students separately to gather information if there is time. Do so when you initially believe that a conflict resolution session is in order.

Plan a time over the next hour or so when two different adults will bring the two students to your office simultaneously. Both students should see the other escorted down the hall and into your waiting room, ensuring that neither thinks the other called for the meeting. If one looks resistant, you want the other to have the opportunity to look equally resistant in full view. It needs to be clear to both students that you're the one who wants the conflict resolution, not necessarily one of them, even if that isn't the full truth.

Invite both into your office and share that you have heard from staff members there may be an issue the two of them need to discuss. If one of them happened to alert you rather than staff, don't let on. Mention the most efficient way to get them back to class is to use the conflict resolution model. You might even ask them, "Are you with me on this?" and punctuate a nod accordingly, even if one or both grimaces. Note you didn't ask permission.

Then you can say something like:

> I wish to thank both of you for sitting down with me for just a few minutes today, and I realize that both of you would much rather be in class right now. I respect that. There may be an issue the two of you are working through, and I need to feel better that you are on a good path. So we'll take a few minutes to share our perspectives, and if we believe we can move forward with the day, I'll get you back to class. Is that OK?

Invariably, they agree. Arrange chairs in a triangle, with the two students facing you on an angle, not toward each other, so that you are the focus point. You do not want them seething at each other while you are talking into both of their ears; rather, they face you with the option of glancing at each other when they feel comfortable.

Set some ground rules. The dialogue might look like this:

> First, let's go over the ground rules for our time together. I want you both talking to me during this session, not talking directly to each other. If you feel comfortable talking to each other, you can do so at the end. Can you do that?

(Their response.)

> I'll do my best to have a balance of conversation today. If I start one question with one of you, I'll start the next question with the other. While one of you is talking, the other is not to interrupt for any reason. There will always be time for a response, and I'll be sure to get one from each of you. You will have your time to talk. You will have a voice and be heard. I hope that I don't have to issue any reminders here, but I will if needed. Do you understand?

(Their response.)

> Finally, let's keep this conversation professional. Keep profanity out of this if you can, unless you are sharing a quote that was said at some point. Even if so, try to abbreviate the bad words so that I don't have to hear them. Can you do that?

(Their response.)

> OK, it's time to get started.

At this point, give the appearance you are starting randomly, but in actuality, start with the person who will provide the best and most accurate foundation for what is happening, with the hope that this person will also be able to provide such without any excessive emotion. This might sound like:

> [Student 1], I'm going to start with you.
> What is your perception of the problem you are having with [student 2], and how do you feel about it?

The latter part of the question is important, as often, in conflict, students do not get vulnerable about their feelings inside, which is key for a resolution. Student 1 shares, and often, you must remind students in this situation to share how they feel about it. Don't let them off the hook. If they don't share a feeling, prod for it. At times, you'll need to settle for an opinion or thought, but strive for the feeling.

Then, alternate and ask the same question:

> [Student 2], now that we have heard from [student 1], what is your perception of the problem, and how do you feel about it?
> (Student 2 shares.)

You then take them at their word that the problem is what they articulate. A brief paraphrase is often not necessary or useful, because the point is that they talk and you facilitate. If what they said is long and complicated, then you might quickly paraphrase, but don't editorialize. This is important. You are not there to fix the problem. Don't offer an opinion.

You then move into what each *needs* from the other. The eventual point is to move from their current emotional state into their cognitive state, but not before paying homage to what they are feeling emotionally. When you ask them what they need from each other, you are targeting their emotional selves. You'll have to get these needs addressed, because I have found that emotional needs must be satisfied before one can attend to cognitive energies. Start this second question with the student who went second in the first question. You're alternating.

> [Student 2], what do you need from [student 1], so that you both can work through this conflict and move forward productively?
> (Student 2 shares.)
> [Student 1], you've heard what [student 2] needs; what do you need from [student 2] so that you can both work through this conflict and move forward productively?
> (Student 1 shares.)

Give these a bit of time to sink in—for about fifteen seconds or so. Try not to paraphrase unless you really need to. The point is to honor their needs through their voices. Now it's time to move from emotional to cognitive perception.

> [Student 1], you've both shared what you need. What can you do for [student 2] so that you can move forward productively and get this conflict behind you?
> (Student 1 shares, typically after a pause to think. You then give that a few seconds for this to sink in and thank student 1.)
> [Student 2], you've heard what [student 1] is willing to do. What can you do for [student 1] to move forward productively and get this conflict behind you?
> (Student 2 shares.)
> (You let this sink in and then thank student 2.)

At this point, you summarize quickly the needs and the willingness of both to do something to get beyond the conflict. Keep your summary brief, and don't editorialize. Again, their voices are important, not yours.

You then say to both of them, "Can you live with this?" Look at both of them, offering a hopeful look and slightly punctuate to both of them with a nod of your head. Move your eyes back and forth hopefully. You'll probably get a yes. Thank them for their excellent work at conflict resolution. But you're not done.

At this time, you'll want to mention to them that despite their best work, there may be folks out in the school wanting the scuttlebutt and even wishing that the conflict will continue. You will need their assurances that if anyone asks, they will simply say, "We worked it out, and it's over." This will be a non-negotiable. You'll share that if they cannot do this, they cannot go back to class. Either you start the conflict resolution over again, *because the problem as articulated was really not the crux of the issue*, or there may need to be a pause, sending them both home. At which point, they'll return to your office before returning to class, to pick up where they left off.

In short, once leaving the office, violating a pact of resolution is serious—it is an immediate *classes closed* for the two students in conflict and trip home for the day or longer, pending a more serious parent or guardian meeting. Also, they must make a pact with you that if they hear anything about the other one saying anything negative beyond this meeting, that these are probably rumors intended to stir up the fire, and rather than go directly to each other to confront, they will instead come back to the office to have you facilitate a professional conversation. They are then welcome to return to class. On rare and very successful days, they may even give each other a hug or handshake, but don't ask for or expect it. Let it happen naturally. You've done your job resolving conflict with consensus in mind. It is all handled within the Chadwick (2012) tradition of how you work with people to value what's inside them, honor their voices, and appreciate their perspectives in order for them to leverage their best selves to engage in collaborative problem solving with others.

TIP

When the conflict resolution ends and the two students are preparing to walk out of your office, stay in your seat as they rise to leave, so that the two of them rise and exit together. At times, this results in them striking up a friendly conversation about other things while walking out and down the hall. In fact, their topic of conversation might even be you, and this is OK.

The How: Strategies to Use With Staff

The following strategies—leveraging compassionate accountability and using the power of the circle—are effective ways to lay the foundation for your work with staff.

Leverage Compassionate Accountability

Great teaching involves great modeling. You have the ability to do this in your role with compassionate accountability, and it makes a positive impact in terms of students and staff learning a new way of being while living professional lives with each other. This strategy comes by way of the work of Next Element Consulting, described more fully in Regier (2016), and has for many years worked to offer the world strategies on how to leverage conflict into productivity. Next Element's work was inspired in part by Stephen B. Karpman (2014), originator and author of the drama triangle, which involves a visual depiction of a triangle and, in the corners, people assuming roles as either perpetrators, victims, or rescuers in situations of distress, and even sometimes switching from one to the other midstream (that is, moving around the triangle). Karpman (2014) explains how perpetrators look to find victims, and perplexingly sometimes victims look for perpetrators; this is known as the "Kick Me" sign syndrome because victims sometimes seem to place a figurative sign on their back to invite more victimization in their quest for role fulfillment. Likewise, rescuers look for victims, and victims will often look for rescuers. It might sound like this would be helpful, but in reality, these roles just keep the drama triangle alive, and never allow participants to step into more positive behavior. When students refer to the drama in school, it's apparent that these three roles are negative and mutually reinforce each other. Your job is to stop the drama by teaching folks how to turn these roles around positively.

Karpman's (2014) discovery of the compassion triangle notes each role on the drama triangle has a corresponding productive role when not in drama: persistence (for those persecutors in drama), resourcefulness (for those rescuers in drama), and vulnerability (for those victims in drama). Next Element created a compassion cycle, as illustrated in Regier (2016), that empowers people to resist the negative pull of drama and allows them to move through conflict productively toward better outcomes. Note the elements are similar, with the characteristic of vulnerability replaced with openness, a construct Next Element found more fitting to a contemporary model. The Next Element compassion cycle is presented in figure 7.1.

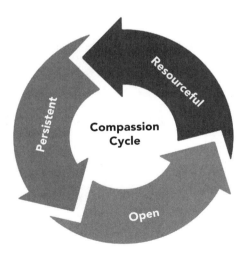

Source: © 2012 by Next Element Consulting. Used with permission.

FIGURE 7.1: The compassion cycle.

The overall idea in leveraging compassionate accountability, which again involves the notion of struggling with and maintaining dignity (Regier, 2016), is to approach situations of conflict with a certain strategy in how you deliver your message. Through such, Next Element (Regier, 2016) notes, you can leverage your openness or courageous transparency, resourcefulness in creative problem solving, and persistence in accountability and consistency between word and deed (Regier, as cited in Duncan, 2018). These three strategies allow you to maintain the conversation with compassion rather than inviting it to spin off into drama.

Note how you can live compassionate accountability and thus teach others how to do so as well through your modeling. You begin your remarks in the cycle at *open*, and then move through *resourceful* and *persistent* and finish back with *open*, using a series of compassionate statements that you apply intentionally in order. Regier (2016) notes in his book *Conflict Without Casualties: A Field Guide for Leading With Compassionate Accountability*:

> The Formula can be used any time you detect a drama role in yourself or another person, or you identify a significant gap between what you want and what you are experiencing and want to pursue a solution that requires conflict. (p. 155)

At *open*, disclose your feelings without pointing out the other's behavior (Next Element, in Regier, 2016). You could say, "I'm feeling a bit of angst as I work with you here," or "I'm sad that we have experienced this turn of events." Do not ask others if they feel likewise; just share what is going on with you. State your own wants. Then, move to *resourceful*, and offer some problem-solving resources or ask for helpful information. Share the gap you are feeling if you wish (Next Element, in Regier, 2016). You could say, "There is a gap between what I'm seeing here and what I'm hoping to achieve; [then provide information on what the gap is]," or "I have noticed that each time X happens, Y is the result." Then, move to *persistent* and state your boundaries and commitments (Next Element, in Regier, 2016). For example: "Please know that as we work to solve this, one thing that I plan to be firm on is civil treatment of our game referees." Finally, return to *open*, where you can check in with yourself and the other person about feelings or perspective (Next Element, in Regier, 2016). For example: "How are you feeling with this?" Be sure to understand that it might take a number of trips around the cycle to get the result you are seeking, all the while inviting critical conversations to move forward productively.

TIP

Keep in mind, as Regier and Next Element note, "The only way forward is forward" (from openness, through resourcefulness, through persistence, and into openness once again), in effectively using the compassion cycle (N. Regier, personal communication, January 26, 2021).

Use the Power of the Circle

Resolving conflict with consensus in mind has a proactive strategy you can teach and model that I call the power of the circle. Adapted from Bob Chadwick (2012) of Consensus Associates, I have used this technique for many years while working with groups to discuss issues, solve problems, and make decisions through consensus. It works well in staff meetings—that is, if you have the time.

The power of the circle works well in groups from about eight to twenty people. It is facilitated by a person who is willing to share equal power with each of the other members in the group. You can do so as the assistant principal if you are willing to assume and actively rectify any power-level differentials. As you have titular authority, you will need to work overtime to assure the group that you will not be making the final decision; then you'll need to follow through and honor that commitment.

First, arrange everyone in a circle or boardroom-style table setting. Everyone must be able to look at one another. Next, ensure that all involved have equitable materials and resources in order to make the decision. Note I specify *equal* power and *equitable* materials and resources. For example, the latter might involve audio materials for someone with visual impairments (thus, equitable access) or a certain more spacious place at the table for a person in a wheelchair (equitable access), yet that person would have no more or less decision-making authority (thus, equal). You then share the norms for group discussion.

Have someone who has comprehensive knowledge of the issue or decision under consideration make an informational presentation. Folks in the group will have the opportunity to ask questions of the presenter when recognized by the facilitator of the group. Keep note of who asks questions, and if it appears that some folks have more questions than others, pause to ask those who are not asking questions. At the conclusion of the presentation and question-and-answer session, the power of the circle begins.

Share with the group that you will start with a volunteer who will offer perspective. Set reasonable parameters for volunteers, such as three minutes. No interruptions or questioning by others is allowed. The folks speaking are not allowed to ask questions of others in the group—simply to share. When that person is finished, move a certain direction around the circle, clockwise or counterclockwise. Invite each person to share similarly. They can pass if they wish, and during the sharing, they will have the same courtesy accorded those who have shared prior, in terms of no interruptions or questions. Again, those presenting will not be able to ask questions of others.

The goal is to have everyone's voice heard around the table and then, as facilitator, move around the table to everyone one more time so that those ideas inspired the first time around but not yet shared are then heard. You might notice that some who have passed on the first circle speak up the second time around and have amazing insight. This happens often with introverts, who may not like to talk as much but sometimes have a talent for synthesizing what has been said.

TIP

Teach that there are ground rules with power of the circle discussions, such as no use of phones or texting, so as to be present in what others are saying. Keep to a minimum nonverbal displays of positive or negative emotions that others can discern, as these can impede the notion of everyone having a voice. The key here is to maintain reasoned temperament, much like a judicial body deliberating.

Once the power of the circle brings in everyone's voice with two circuits around, open things up for discussion. The extroverts will probably monopolize as it is their nature, and this is OK. The point is that the circle has brought power and voice to all in the room. When it appears that discussion is settling, work to craft a consensus decision statement with all involved. The goal is to put together something you all can live with. If this is too difficult, a smaller group can work on the problem, and you can reconvene the group to ponder the smaller group's conclusions. When doing so, embrace the power of the circle once again and discuss the consensus statement similarly: two times around the circle and open discussion. That hopefully results in a decision that you all can live with, via consensus.

The How: Strategy to Use With You

Teachers prepare for the lessons they teach; so should you as an assistant principal. Have a lesson plan template available that serves as a guide for how you'll teach the important life lessons you wish students will learn from you. Your template will include, at minimum, the following elements: what you will teach; the goal you wish to achieve; what you will share and model; how you will monitor a student's attempt; circling back, discussing, and assessing; and then trying things out a next time. The reproducible tool for this chapter (page 129) is an example of what this could look like.

These elements are a throwback to the work of education professor Madeline Hunter (1982) on objective, input, modeling, guided practice, and independent practice; they also echo techniques for gradual release of responsibility (Pearson & Gallagher, 1983), as I do owe a debt to these experts and those methods.

Instructional design experts Douglas Fisher and Nancy Frey (2013) contribute important thinking about the effectiveness of the gradual release of responsibility; they note the importance of students experiencing four phases of learning, including focused instruction, guided instruction, collaborative learning, and independent tasks. In such, focused instruction is recursive and can occur anywhere in the lesson; guided instruction involves high expectations and providing student support. Collaborative learning helps students develop critical thinking skills and inquiry, and independent learning focuses on application (Fisher & Frey, 2013). Applying these phases to your work as an assistant principal, your focused instruction is the advice you deliver; guided instruction is helping facilitate with students a demonstration of how they could handle things correctly. Collaborative learning is the student's opportunity to try things out their own way while working with peers, and independent learning is where the rubber meets the road with students trying your advice on for size, with real teachers or staff or other students.

So, while all of this teaching and facilitative learning is going on, do something all the while that seems obvious, if not counterintuitive. Plan to be you. Project a style that is still much the same version of yourself as when you were a great teacher. Ensure that your vibe projects unconditional positive regard for students and those with whom you work. Couple your high standards with consistent care and a road map for success, just like in parenting. This will resonate with others and invite respect. Again, it might seem that all these things are natural, and you can do them without even thinking. But in the midst of a busy and sometimes harried day, it's easy to derail. Have the plan so that you can model a definite path to success for students. Compare this idea to being in the military, in that one can fall back on training in stressful situations. Ensure that your students not only practice but practice more perfectly when they don't have things just perfect, but close. Pay attention to the little details of your lessons and what they are doing with them. Reteach as Fisher and Frey (2013) suggest. And reteach again if necessary. It works.

The following are lessons that assistant principals can teach students regarding the students' own life skills that typically bring them to your office in the first place. Have a plan for how you will teach them.

- Prioritize social-emotional regulation.

- Solve problems with others.

- Get along with the teacher.

- Make good decisions.

- Stay in school and don't leave when stressed.

- Do difficult things, especially those that are academic, in front of friends you wish to impress.

Prepping like teachers do involves planning ahead. Sit down with a laptop, device, or lesson-planning book on an evening or weekend and think deeply about what you will teach, how you will teach, and then visualize success. More than anything, write things down. Commit them to a document, a file, or a notebook. Read it over and over again to become familiar, just like teachers getting ready to teach their classes. This is high-stakes stuff; make the most of it through deft planning and preparation.

Toolkit for Tomorrow: Next Steps

These next steps provide some suggestions for how you can put the ideas in this chapter into action.

- Get something subtle that will alert others that you are in a teaching role in your assistant principalship. Display it in your office. Mine was a desktop stand that said "An Apple for the Teacher" that I had since my first year of teaching. It always reminded me of my place as a teacher, and it reminded others of the role that I respected and tried to carry out. Do you have something in mind that could represent the forever-teacher in you? If so, display it beginning tomorrow. Subtlety is a nice way to go about it.

- Strive to find parallels in your role that require academic tenacity, much as you are trying to build in students. Then, find five role models that students wish to emulate, and identify five aspects of academic tenacity in each that allowed them to reach their goals. Be sure you can rattle these off when students visit your office, and don't stretch to make connections; if they're not clear and compelling, students will not respond as well. For example, countless young people identify attorney and former First Lady Michelle Obama as a role model. I believe her aspects of academic tenancy would include the following.

  - **Self-efficacy:** Without a single hint of entitlement, she made things happen for herself to get where she is in life. Nobody overindulged her.

  - **Curiosity:** She wants to learn more about people and circumstances of all kinds.

  - **Empathy:** Her desire to help uplift others helped her champion many important causes, such as good nutrition for children.

  - **Resilience:** In spite of obstacles, she displayed calmness, coolness, and collectedness when it was probably pretty challenging to do so while living in the public eye.

- **Deferred gratification:** She supported her husband and partner's career while having many gainful areas of expertise herself. Now, she is able to leverage all she has, in the way she wishes to do so, for the rest of her life.

- Some of these ideas for academic tenacity might need some work in terms of your own awareness of them or the examples you could provide before you're ready to roll them out to students you talk to, but there's no time like the present to start getting them ready. When you have students' rapt attention, you'll be glad to have some examples ready to go.

- Practice your conflict resolution skills on a few relatively docile pairs of students who are having minor disagreements with each other. If you have not facilitated these meetings before, don't jump into the deep end right away with two potentially volatile individuals, for example. Know that for the more explosive situations, you can always add a fourth chair—that of an adult both students in the room respect. This person sits opposite from you so that triangle formation becomes a diamond. The extra adult has no formal role other than to keep the collective blood pressure down for all involved. When inviting other adults, let students know they are present because they care for both students, and for no other reason.

- Facilitate by using the power of the circle in your next consensus-based discussion. Try it with an issue that is not high stakes but is important enough to take people's time in the activity.

- Practice in the mirror the compassionate accountability strategies until a trip around openness, resourcefulness, persistence, and openness feels and appears natural to others (that is, you in the mirror).

- Complete the professional development activity on page 129. This will give you an opportunity to actually set out a playbook for how to capitalize on teachable moments when you encounter them.

Professional Development: A Deeper Dive—Capitalizing on Teachable Moments

Instructions: In this professional development activity, take some time to plan ahead for the teachable moments mentioned in this chapter's strategies. Fill out the following lesson plan chart for teachable moments you will undoubtedly encounter. Consider this a playbook for when you have students visit you, so that you know what to do, what to say, and how to assess the quality of your teaching.

Capitalizing on Teachable Moments: Your Assistant Principal's Lesson Plan					
Prior to Student Implementation				**Post-Implementation**	
Topic you wish to teach (your teachable moment)	What is the goal of your lesson?	What specific skills will you share and model for the student?	How will the student use these skills, in what context, and how will you monitor the attempt?	As you circle back, discuss, and assess, how did things go?	How might the student adjust, or not, in trying things out next time?
Prioritizing social-emotional regulation					
Solving problems with others					
Getting along with the teacher					
Making good decisions					
Staying in school and not leaving while stressed					
Doing difficult things (academic) in front of an audience					

CHAPTER 8
SAFEGUARDING AN EQUITABLE EDUCATION FOR ALL

Sitting inside the historic and picturesque Greensky Hill Indian United Methodist Church in Charlevoix, Michigan, I was honored to attend a milestone event for one of my students. One of my assistant principal roles was to work with our school's Title VI Indian education coordinator to help ensure excellence in education for the Indigenous students and families with whom she worked. I had first met this student when he attended my summer school class as a young middle schooler. He and I immediately connected, and years later in high school, I often would seek him out and ask how he was doing. I felt it important to work closely with the local communities, and I believe folks knew how much it meant to me. Experiences brought me closer to local traditions, such as suppers honoring loved ones and powwows with joyous singing, dancing, and feasting. Mine was an opportunity to serve as a special advocate for students of Indigenous descent and to understand that communities have differences among them. Yours may be much different, yet the universal idea for assistant principals is that you make intentional your involvement with students from diverse backgrounds. Learn from them and their families. It's important to share openly with colleagues that we are especially willing to safeguard and champion the rights of underserved students, and we encourage them to join us in our efforts.

In this chapter, I discuss how to ensure that all students in your care receive an equitable education. After discussing the what and the why of championing all students, I'll move on to how to do so with strategies for use with students, staff, and yourself.

The What and the Why

Assistant principals safeguard an equitable education for all. They must be effortful to ensure the fair acquisition of resources and opportunities so that students and families are aware of what is available. This includes educational opportunities and coursework, informational resources and materials, and the time and effort of adult educators on their behalf. All students and families must receive a level playing field when resources are limited and tough decisions are necessary.

In championing all students, it is necessary to develop an operating definition of what *all* includes. *All students* includes students who are diverse in terms of their physiology and personality as well as those with differing levels of academic aptitude and proficiency. Diversity of race and ethnicity is also key as we seek to recognize and embrace differences, not minimize them. The notion of *all students* includes those with different identities, such as gender identity, sexual orientation, and factors pertaining to student self-concept, self-esteem, and self-efficacy. Circumstances work into the definition of *all*, including socioeconomic status, the functionality of homes, available community assets, and peer relations. Our definition of *all* should also take into consideration those who have been successful in navigating school and those who have not. Finally, *all* includes students who miss our attention for whatever reason.

Safeguarding an appropriate education for all ensures we are doing things right on behalf of students. When assistant principals ensure schools are doing things right, they see that the proper allocation of materials, resources, and talent is finding its way into the lives of all students. From a legal standpoint, doing things right is offering a free and appropriate public education in the least restrictive environment for every student. Gleaned definitionally from special education, this applies to all students. Assistant principals should ask themselves, "Are all students placed where they learn best?" If the answer is "No," then schedules should be rearranged. Let's take, for instance, students with exceptionalities, such as those with high abilities (formerly called *gifted and talented* in many locales), those in special education, and those who qualify for Section 504.

Your role with high-ability students is critical in that with the pressures of school accountability, as some have contended over the years, there exists a systemic incentive to pay more attention to students who must pass a standardized test and might not be able to do so, if left alone, than those who can pass with ease. Literature has referred to the students near any given test cycle's cut score line as the *bubble kids*—the ones who will help the school's average grade if we just give them a little bit more of our time and attention (Lauen & Gaddis, 2016). Findings suggest educational triage is more probable when states couple high accountability measures with an increase in standards expectations, because schools find more of their students are in danger of adversely affecting performance results (Lauen & Gaddis, 2016). They then can be pressured into paying attention to the students who they perceive have a shot.

The risk, however, is that the students who are high ability can be forgotten in the process. So can those who have already passed the test the year prior. One hazard for schools and high-ability students is that, according to the National Association for Gifted Children (NAGC, n.d.), educators often buy in to certain myths that work to the students' disadvantage. These include that gifted students need no help, so they'll do fine on their own; teachers challenge all students, so gifted students will be just fine; and Advanced Placement (AP) classes fit the bill in terms of gifted programming needs (NAGC, n.d.). High-ability students also have unique social and emotional needs where their "'gifts' can be both positive and negative" (Pederson, 2009, p. 280), and in some cases can increase in degree, in proportion to giftedness. In students, "perfectionism, extreme self-criticism, and disruptive, self-destructive, or delinquent behavior may affect school experiences and well-being" (Pederson, 2009, p. 280). Many squandered opportunities come about if someone is not safeguarding an appropriate education for high-ability students, which means appropriate challenge—in many cases, creatively designed learning situations that require much effort on the part of the school to create, monitor, and assess.

Your role with students in special education is critical because someone must take the lead in seeing students with talents, dreams, and value first, and their disabilities as something wonderfully unique about how they experience the world around them. How often over the years have we heard students labeled with their disability first, and their student status second? An example would be *special education students* rather than *students with exceptionalities*. We must adhere to what's called person-first terminology. Students in special education are guaranteed under U.S. law to receive a free and appropriate public education in the least restrictive environment and be "educated with their peers without disabilities to the maximum extent appropriate" (Yell, 2019, p. 62).

International research on free, inclusive, and appropriate public educational practices has been undertaken in Canada, China, Denmark, Germany, Japan, Mexico, the Netherlands, Singapore, Taiwan, and the United Kingdom and has determined "variability and lack of consistency exists in the assessment, identification and services provided to students with [learning disabilities] across countries in the three subcontinents as compared to the United States" (Agrawal, Barrio, Kressler, Hsiao, & Shankland, 2019, p. 110). These findings suggest that educators and parents using collaborative approaches in decision making can make a difference, especially with the support of school administration. You are a big part of student success in these instances. Parents of students who qualify for special education services need an advocate within the school administration. They need to know that there is someone who sees their children with affection and will work valiantly to ensure that they are receiving excellent developmental experiences that cherish their interests, aptitudes, and abilities. They need to know that someone is on their team and that you respect the fact that the parents are team captains. That is where the assistant principal shines.

TIP

Categories of special education disabilities under the Individuals With Disabilities Education Act (2004) include autism, deaf-blindness, deafness, hearing impairment, intellectual disability, multiple disabilities, orthopedic impairments, other health impairments, emotional disturbance, specific learning disability, speech or language impairment, traumatic brain injury, and visual impairment, including blindness. The *World Report on Disability*, published by the World Health Organization and World Bank (2011), estimates numbers of children up to fourteen years old living with disabilities range from 93 million to 150 million worldwide. The report categorizes students broadly as those with "learning, cognitive, behavioral, or emotional impairments," as well as "intellectual impairments," "visual or hearing impairments," and "emotional disturbances" (World Health Organization & World Bank, 2011, p. 214), and notes the United Nations Convention on the Rights of Persons with Disabilities "recognizes the right of all children with disabilities both to be included in the general education systems and to receive the individual support they require" (p. 205). Countries with policies and documented processes for implementing IEPs for students with disabilities in the least restrictive environments include "Australia, Canada, New Zealand, the United Kingdom and the United States" (World Health Organization & World Bank, 2011, p. 220).

Another group of students to think about is those who, in the United States, qualify for accommodations and programmatic considerations under Section 504 of the Rehabilitation Act of 1973. Comparable protections internationally may be found in Article 26, Habilitation and Rehabilitation, of the United Nations Convention on the Rights of Persons with Disabilities (World Health Organization & World Bank, 2011); however, it seems implementation can lag behind legislation and policy in many locales. It is critical that you champion these students as well because in some communities, there is a general lack of awareness of Section 504 and what it provides for students in need. In others, it seems only more well-connected or socioeconomically savvy parents leverage the services available. Section 504 protects "any person who (i) has a physical or mental impairment which substantially limits one or more of such person's major life activities, (ii) has a record of such an impairment, or (iii) is regarded as having such an impairment" (U.S. Department of Education, n.d.). One of these major life activities, of course, is *learning*. Many of the impairments covered by Section 504 have just as much adverse impact on a student's ability to navigate school, and much to the surprise of teachers, it is not a special education teacher's responsibility to provide classroom accommodations; the general education teacher is required to provide them. These could include testing accommodations, instructional accommodations, and even environmental accommodations. As an assistant principal, you understand and share with your general education teachers that if parents are dissatisfied with what the educators are doing, they can file a complaint with the U.S. Department of Health and Human Services Office for Civil Rights.

Schools, as much as society, inherently contain a certain amount of power, privilege, domination, and inequity that has developed over time. You must safeguard against this. Safeguarding an appropriate education for all involves empowering those who have been marginalized and understanding that issues of racial, ethnic, and cultural difference have been challenges in our profession as they are in our society. I would argue, inspired by best-selling author and historian Ibram X. Kendi (2016), these issues are more the result of the system in place than of the flaws of the people within. Over time, inequitable practices have developed as a byproduct of our education system's architecture, history, and current attributes to perpetuate through policy and practice what we now experience. Assistant principals can have an impact here directly, as they can "foster equitable environments through deliberate attention to cultural inclusivity in their daily work" (Goldring et al., 2021, p. 76).

One example is how often educators profess to embrace diversity, even though according to the National Center for Education Statistics (2020), 79 percent of educators in the United States are White. In Canada, teachers not in a visible minority were at 93.1 percent, according to the 2006 Census (Ryan, Pollock, & Antonelli, 2009); in England, 85.7 percent of all teachers in state-funded schools were White British, according to the United Kingdom Department for Education (2021). Additionally, research on bias has shown that teachers reflect the same pro-White racial attitudes of nonteachers, both explicit and implicit (Starck, Riddle, Sinclair, & Warikoo, 2020). If we do not explore whether current structures that run schools have been built upon implicit biases, we're not going to be positioned to champion all students.

Take school discipline, for one. Research published by the Mid-Atlantic Regional Educational Laboratory notes while exclusionary discipline rates have declined since 2010 for all subgroups, Black students and students with disabilities continue to be suspended and expelled at more than two times the rate of other students, even with the same types of infractions (Lacoe & Manley, 2019).

Infractions were in six categories: (1) attendance, (2) conduct, (3) drugs and alcohol, (4) health related, (5) sex, and (6) violence. In terms of disproportionality, Black students in the study in 2017–2019 were cited for 58 percent of all incidents while they comprised 45 percent of the population. White students were cited for 25 percent of incidents while they comprised 37 percent of the population (Lacoe & Manley, 2019). A redoubled focus on equity is long overdue.

Another study notes the challenges school leaders face in having authentic conversations with their faculty and staff. Researcher Alison C. Tyler (2016) finds White educators are hesitant to talk about race and often suggest deficits, such as lack of parental care for an education, as the reasons students are unmotivated or uncooperative, and they project a lack of literacy experiences in the home upon the students and communities in which marginalized students live. Using terms such as *those populations*, White "saviors" then adopt the roles or perspective of missionaries (Allen & Liou, 2019). Let's take, for example, standardized tests "that empower Whites to affirm their intellectual and material superiority and use standards as property to subjugate students of color to an inferiority status" (Allen & Liou, 2019, p. 691). These tests determine *who* has access to *what*, next, in terms of educational opportunity.

Beyond issues of race and ethnicity, assistant principals must champion rights and opportunities of those who have diverse identities in terms of gender or sexual orientation. Teachers need to be equipped with understanding of both theories and practices related to inclusion, and—most critical—a layered approach of dialogue and empowerment, including such things as a commitment to equity, modeling democratic practice, noting power and privilege, questioning the status quo, offsetting asymmetrical power relationships, developing critical thinking in students, and having deep care for students and community (Page, 2016). Students must feel safe to be OK within their own identities, and this is where you are key as an assistant principal.

In your role, you must honestly recognize whether your school has fallen short in terms of access, equity, diversity, and identity. It involves an honest appraisal of historical and contemporary power imbalances inherent in our systems. Doing the right things has to do with who you are as a person and as an assistant principal. You can be the change agent and have courage to take risks with your words that may bump up against the power structures that have been built by those who have benefited from the systems. In short, as an assistant principal, you have privilege, which includes status privilege and power privilege. It also may very well include White privilege. And even though some may believe we are now in a world that is post-racial or all-inclusive, racial inequalities and racism remain rampant (Carr, 2016). In fact:

> Race matters because of the lived experiences and historical realities that have placed racial identity at the center of how countries and peoples have been organized in relation to socially constructed racial hierarchies that have always placed the White race as the pinnacle. (Carr, 2016, p. 54)

Thus, if you're White, and many assistant principals are, you have White privilege. National estimates based on Wallace Foundation research estimate that 24 percent of assistant principals are people of color, compared with 13 percent of teachers and 19 percent of principals (Goldring et al., 2021). The flip side would indicate 76 percent of assistant principals are White, with the privilege that comes with it. The point here is that as a member of the societal power structure—even of the perceived power structure—you are positioned to wield influence to make changes when needed. Use these opportunities.

Safeguarding an appropriate education for all is difficult work, and someone at school must be the one to begin or reinvigorate it, if it is not ongoing. As an assistant principal, you are the one standing between someone's successful education and someone's future circumvented by circumstance. You've got to remove the barrier. Some families have built up generational resentment toward school as an institution, the teachers within, and certainly those in educational leadership. This resentment typically is borne of prior negative experiences in school. You can bet on many trips to the assistant principal's office for the parents from these families, chips on their shoulders, grudges to fuel, and a sense of desperation. You need to do the difficult job of receiving these parents, describing the situation, and working effortfully to foster a connection. They are counting on you to safeguard what is important to them.

Safeguarding an appropriate education helps reduce the negative influence of assumptions on student success. Assumptions exist for the most part in our blind spots. They are an invisible filter through which we perceive the world, and they whisper in our ear subliminally to rationalize the decisions we make. As people, we have behaviors, and undergirding our behaviors are our beliefs about what we should be doing. Our values influence our beliefs, acting as arbiters when our beliefs conflict or contradict each other. Assumptions lie even more deeply embedded, making things even more complicated. This is where we can get tripped up as assistant principals because we often do not realize assumptions are influencing what we do. This includes both the assumptions of those with whom we work and our own while we are working with them. It is almost as if there are multiple mini-dialogues going on just outside our awareness, as assumptions put us on automatic pilot, thinking we are heading in the right direction yet with a veil over clear thinking. An excellent resource on this topic is *Finding Your Blind Spots: Eight Guiding Principles for Overcoming Implicit Bias in Teaching*, by curriculum designer and edtech expert Hedreich Nichols (2021), which involves uncovering your own assumptions, recognizing those of others and those inherent in our profession, and working as an educator to ensure equitable outcomes. Particularly insightful is knowing when you're ready for change and others are not (Nichols, 2021) and, thus, knowing how this knowledge could serve as that lens for clear thinking and informing what we might do, given the developmental reality among colleagues.

Our assumptions also give rise to microaggressions. While *microaggressions* (words or actions that discriminate, usually subtly or unintentionally, against marginalized groups) is the well-known term, Ibram X. Kendi (2019) shares that there is really nothing minor about them. Nichols (2021) refers to a subset of these called *microinsults*, which I concur aptly describes what happens frequently in the society in which we live. Influenced by Kendi (2019), I developed my own term—*assumptive aggressions*. What are they? They are certain statements or behaviors we project on members of marginalized or other social groups that are not in good form; in fact, they can represent underlying assumptions rooted in societal classism or systemic racism. When we are made aware of our microaggressions or assumptive aggressions, our response might be that we didn't intend them, and that we just simply wouldn't do that. At times, we might even take offense to being called out on them. An example of a microaggression or assumptive aggression might be, "I had this wonderful conversation with a person who was [insert marginalized race or ethnicity], and he was so intelligent. I was truly impressed."

Another could be, "You really set yourself apart from the other [gender-specific insertion] in class; it's impressive you're doing so well." Another would be a ticket taker at the student job fair greeting a student with a ruddy complexion and camouflage jacket, saying, "Thanks for coming. We're glad you did. The trade schools start over there, on your left."

On the surface, the behavior to the casual onlooker could be pleasant and well-intended. To the person or group on whom the microaggressions or assumptive aggressions are levied, they can be insulting. Why is it impressive that a person of a certain race, class, appearance, or marginalized group is intelligent, unless your assumptions tell you it is typically otherwise? Why would one gender's class performance be impressive, unless assumptions tell us that it is typically otherwise? Why does one style of jacket or one's appearance symbolize someone who is typically not college-ready? Your assumptions, of course. While moving to unearth any assumptions you might have developed, don't be too hard on yourself; instead, be curious about how they may have come into play for you, and be open to what you find. Discuss them if you wish with someone you trust, and get a different perspective on what you might do next.

TIP

If you hear from others that what you have said or done is a microaggression or assumptive aggression, resist the temptation to say, "But I didn't mean it." After all, your surface self may not have meant it, but your assumptive self, inside self, certainly did. Move into that assumption and address it, rather than try to outflank or minimize it. Don't leave it comfortably inside. Be curious about what the other person said. It can take courage for others to tell you that you've just used a microaggression, especially when you're in a position of authority; thank them for it. If they are willing, ask them to kindly help you understand. Don't beat yourself up. Just learn, move on, and be effortful as you get to know yourself better over time.

The How: Strategies to Use With Students

The following strategies—leveling the playing field and cultivating your counterspace—are effective ways to lay the foundation for your work with students.

Level the Playing Field

Leveling the playing field means that each and every student should have access and equity in terms of offerings and opportunities, both academically and in extracurricular activities. Simply saying that all students have opportunities for this or that is not enough. Some families are more well networked than others. They know which teachers are desirable, how to get a leg up with coaches (which camps to attend; which equipment to donate; which contributions to make from their own businesses, such as the student's dad who is a banker, for example), and how to work the system (in the local civic organization with the superintendent). Access and equity means having an intentional plan to let students and families know not only what opportunities are available but how best to prepare to get those opportunities.

TIP

Have a staff member in touch with what the well-networked parents know and are saying about opportunities in your school, whether it is the teachers to get, the grade-level teams to join, or the way to get things done. Encourage this person unofficially to share this information with parents who are not so well connected.

Develop your game plan to message opportunities in a way that works for *all* students and families, well before the time to apply for or schedule those opportunities. Key here is augmenting what your guidance counselors do with families you work with particularly—for example, to share opportunities for taking the more rigorous courses in high school to obtain college credit. Your goal should be to target some of the frequent flyers to your office early in their high school careers. This is easier said than done, because sometimes when students avail themselves of the courses that stretch them, they experience difficulty with the receiving teachers whose tolerance wanes. In leveling your playing field, ensure your teachers do not demonstrate "the soft bigotry of low expectations," as President George W. Bush (as quoted in the *Washington Post*, 2000) puts it and expressed concern about in his No Child Left Behind speech to the NAACP's 91st Annual Convention. This happens when your colleagues profess the desire to protect students from failure while unintentionally depriving them. Saying, "Wouldn't this student be better suited for the general education class?" is one example.

Have a discussion with your principal and counselor about who is teaching the AP and International Baccalaureate (IB) classes. How long have they been doing so? If they were to experience an influx of diverse students into their classrooms, would they have the ability to connect, challenge, and motivate? Put the teachers who are connecting best with *all* students into these assignments one or two class periods per day. Have them teach your most rigorous courses, and by doing so, strategically encourage more of the students visiting your office to take those classes. Shatter the ceiling, and thus by doing so, level the playing field.

Reach out to counselors; let them know you are paying attention. Give them the names of students you want placed in these classes and challenged. Share your rationale, and be confident. Remember you must embrace the role of watching out for the underdog in access and equity. Students will be better off because you did things right.

Cultivate Your Counterspace

Think about the wide array of students you have in your school and how some seem to fit in more seamlessly and function better than others. Whether these are the popular students and those not so popular, or whether certain students run in cliques and others move between and among them, the bottom line is that some students feel more connected with school as you have designed it, and others feel less connected, or *othered*. This is particularly true for students who are members of minoritized or marginalized groups, those who don't feel they're a part of the dominant narrative or in sync with the way things are done, and accessed, in your school. Over time, this means these students are likely to lack access to valuable information adults provide, such as college preparation information. Some students may tune out of school altogether. Some students have more privilege in the way school is advertised to, communicated to, and shared with them. Some have the confidence to walk into the guidance counselor's office to get information, and others are more apprehensive.

As an assistant principal providing a safe and appropriate education for all, you have an obligation to create a sense of place and belonging for all students so that they develop the confidence to feel they're a part of things, self-advocate, and avail themselves of all school provides. Andrew D. Case and Carla D. Hunter (2012), writing for the *American Journal of Community Psychology*, note what you want to do is to foster within individuals their abilities in adaptive responding, a dynamic interplay of self-protective and self-enhancement mechanisms that muster psychological resources and bolster self-worth.

A powerful way to do this is to cultivate your counterspace, the notion of creating a certain amount of separation of certain groups from others in order to bring them closer together. The notion of counterspace is common in higher education, but it can and does exist in K–12 as you think about your own school. Author Micere Keels (2019) in *Campus Counterspaces: Black and Latinx Students' Search for Community at Historically White Universities* shares, "Counterspaces are those 'exclusionary' spaces where those of a similar social identity gather to validate and critique their experiences with the larger institution" (p. 11). Case and Hunter (2012) note that counterspaces challenge the "deficit-oriented dominant cultural narratives and representations concerning these individuals" (p. 261). Counterspaces create connectedness amidst stereotyping and feelings of alienation. Essentially we can define counterspaces as not only safe spaces but as "brave spaces" (Keels, 2019) because students who use them create bonds with each other and have each other's backs.

I think back to one example when I was in school administration, where each day after lunch, we would open up the gymnasium to students who wished to play basketball and other things. Many students would show up each lunch period, and others avoided the gym like the plague. A group of students, ones we might say were more the rock 'n' rollers or concert-goers, with longer hair and proudly on the fringe in their appearance, asked if they could use the school mezzanine, the area above the gym, to gather and play music through a portable PA system that I had access to. It was a great idea. The mezzanine became their place. It was a safe place for them to go; I could still supervise them as I could the others, and a really cool thing happened—some of the athletes on the court below started making requests. Two very different groups made a connection. It gave the rock 'n' rollers a sense of place, and brought them more into their school with other groups.

Counterspaces need a physical element to them, a demarcation of territory where certain students are allowed and encouraged to go to be with their group. They can be created by those who self-identify with similar interests such as the ones in my example; they could comprise those who wish to disconnect from "the scene"; or they could be organized by those who bond over issues of social justice or advocacy, or even those who in other ways feel marginalized or disenfranchised yet are comfortable around each other, such as gamers, budding disestablishmentarians, or self-proclaimed odd ducks. Counterspaces can pop up organically in certain locations, but it can be validating if the school provides actual space structurally for their use.

Students who have had similar experiences are in need of counterspaces as well. In these situations, it pays dividends to have an adult coordinating the initial coming together. These might include students experiencing divorce, homelessness, food insecurity, or even addictions. One of the best counterspaces I ever saw was a staff-facilitated tobacco cessation program that brought students and staff together each week, with both groups working toward their own personal goals of tobacco usage reduction and elimination. There was ceremonial sage burning and other elements of support-group membership, and overall, it created a group committed to supporting each other with an addiction sometimes vilified and disciplined by school officials rather than recognized and treated. Over time, the adults might even step back and allow the students to facilitate their counterspace.

So, what are you to do? Do something. Get your principal's permission to cultivate your counterspace. Carve out time each day for counterspace opportunities. Focus on the time you have during nonacademic periods, and make available space for students to congregate. Look for spaces in the library, at the ends of certain hallways (nooks and crannies), in the gym mezzanine, in school courtyards, and on school grounds if weather permits. Ask your maintenance crew to landscape with purpose; create walkways and patios. Encourage students to start daily video news programs about their school and provide them a small recording studio. Create spaces for your artists after lunch and before their next class. Build a pickleball court or a few putt-putt golf holes. Designate a laptop lounge with device-charging stations, and when you do so, arrange seating in a circle. Create intentional learning spaces with comfortable chairs and lounge-like seating in common spaces. Encourage staff who are respected and connected to advertise and put groups together based on student or staff issues and needs. Create a chill room in your school for students to go when they are frustrated with what is happening around them, and empower the adult staff member within to suggest that students get together and create their own counterspace. Prioritize and pay particular attention to the value of racial or ethnic affinity groups and counterspace, and ensure that they know what opportunities are there for them. Keels (2019) notes, "Contrary to what many assume, in racially-ethnically oriented counterspaces, race-ethnicity often recedes into the background enabling minority students to relax and lower their cultural defenses" (p. 94).

Creating counterspace admittedly provides for a certain degree of separation and some might say segregation, yet in the end, with your intentional support, what it does is bring students together in engagement around their own identities, which actually furthers your school's main purpose if it is to be inclusive. Keels (2019) cautions about what can happen without counterspace: "Classroom learning is the result of many successful interpersonal interactions among teachers and students. Thus, when students feel disconnected or misunderstood, their learning is negatively affected" (p. 85). Counterspace first of all fosters identify affirmation and a sense of safety; what happens over time is belonging, support, advice, resource sharing, and empowerment, with a feeling that together, we can do this thing! Keels (2019) shares that counterspaces "allow students to share empathy as well as information. As a result, students were better able to cope with the challenge of being othered" (p. 162), while Case and Hunter (2012) note that with counterspace, members can reimagine their own personal narratives through identity-affirming experiences.

The How: Strategies to Use With Staff

The following strategies—protecting safe zones and lifelines and doing difference differently—are effective ways to lay the foundation for your work with staff.

Protect Safe Zones and Lifelines

No matter how many structures and supports you put in place to help students navigate problems when they are occurring, there is a chance that these are still seen as a tool of the school to control students, at least from the student's perspective. Invariably, students and the staff who advocate for them most will create informally safe zones and lifelines to resolve issues that fall outside of what is prescribed, sanctioned, and staffed officially. Your challenge is to work effortfully to learn what is really going on when some students are having a tough day outside of your radar. At times, how things are accomplished and what deals are made to keep students in a good place are not what you would have wished. I encourage you to step back and respect these alternative avenues as long as they are not putting anyone at risk or increasing school liability uncomfortably.

Often, you will have a paraprofessional, administrative assistant, or member of the staff situated somewhere in the building who gathers students like chicks in a nest. Examples I have seen would be the reading aid who gathers many more students than would qualify for those services, the computer lab supervisor who has many more students hour by hour than the room has capacity for, or the itinerant school social worker who has students looking out the window for his car to arrive. We might also see here the attendance secretary whose desk and office space off the beaten path has a seemingly continual flow of students sitting alongside, often doing their work quietly. A couple of students might help the custodian unload a small truck for an entire afternoon, or a librarian has a student sitting with head down on a desk, taking a quick nap behind some shelves in the back of the library.

On the surface, you see students who are not where they are supposed to be, or at minimum dawdling to avoid class. There might be a problem at school or home that your radar has not picked up, and while you are doing the good work of solving other problems of which you are aware, informal lifelines have provided a way to keep these students from leaving school or making bad decisions and also, in many cases, have solved problems that many don't even know existed. Or, there might not be a problem going on, except that because of the systemic issues discussed earlier, no space is available for these students, and they are seeking their own counterspace. These safe zones not only provide a safe place to be but they also prevent problems; for example, when students take a moment to proceed to their own self-designated chill room, they often prevent themselves from staying somewhere that will push their buttons and increase their tendency to make bad decisions. It is a strategy for self-correction, really, that works. And it has happened in spite of you.

I have seen school administration handle this well and not so well. Admonishing these staff members that students are not supposed to be where they are not supposed to be is not a good response. Neither is reminding them that they are not in the role of interventionists requiring students in every case to get permission officially before seeking the advice or counsel of those they have designated as lifelines. But when school administration offers a positive observation to those staff members whom students are seeking out, letting them know it is nice that they are providing a lifeline, that's handling things well. You can also ask for your colleagues' help in giving teachers a heads-up that students are with them so that the school can fulfill its attendance-tracking obligations. Another way to handle things well would be to establish a trusted partnership with your lifelines and informal safe zone sponsors so that if students with bigger issues seek them out, they will let you know what is going on if safety is in question, enabling you to help keep an eye on these students for their own sake. Student care is a team sport.

When you find that despite your structures and support, as well as your good-natured offer for help with problem solving, students and staff have their own work-arounds that don't directly involve you at first, don't get offended. Instead, take a step back, let the situation move forward if things appear to be working, and help with the necessary alerts so no one is making phone calls home thinking the students are skipping school. After doing so, follow up with your lifelines and safe zone sponsors, letting them know you appreciate them for doing what they are asked to do regularly and well, and above that, for caring enough to take some extra time and unconditional positive regard to make a difference. Do all this, even if it is difficult.

Do Difference Differently

To do difference differently, identify practices, policies, materials, structures, expectations, and systems currently in place that are Eurocentric or otherwise support an inequitable status quo, and widen the gate of how your school can be more inclusive to diverse perspectives, practices, and people. One key step toward doing the right thing is to work with your principal and hiring teams to make every effort to ensure your new teachers look more like your student body than your existing teachers.

To do difference differently, you must first change the dialogue. It is not acceptable to be "color blind" or to say we are all the same as one human race. The impulse to think this way often arises from good intentions, but in reality, this allows White people to ignore the problems of racism, and it erases the identities of marginalized people (Wingfield, 2015). It also means that naturally curious students of the dominant culture don't have the tools they need to address misunderstandings and avoid microaggressions, and people of nondominant identities may feel singled out and self-conscious (Rogin, 2022). I once heard in a faculty development session, "I don't see Black and White. Everyone's the same to me." This is an example of *difference* done from a well-intended place but not one that is developmentally appropriate. It lacks sufficient racial and cultural humility. Of course, we see color. Of course, we see social class. Of course, we see differences in how we worship. Big differences. Not only is this OK; this is necessary. Students and staff need to see differences—to see color—because it's important that they understand the historical, ongoing, and tragically current social injustices that people of color and other marginalized or minoritized people have faced, and continue to face, each and every day. Recognizing, identifying, naming, and acknowledging difference is a first step toward positive change; doing something about injustice or inequity when you see it is a necessary step in moving further in that direction. You must remind your colleagues of this. The key is being curious, effortful, transparent, reflective, and humble.

Next, identify exclusively binary structures in your school that make some students and staff uncomfortable. Be mindful of *intersectionality*, which is the interconnected way that social categories or identities can overlap to create systems of discrimination or disadvantage. Intersectionality is the notion that many parts of our lives influence the sum total of who we are and what we need as people and individuals. It happens at the intersection of race, ethnicity, sex, gender identity, social class, academic aptitude, athletic prowess, and many other things that influence who we are and how we see the world. Ensure current conversations take place regarding facility-usage options that do not cause discomfort for nonbinary individuals and how intersectionality can broaden our plan of how we define who we are and the human experience.

Further, engage in conversations regarding the limits of Eurocentric teaching practices and their impact on who is sent to the office. Inclusive education authority Dianne Bradley (2007) in the *Journal of the Alliance of Black School Educators* shares that cultural norms in the Black community, such as the practice of call and response and the energy level of families in learning and spiritual situations, can pose problems for Black students in the classroom. White teachers may see Black students as disruptive and send them to the office, when they simply need to be understood and valued. Teachers in this case are not seeing what they must see.

Finally, conduct an equity audit. Lauryn Mascareñaz (2021), culturally responsive instructional expert and author of the book *Evident Equity: A Guide for Creating Systemwide Change in Schools*, asserts that equity audit tools "provide a large- or small-scale view of what exactly is happening in your school or district environment" (p. 16). Mascareñaz (2021) recommends Mid-Atlantic Equity Consortium's tool (https://maec.org/resource/equity-audit-materials), which is customizable. Researchers have studied whether educators ask themselves the following questions: "Do we frequently have conversations about race? Do we conduct equity audits that include disaggregation of face data?" (Amiot, Mayer-Glenn, & Parker, 2019). They envision an equity audit as "a process that addresses systemic inequities. Systemic inequities are those internal causes of inequity that have become part of the norm inside a school" (Amiot et al., 2019, p. 9). Doing so helps trigger improvement processes around race and racism. Teachers often evade or avoid the possibility of racism by blaming external factors for underperformance (such as poverty, family interest, and so on), not systemic factors inside. Researchers also found that failure of students of color was part of the school's norms. Racial deficit thinking abounds (Amiot et al., 2019). Strive to do something about it.

The point here is not to criticize or disavow the historical foundations on which our schools have been built but rather to recognize that to some, schools privilege certain students over others, even unintentionally, through their policies and practices. *Privilege* is defined as how members of a majority race, ethnicity, or ruling class are able to move through each day not burdened with connotations ascribed pejoratively to members of marginalized groups. They receive deference and, to use school parlance, a hall pass, on many of the things they do because people do not judge them negatively for the way they look. There are implications regarding which students are sent to the office, toward which students the teachers are constantly watching out of the corners of their eyes, and which students are reminded of yesterday's behaviors as they enter a classroom, even before today's behaviors begin. These pernicious realities are important for an assistant principal to closely consider as you do the right thing by your students.

The How: Strategy to Use With You

Safeguarding an appropriate education for all requires that you recognize your lived reality is not shared or embraced by some of your students. You may at times be uncomfortable that you are judged negatively because of your professional position or place in the majority, if that is where your identity lies. This is not where I am going to tell you not to take it personally; rather, I'm going to encourage you that it is a deeply personal experience and one from which you can learn and grow. Nichols (2021) emphasizes that guilt is normal and should not tip over into shame or defensiveness because these can cause you to cover up behaviors or avoid the topic. She asserts, "The only standing up you need to do as you explore your comfort level with race, gender, sexuality, belief systems, and so on, is to stand up for your students who need your support" (Nichols, 2021, p. 22). I share the following strategy with encouragement to go where things feel a bit difficult and explore more about you and your position, as well as how the expression *Where you stand depends on where you sit* applies. Once you have done so, strive to understand others from a place closer to them. I call this strategy *moving to the edge of discomfort.*

Doing the right things involves going somewhere challenging. It is about moving to the edge of discomfort. Moving to the edge of discomfort is where your most impactful learning can occur. It means actually moving a bit beyond your psychological, intellectual, and social-emotional zone of proximal development (Vygotsky [1978] would be proud), where you are just at the edge of what you can handle successfully and build on such for quality learning; it is going a bit further into a place authors have described as a productive zone of disequilibrium (Heifetz, Grashow, & Linsky, 2009), where over time, people sort through what they must determine is the essential and expendable, within the adaptive challenges they face. As the assistant principal, you need to be able to manage your own discomfort during these processes, while at the same time help others manage theirs, as you will readily witness that adaptive processes include distress, and it behooves you to have compassion for those struggling with expected change. Productive disequilibrium, thus, exists at your edge of discomfort, or limit of tolerance as authors Ronald Heifetz and colleagues (2009) note, where a productive zone of disequilibrium exists and some really cool things are possible. Here are a few ways to move to the edge of discomfort.

First, be vulnerable, and be OK with that. Confess to those with whom you are working when you are worried, have a bit of angst, or feel some trepidation with the situations you are navigating or with decisions you are about to make. Disclose your intentions. Vulnerability does not equal weakness. Vulnerability gives you permission to be imperfect, which is an essential part of being an effective educator (Boogren, 2018). Everyone with whom you work would do well to let down their walls and share honestly with colleagues what they are feeling. Once others can see you in your position of authority take the difficult step of sharing vulnerability, then acting with resolve, they will see that the two can work in tandem rather than in opposition.

Next, move to the edge of discomfort by examining your own privilege to the degree you have it and what it has allowed you to do more easily than others. Are you White, for example? If you are, you have gone through life without experiencing racial profiling. If you have status privilege, you probably get a deferential nod while in a meeting with bankers for a consumer loan rather than having them treat you much differently before and after they pull up your credit score. If you are a man, you probably have had an advantage competing for jobs with a higher starting salary than what's accorded to those without such privilege—that is, women (especially women of color), who have consistently earned 16 cents fewer on every dollar than men, according to ongoing Pew Research Center reports (Barroso & Brown, 2021). When you're able to do the admittedly uncomfortable work of recognizing these realities, you then have a social responsibility to leverage them for equity for all.

Finally, move to the edge of discomfort by getting input on how you are doing as an assistant principal from two groups of people: (1) those who *do not look like you* and (2) those who *do not like you*. Both are key in ferreting out a part of you that you must address. Reaching out to those who are different in terms of life perspective and preconceived notions of your value and performance can provide a wealth of information of how you are doing, albeit uncomfortably if you let it. It can also help build connections with these groups, which is well worth any discomfort involved.

Toolkit for Tomorrow: Next Steps

These next steps provide some suggestions for how you can put the ideas in this chapter into action.

- To unearth your assumptions, try thinking back as far as you can and recall what your parents and grandparents taught you about people and groups. Then, even if they did not teach you this directly, what did you overhear them saying, and how did they act, especially when they thought you were not around? What reading materials did you have around the house, and did these reflect any judgment on certain groups or others? To which organizations did your parents belong, and what group congregations, outings, and events were you taken to? What type of church did you attend if you did, and what did you learn in your early years? What cartoons did you watch or books did you read as a child, and how did they depict the characters in terms of who had influence and how they were caricatured? This will help educate you on things that may have influenced you that have escaped your radar.

- Seek out professional development opportunities that offer current information, expert presentations, and readings on issues of difference, diversity, inclusion, and the concept of identity intersectionality.

- Work with your principal to recruit and hire a diverse team of teachers, and strive to ensure your school does not have a disproportionate number of marginalized professionals working in support staff positions as opposed to working as teachers.

- Actively read new books that offer positions on history and historical contributions to society that fall outside the dominant Eurocentric perspective. The key is to read them for your own awareness and expansion of thought in terms of a larger conversation about diversity and the world around us. You will find that what we learned in school about American history, in particular, is told from one perspective, and there are other viewpoints and anecdotes out there that are helpful in developing your own understanding of what others in your school community might be thinking, valuing, or acting upon. Examples include *Lies My Teacher Told Me: Everything Your American History Textbook Got Wrong*, by James W. Loewen (2018), and *Stamped From the Beginning: The Definitive History of Racist Ideas in America*, by Ibram X. Kendi (2016). The point is not devaluing, debunking, or dismissing what we have been taught; it is just to expand on it educationally.

- Complete the professional development activity on page 146, which gives you some ideas about how to conduct your next special education case conference or disciplinary hearing in an equitable way. If a student moves forward unsuccessfully after such a meeting, then everyone at school has failed the student and family. I realize this sounds harsh, as families at times resist the services we offer, but we have to plan for that too. Keep in mind that with the right team and the right intentions, we can provide life-changing services.

Professional Development: A Deeper Dive—Safeguarding an Equitable Education for All

Instructions: As an assistant principal, you must do your homework before each meeting. Study and use the following cue card. It will help you get in the zone for what must be done.

Suggestions and Questions for You	Things You Have Done, Have Learned, and Must Keep in Mind for a Successful Meeting
Suggestion: Study Students' Grades and Attendance	
What do they tell you about current performance?	
Who could be an adult ally focusing on the positive?	
Suggestion: Check Transcripts and the Path to the Next Grade or Graduation	
What is the trend in grades over the past year or so?	
If there are any deficits or roadblocks, what are they?	
What could be an idea to overcome those challenges?	

Suggestion: Gauge Services Provided	
What is the student's disability?	
Do services appear to be thorough and appropriate based on the reality of limited resources?	

Suggestion: Make a Round-About With Colleagues Prior to the Meeting	
What does the student's caseload manager say is working and not?	
What is the sense of parental and family support with the school?	
What is the student's level of general effort and cooperation, and if lacking, why?	
With whom do the teachers say the student is doing well, and with whom not? Does this vary by content area, teacher disposition, or time of day?	
What activities is the student involved with in school or outside of school?	
Are peer relations positive or negative, and who are their peers?	

Suggestion: Plan Ahead for Meeting Day Logistics	
Who must be present by law in order for the meeting to go forward?	
Who will facilitate the meeting and ensure all have a voice and equitable involvement? Can this facilitator ensure proper greeting, welcomes, housekeeping, transitions from one person to another on the agenda, and appropriate closure and next steps?	
Who will drive the meeting and discuss the details of programs and services? They will typically contextualize what each expert says, in terms of how their input influences the overall program and educational experience.	
Who will drive the keyboard and populate the actual plan when folks are providing input, typically projected on a big screen? Do they have the capability and detail orientation to synthesize verbal comments while discussions are taking place? They will need to ask questions for clarification and solicit input from the audience on the accuracy of what they type.	
How will you as the assistant principal ensure that the student and family walk out of the meeting feeling better than when they walked into it?	
What supports and structures, or follow-up, will you put in place to help the family build capacity to follow through with what was agreed upon?	
Suggestion: Ensure Preparation of Space	
Is the room or office space arranged for collaborative discussion where all can see one another, as well as a projection screen with the paperwork prominently displayed?	
Is the room comfortable in terms of temperature, light, and space?	

Suggestion: Ensure Preparation of Space	
Is the room free of materials and debris that parents and visitors should not see, such as student performance charts on walls or private paperwork lying about or in mailboxes?	

Suggestion: Ensure Preparation of People	
Is there a staff member who can get necessary colleagues in and out of the meeting and ensure coverage of their regularly scheduled classes if they step away to attend?	
Which student-ally colleagues will you invite, and what will you need to do to prep them? If you have colleagues you must invite who do not appear to be student allies through either their behavior or dispositions, what will you do to prepare them for a successful and productive meeting, given those obstacles?	
Which colleagues will ensure the student and family are comfortable and relaxed while waiting on others to arrive? (It might be best to call in the student and family once all are sitting and then welcome them warmly.)	
Do colleagues ensure that they will talk to the student, not about the student, while the student is present, and the same for the parent?	
Do the parent and student understand that they are as much empowered to offer input and suggestions as the faculty in the room? How will you ensure this?	
Do all understand these meetings, by design, require consensus to be reached? They are not in place to hold democratic votes or to offer suggestions and let the administration or special education teachers decide what will happen next.	

page 4 of 4

CHAPTER 9
TAKING TIME FOR TEACHING AND LEARNING

I once served as a secondary school administrator in a one-building, K–12 school district, with no assistant to speak of, so I handled all things leadership and management: safety, order, discipline, attendance, and even athletics. During that time, I had the opportunity to take time for teaching and learning through many classroom visits, particularly through amazing experiences watching our band teacher, Robert (Bob) Gulash, with the high school concert band. He was not only a deft musician but a true master of student-centered teaching.

Even the students who gave most other teachers difficulty were no problem for Mr. Gulash. I learned volumes about how to connect with our most challenging students by watching the way he approached conversations and microcorrections. Students hung on his every word and were willing to try difficult things in full view of their peers, which would have brought about certain disruptions in other classes. This didn't necessarily stem from a love for music; many of these students were required to take band by their parents. Others shared with me they only took the class because of the magic and care of the teacher in front of them. They didn't want to let him down.

In commenting on his secret of success, Gulash shares, "Think about this: I've had every single one of these kids since they were in kindergarten, each year. I've known their parents since they were in school" (R. Gulash, personal communication, September 7, 1999). The band teacher paid attention to what they needed, what they knew, and what they cared about. It's not about band, I thought; it's about life. That's what excellent teaching is all about. It makes other problems go away, or at least invites them to be set aside temporarily. Over the years, I have learned volumes about students and my own craft by taking time for teaching and learning, and I hope you do too. You have so much talent in schools—teachers finding unique ways to connect with students. Go to school, yourself, in their classrooms; add to your repertoire. It turns out that our best teachers can model many of the skills assistant principals need for success. A few years after I moved on to another school, the new principal asked Mr. Gulash near his retirement to embrace a new role, to handle school discipline, attendance, and family intervention as a dean of students. Great teaching continued.

I now present what good teaching really is and why it is important for you to focus on it in your role. What does it actually entail, particularly your service as an extension of your principle to support and facilitate outstanding classroom instruction? Then I'll get into strategies for how you can enact this work with students, staff, and yourself.

The What and the Why

Our best teachers know what students need, and foundational to this is effective and proactive classroom management and sound discipline. As an assistant principal, you can facilitate this by keeping a few things in mind as you observe and talk with teachers. Todd Whitaker, Madeline Whitaker Good, and Katherine Whitaker (2019) use a house metaphor in their book *Classroom Management From the Ground Up*, with a foundation of relationships, a structure of high and clear expectations, and the maintenance of consistency. Teachers with effective classroom management put relationships first by using what I call their *invisible time* efficiently. This is any time that they can handle responsibilities—typically clerical, preparatory, or organizational—when they are not in front of students or others, or, in other words, private time when they are handling tasks outside of others' visual views. They are not scurrying about finishing up tasks as students enter the room, as these have already been accomplished before the students arrive. Teachers are greeting students enthusiastically by name, often with a handshake, high five, fist bump, or individualized greeting that they have manufactured together. It is all about relationships as class gets started, as this is what fills the students' gas tanks and readies them for learning. Ideally, students will connect with your teachers' content because it is presented so well, yet it doesn't hurt to have them want to connect with your teachers first. Whitaker and colleagues (2019) note, "Remember, it is important to build a relationship before you need a relationship" (p. 92).

TIP

Discuss the notion of *invisible time* with your teachers, and use a performance metaphor. When the curtain (classroom door) opens, invisible time for setup must be over. The prop setting and stagehand activity should be complete. You're now on stage with the audience— at your door, meeting and greeting—and it is time for the show.

High and clear expectations are a part of effective teaching. Everyone in the class must understand them. One such expectation is what students must do upon arrival. The best-managed classrooms have routines that students know well. They know what is expected of them when entering, how to organize their materials, and how to get started. Taking classroom attendance should be seamless for the teacher and must not interfere with the cadence of settling in productively. One option might be a classroom schematic or overhead view of desks and tables on a piece of paper, with names for each student. The teacher simply has to look to see which desks are empty, glance at the schematic, and enter in names of those absent while the students are readying themselves for learning with a prompt activity on the board. For students who have been absent, systems and strategies are in place for them to find what they missed without the need to interrupt the teacher. This could be a lesson plan booklet for them to peruse, posters with notations on the wall, or what I call *study buddies*, designated go-to students who can huddle with them during the pre-lesson activity. Teachers can provide clarification later on one to one, as needed. Students know what to expect each day because the routine is fairly consistent.

Our best teachers know how to get students into learning readiness with deft precision in terms of task and technique. They can use prework activities to connect schematically with the day's lesson objective. Efficiency and productivity with an academic focus is key (Whitaker et al., 2019). Teachers must consistently ensure they strive to connect effectively with students' interests, aptitudes, and abilities. In short, they try to reach students wherever they are, and they do so with the variety of students they have in their class.

Effective teachers are intentional with their efforts to reach students. Some do it through instructional differentiation, such as to mix the ways of presenting information, varying didactic instruction, collaborative learning, individualized exploration, group discovery, and other methods for initial content exposure. Others ensure they differentiate by way of students' personalities, by asking key questions when designing lessons, such as the following (Pauley, Bradley, & Pauley, 2002, p. 144).

- "How can I ensure the task is meaningful?"
- "How can I give recognition for work and provide time structure?"
- "How can I make this fun?"
- "How can I provide personal recognition?"
- "How can I provide reflection time?"
- "How can I incorporate action?"

TIP

In enacting students' learner readiness, our best teachers realize that students enter at different places, so differentiation in the warm-up activity is often not just a luxury but a necessity. You'll want to watch for this in your observation.

Our best teachers know how to put things together with focus. You can gauge the fidelity of instruction by paying attention to whether your teacher knows what's important. Schmoker (2011) in his book *Focus: Elevating the Essentials to Radically Improve Student Learning* notes the importance of simplicity, clarity, and priority not only in what we teach but in how we teach. With the *what*, Schmoker (2011) notes a need for adequate amounts of content, coupled with thinking skills and authentic literacy, no matter the subject or grade level. This involves reading, writing, and discussion as primary modes of learning. Teachers should not chase endless sets of standards, as the result will be superficial coverage and a pacing guide tether. Students will not learn under these conditions. Regarding the *how*, Schmoker (2011) shares that a lesson's core structure should include a clear objective, creating interest by connecting to background knowledge, teaching, and modeling; guided practice with checks for understanding; and independent practice and assessment. Basically, look into students' eyes to see if they're learning what's being taught, ensure gradual release of responsibility toward that end, and you're in the zone of good teaching.

TIP

Sometimes you'll find teachers so tethered to their pacing guide and external pressures that they hold fast to their cadence and move on before learners are ready. Stress to your teachers that they sometimes need to use their own wait time, beyond what they provide students, when answering questions. They need such before they move on. This allows them to look more deeply into the students' eyes, and even to look around and see who is hesitant in answering truthfully when asking if everyone is ready to move forward.

Excellent teachers connect their world of teaching with the students' worlds of learning. This involves leveraging technology and embracing and empowering diversity for the best learning outcomes. Regarding technology, authors Todd Whitaker, Jeff Zoul, and Jimmy Casas (2015) in their book *What Connected Educators Do Differently* note that connected educators "learn what they want, when they want, and how they want" (p. 17). I think we can apply this same notion to students in schools, as they are in fact very much connected. That's their world. Thus, teachers must ensure their instruction is mindful of what students want, when students want it, and how they want it delivered. Just look around. Are your teachers doing so, or not? I'll bet this involves deft use of technology to leverage learning. If so, it's effective teaching; if not, probably not.

Think about the considerations raised about equity in chapter 8 (page 131). When connecting to their students' worlds, are your teachers teaching inclusively in terms of culturally sustaining pedagogies, or are they coming at everything from a Eurocentric perspective? What do their materials represent? Who are they placing on historical pedestals? Do they understand contributions from races, ethnicities, and cultures other than their own? One way to check this is to see if they are teaching the same sorts of things they learned themselves, as students; these things are probably woefully inadequate in terms of being culturally sustainable. Further, as Django Paris and H. Samy Alim (2017) caution against in *Culturally Sustaining Pedagogies: Teaching and Learning for Justice in a Changing World*, they are centralizing Whiteness and using a "White gaze–centered question . . . how can 'we' get 'these' working-class kids of color to speak/write/be more like middle-class White ones . . . ?" (p. 3), they are not teaching in the same world where their diverse students live, and they are doing students a disservice.

The best teaching aligns with what research has shown works, and for you as an assistant principal, it is easy to spot. You can see certain strategies that make a big difference in walkthroughs of only a few minutes. John Hattie (2012) notes teaching strategies with high effect sizes that include the following, here using one of a family of effect sizes derived from statistician Jacob Cohen (expressed as $d =$); it's my favorite to use, as it is easy to explain in terms of before and after using a strategy.

- Classroom discussion ($d = 0.82$)

- Teacher clarity ($d = 0.75$)

- Feedback ($d = 0.75$)

- Teacher-student relationships ($d = 0.72$)

- Metacognitive strategies ($d = 0.69$)

- Problem solving ($d = 0.61$)

Robert J. Marzano (2017) shares research-based strategies that can be part of any type of lesson, whether it's direct instruction, instruction that practices and deepens knowledge, or instruction that applies knowledge. These include the following.

- Previewing strategies to activate prior knowledge (such as information hooks or preview questions)

- Highlighting critical information (such as pause time or advanced organizers)

- Reviewing content (such as summary or demonstration)

- Revising knowledge (such as peer feedback or assignment revision)

- Reflecting on learning (such as journaling or exit slips)

- Assigning purposeful homework (such as homework to deepen knowledge or practice a process or skill)

- Elaborating on information (such as inferential questions or elaborative interrogation)

- Organizing students to interact (such as think, pair, share or cooperative learning)

Marzano (2017) notes educators must view learning with these strategies as a constructive process: "This requires iterative and multiple exposures to the content" (p. 64). Teachers also need to intentionally integrate new knowledge with the knowledge students already have.

Finally, our best teachers are diagnosticians of learning. When students are not learning, these teachers embrace it as their own fault, and design other ways to make learning happen. This starts first with an understanding of brain research and student learning, particularly with implications for the classroom environment and teacher-student relationships. What is concerning is the number of *neuromyths*, or misconceptions or misunderstandings of scientific research, that exist in our profession. These pertain to things like the existence of distinct learning styles for students, the Mozart effect of classical music on achievement, the negative impact of sugary snacks, right-brain or left-brain dominance determining how you learn, and the notion that students are only using 10 percent of their brains (Gabrieli, 2020).

TIP

Researchers Wilhelmina van Dijk and Holly B. Lane (2018) from the University of Florida discovered that large numbers of K–12 teachers, preservice teachers, higher education faculty, and educational leaders believe and perpetuate neuromyths related to environmental stimuli, nutrition, exercise, learning styles, and brain development. Respondents were only able to answer correctly about two-thirds of questions about the brain.

Teachers who are diagnosticians of learning stay current with what brain research is actually reporting regarding teaching and learning. One such finding would be that "children's cognitive, emotional, and social domains are integrated and mutually reinforcing" (Rimm-Kaufman & Jodl, 2020, p. 4), meaning that classrooms must have not only cognitive stimulation but also emotional safety and relationship-based intentionality from teachers. "Learning is not a separate part of our physical, mental, and emotional being but a composition of the trinity, each part deeply interwoven into the next" (Holmes, 2019, p. 450). I recommend browsing through resources on learning and the brain from quality sources, including the website of the American Psychological Association (www.apa.org). I particularly like neuropsychologist Margaret Semrud-Clikeman's (2010) research overview. Education neuroscience experts Ian Kelleher and Glenn Whitman's (2020) article, "Every Educator Needs to Know How the Brain Learns," is also a great resource, as is Jay McTighe and Judy Willis's (2019) book *Upgrade Your Teaching: Understanding by Design Meets Neuroscience*.

Diagnosticians of learning know from brain research how curriculum and instruction best connect to the higher regions of the brain: through a student's emotions. Carol Ann Tomlinson and David A. Sousa (2020), writing for *Educational Leadership*, note that "emotions are a gateway to cognition and learning. When curriculum and instruction evoke enjoyment, surprise, empathy, personal relevance, and so forth, the gateway opens and learning is likely to proceed more effectively and durably." Tomlinson and Sousa (2020) share that learning the physiology behind the psychology can be helpful to teachers, and that as educators, we teach students, and we also teach brains. Bryan Goodwin (2018), president and CEO of McREL International, points out that teaching is a noninvasive form of brain surgery, and notes that forgetting is as important as remembering, in that it prunes our brains and makes way for new information. It is through these emotional gateways that strategies for learning can be built, with a new partnership of researchers and teachers in terms of taking the science of learning and moving from research into practice (Jamaludin, Wei Loong, & Xuan, 2019).

A key ingredient is now a newfound focus on the learning taking place and on the learner, as opposed to the teaching taking place and the teacher. Teachers best design their lessons through learning, not teaching, and looking through the eyes of their students (Goodwin, 2018). As an assistant principal, all you have to do is to look for six things. One research-based model, the Six-Phase Model for Student Learning, is designed as follows with segments of information gleaned from Goodwin (2018).

1. **Interest:** Engage students emotionally, and spark their curiosity.

2. **Commitment to learning:** Make sure students know why they're learning something, and set goals.

3. **Focus on new knowledge:** Give students space to be thoughtful, and support visual learning.

4. **Sense making:** Allow students time to process and categorize what they have learned.

5. **Practice and rehearsal:** Help students refine and deepen their learning with reflection.

6. **Extension and application:** Guide students in applying what they've learned to new challenges and demonstrating their deeper learning.

Again, the *what* of excellence in teaching includes knowing what students need and seeing to it that teachers do too, gauging fidelity of instruction and providing quality feedback, and ensuring and equipping our teachers as diagnosticians of learning. *Why* this is important includes the fact that it creates cultures of thinking, supporting what Robert J. Marzano, Phil Warrick, and Julia A. Simms (2014) call High Reliability Schools to reach and inspire students.

A High Reliability School has five levels of operation (Marzano et al., 2014).

1. A safe and collaborative school culture

2. Effective teaching in every classroom

3. A guaranteed and viable curriculum

4. Standards-referenced reporting

5. Competency-based education

These levels are hierarchical, with higher levels only able to exist when the more foundational levels are present and operating fully (Marzano et al., 2014).

Your role as an assistant principal is critical at level 1 each day, and in taking time for teaching and learning, it's critical at level 2 as well. In short, your role is instrumental in providing what Marzano and his colleagues (2014) call the leading indicators that make level 2 possible. These include support for "teachers to continually enhance their pedagogical skills through reflection and professional growth plans" as well as for "clear, ongoing evaluations of [teachers'] pedagogical strengths and weaknesses that are based on multiple sources of data" and through your efforts and willingness to substitute or co-teach, providing teachers "opportunities to observe and discuss effective teaching" (Marzano et al., 2014, p. 37).

Ron Ritchhart (2015) in his book *Creating Cultures of Thinking: The Eight Forces We Must Master to Truly Transform Schools*, shares that school is now a place where we can think differently about outcomes, more like we do when we think about what we want our own children to become as adults. We want them to be curious and inquisitive, with a willingness to solve problems, take risks, and collaborate. We want them to have empathy, good listening skills, and a willingness to be helpful. We hope that they can deal with complexity, be critical thinkers, and contribute as positive members of communities (Ritchhart, 2015). Taking time for teaching can transform your school into a place where this is possible.

Taking time for teaching will move your school's educational experience into one that encourages students to focus more on their learning than on their school work. Ritchhart (2015) notes research where teachers were heard using the term *work* forty-nine times more than the term *learning* while teaching. Students will ask, "How long does this have to be?" or "Will this be on the test?" (Ritchhart, 2015, pp. 44–45); and imagine the inverse, as in the classrooms noted earlier where teachers focus on quality feedback and descriptive clarity in terms of objectives and making sense out of things. Learning tends then to be the focus, and this is a natural byproduct if you are there taking time for teaching.

TIP

Our best teachers and those observing them keep their eye on the ball; they focus more on what the students are doing than on what the teachers are doing.

Ritchhart (2015) also shares that schools where cultures of thinking are present are filled with teachers who make their own thinking visible to students, empower disenfranchised learners, create new patterns of discourse, and build the capacity of teachers to teach one another. The latter involves teacher collective efficacy, Hattie's largest factor influencing student achievement, with an effect size of 1.57 (Donohoo et al., 2018).

Taking time for teaching is important because it inspires students. The school experience, no matter its quality, starts students on a pathway to their dreams. Either it is a well-paved pathway, or it is not. Everything attainable for students in life comes by way of a learning process, and our business is to teach them how to learn. Either we do well and provide them these skills, or we fail in our attempt and they have difficulty doing such an important thing in life, a problem that could very well continue for a lifetime. Where this is particularly powerful is in the notions of student mindset, student efficacy, and student agency.

We teach and students learn either to have a fixed mindset, where they have a determinant amount of skills and smarts, or a growth mindset, wherein they can leverage challenge and even failure into success through effort and the assets they bring (Dweck, 2016). We teach and students learn to have self-efficacy—the quality that allows them to understand that through hard work and effort, they can gain control of their lives and have success—or not. We teach and students learn either to have agency—an ability to take charge of their own lives and work to change the paths of others and of the world—or not. These qualities are what students develop each day in class when teachers do what they do and do it well. Doesn't it make sense that more eyes need to be on exactly what is happening in our classrooms, and more hands need to be involved in making sure this development succeeds? Of course it does. And your role in taking time for teaching and learning as an assistant principal is pivotal in it.

Taking time for teaching—being inside the classrooms—allows you to be able to answer the "Why?" question from your principal, put things into perspective about why learning is optimal or not, and make recommendations to administration when necessary about what to do next. For students and families, taking time to be in the classroom ensures a quality control mechanism is in place that engenders a feeling in them that school is doable, even when it's difficult.

The How: Strategies to Use With Students

The following strategies—empowering through teacher cadets, establishing a learners' lounge, and housing a student success center—are effective ways to lay the foundation for your work with students.

Empower Through Teacher Cadets

Teacher cadet programs are programs for students interested in teaching as a career, typically delivered in high schools in partnership with colleges and universities as part of educational career pathway programming. At times these programs also offer certain college credits. I'm proposing that no matter your level, you establish a teacher cadet program for students who are willing. At the elementary level, it could involve fourth and fifth graders helping in kindergarten through third-grade classrooms. Middle school students could visit elementary classrooms, and high school students could work in elementary school or middle school classrooms. The experiences students receive include one-to-one tutoring, small-group assistance, materials preparation, room décor and functionality, and floating assistance during center-based activities. One benefit from these experiences is the potential career interest that students may develop from an early age. For your purpose of taking time for teaching and learning, an additional plus includes the investment necessary by teachers and staff to have this be a success.

You'll want to place your cadets only in the classrooms of teachers who are respected, connected, student centered, and positive in disposition. They should have the ability to sell our profession to those showing interest. Cadets will model what they see, in deed and nuance, so ensure that they do not eventually have to unlearn anything learned on your watch. Take charge of your cadet program so that you are intentional in providing certain experiences for students and teachers alike.

At the secondary level, you could have weekly themed topics for your cadets to learn about, including setting high expectations, creating clear learning objectives, checking for understanding, using proximity in proactive classroom management, differentiating instruction, using wait time in questioning, managing discipline in a positive manner, implementing instructional groupings, and applying gradual release of responsibility. At the elementary level, you could have weekly themed topics, such as giving praise, being kind in redirecting, working together effectively, using play time productively, using helpful routines, practicing attention-getting strategies, and learning to disagree kindly. You might think this is educationally helpful for the cadets involved, and it certainly is. Yet your hidden curriculum is that these topics are being reinforced by staff and *in* staff as well. The pact teachers make when they agree to adopt a cadet is to stay current in their learning, be the best versions of their teaching selves, and use the foundational aspects of pedagogy that make quality teaching quality.

As you grow your group of cadets, have monthly meetings in which you bring them and their teachers together and show new ideas for classroom lessons and pedagogy. Model strategies that you would like the cadets to try with their supervising teachers. If you are partnered with a college or university, make clinical supervisors and professors a part of these experiences, and more than anything, create a curious and engaging learning community centered on quality teaching and pedagogy.

A growing awareness in students of what good teaching looks like and feels like brings heightened obligations for adults in the building to step up and be a part of it. The gold standard would be if the cadets take part in clinical supervision of each other's best efforts or even their teachers, if teachers would be open to this approach to learning. The use of video technology to review lessons, strategies, and relative levels of success, facilitated by master teachers or you as assistant principal, would allow groups of cadets to learn together, much as medical fellows do on rounds with teaching physicians. What you are trying to create is a shared awareness, responsibility, and delight in the best teaching possible, and sometimes the best way to go about it is through the eyes and mouths of babes, who watch with rapt interest what the respected adults around them are doing.

Establish a Learners' Lounge

As teachers have teachers' lounges—with materials and comforts to help them do their jobs as best they can while building community—so should students. Where is the learners' lounge in your building? What could it be? It could be a place students could go that allows them to sit comfortably, in pairs, small rounds, or even alone, to connect with their learning. Ideally, it would have glass walls so that you could supervise from a respectful distance and not be right on top of the students. It would not have an adult monitor on the inside; that would remind students too much of a library or media center. It would be a place for them.

Your learners' lounge would have ports where students could plug in and charge or use their laptops or other devices. It would have wireless internet accessibility with a school-sponsored firewall for appropriate research and web usage. It would have machines to dispense healthy drinks, cold and hot, and nutritious snacks. The best brain research would influence lighting and color scheme, and in keeping the needs of all students in mind, it would connect to an all-gendered, single-space restroom, so that your nonbinary students have a place they can go and feel comfortable. Your student organizations could meet in your learners' lounge, and you might even provide lockers, cabinets, and cubbies for their storage of materials and décor for their events.

It's essential that a learners' lounge provide materials for learning. This would include homework help line telephone numbers; helpful websites for online tutoring and guidance; and information on techniques they can use to learn, study, prepare for classroom or standardized tests, and write quality essays. An excellent model for a school's homework hotline is one provided for local Indiana schools by the Rose-Hulman Institute of Technology in Terre Haute, Indiana, called AskRose Homework Help (https://askrose.org). Leveraging what is available in your area and understanding what might be available online is key, as these services are no longer geographically dependent in many cases.

Learners' lounges should also include motivational materials from high school graduates on why it is important to be effortful in school, such as videos playing of the kind you would find before movie productions or even at the pump at your local gas station. Schools can elicit the aid of their own students to interview interested people or alumni, perhaps using a talk show format or other engaging setup. Questions might include how these local (or former local) celebrities are successfully applying academics or the things they learned in school to their current lives or to their lives as recent graduates. I have found that in many cases, students uninterested in traditional academic tasks in English class excel when the parameters of communication are broadened to allow for audio or video interviews and other creative mediums that can be showcased.

Most of all, your learners' lounge would reflect the needs of the students in your care. I suggest you find a space, but ask students to help you design it with possibility. You want the space to be relevant and accessible; most of all, you want it *used*. If your building allows, you might consider creating this space adjacent to or as part of a spacious student commons area or cafeteria. This way, natural traffic patterns emerge nearby, and students will start creating community, their own way, in a space that has environmental intentionality for their school success.

House a Student Success Center

Moving beyond models of detention or in-school suspension rooms, past what I call time-out or chill rooms, I encourage you to reframe the way you look at student supports and work with your students to design, staff, and support a student success center. The center is a room for focused academic tasks that provides students a place to work quietly with supports when it is in their best interest to separate them from their regular classroom because of either a suspension, the necessity to stay after school for detention, or a situation in which they are unable or unequipped to stay in class because of various circumstantial reasons having to do with emotional regulation, social challenges, or behavioral difficulties.

Key in a successful student success center is a combination of branding (for example, the name), supports provided while students are inside, the stories students tell once returning to class, and, most particularly, the person you hire to staff it. We'll start first with the staff member. You want to designate a staff member who is poised and professional, with a calm, serious demeanor, but who is approachable by students and staff alike. You want someone with genuine affection for students in challenging situations yet not someone to get caught up in the drama of the moment or prone to be sucked in to sympathy. You're looking for someone who is emotionally regulated and has an assets-based perspective on students and families, no matter their circumstances. You want someone who will see the good in the students who visit but will not be blinded by charisma or charm.

In terms of academic qualifications, you do not necessarily need someone with a bachelor's degree, but keep in mind that in the United States, in some states, you cannot count time spent in your student success center as instructional time unless you have a certified professional in the room. That said, minimally, you want someone who can help students with their mathematics, probably through mid-level algebra at least, and you want someone who can help with the writing process, particularly to copyedit written assignments and papers. You want someone friendly, yet not a friend and certainly someone who will be able to maintain quiet conversations with students about their circumstance without allowing others to jump in or feed in to those situations with unwanted opinions. Good relations with other teachers is a plus, as this person can help gather assignments for students or caucus with teachers to find out if the student is on the right track midway through any given assignment.

Ensure that your student success center is a place that is consequential, academic, and restorative. What this means is that students would rather be in class with their friends than in the center, and thus, it serves a consequential purpose or at least one of mild deterrence. The center should be academic in that students can move forward with their schoolwork under the tutelage of your staff member, with appropriate methods of receiving textbooks, materials, and supplies each day, sometimes each hour. It often helps to have a student aide assigned to the center to gather materials from teachers for students, as your staff member can only leave periodically when substituted by another adult.

Ensure appropriate technology that is comparable with classrooms, and, ideally, each student would have a station in order to access the internet, complete assignments, and connect with whatever student management system you are using. The center can be restorative in that students are guided through reflection and rectification processes for most (if possible) situations that caused discomfort, harm, or a disruption of the educational process. Often, schools have certain guides or question sets that students can work through, along with follow-up discussions with your staff member to process what happened and what needs to be done before returning to school or to class. At times, these experiences are coupled with conflict resolution processes with people more directly involved, and you can be instrumental in inviting students from the center to your office for those purposes, after which they can return to the center for the balance of the necessary time. In establishing a student success center that is consequential, academic, and restorative, you are actually providing key learning experiences in choice and consequence, emotional regulation, and personal responsibility that are personally meaningful and developmentally relevant for students.

Know ahead of time that no matter your efforts at providing a place that, in part, incentivizes positive behavior through appropriate school consequences, some students will be more comfortable in that environment than in their regular classroom. In fact, a select few might intentionally misbehave in order to be assigned to their favorite space with their favorite staff member. This is where you rely on your staff member to take extra time and effort to provide guidance to those students about how they can accomplish the goals they have in mind (that is, being in a comfortable place with someone with whom they feel safe) and do so in a socially responsible fashion, within acceptable guidelines. This might be the case where you make a deal with specific students that they can attend portions of their day in your student success center if they set behavioral or academic goals for themselves and exhibit proactive behavior and personal growth. A final note in establishing a center that works: personally relieve your center staff member for breaks or for lunch at certain times each week. This keeps your finger on the pulse of what is happening each week in your center, and it puts you in contact with students who need to see you in a supportive light as part of the team they have in place rooting for their success.

The How: Strategies to Use With Staff

The following strategies—modeling a monthly method; connecting with co-teaching; and visiting, just because—are effective ways to lay the foundation for your work with staff.

Model a Monthly Method

Ideally, your school has a monthly staff meeting with appropriate time for discussions of items of importance, and it's not something that could be replicated by an email or weekly bulletin. If not, I would suggest as a first step you and your principal work to get this right. And if you do hold this meeting each month, request that you carve out fifteen minutes of time during the meeting in order to model a monthly method. This is where you and your teachers actually take time for teaching by highlighting a new teaching method each month, talking about it together, and showing each other how it is done.

One way you could go about this is to ask a small group of teachers who are respected and connected with their colleagues if they would be good sports with you and do something that's possibly different at a staff meeting. You don't necessarily need your best teachers, and in some cases, these are not the ones who are most respected and connected. You want the ones who spend a lot of time with their heads together, because they have a pretty tight alliance. With this small group, divvy up the next few months, and have each, individually or some in pairs, model a monthly method for only fifteen minutes—something in their bag of tricks that really works and is grounded in research. You could serve as the emcee, saying that you saw them in action while out and about talking with students.

Their chosen monthly method could be something that has worked for them for many years, or it could be something new they have found or tried. One of mine might be the use of a technique that I called writing roulette, where students sit in a circle, begin a creative writing piece, then at the sound of the bell, pass their paper to the person on their right or left, who would read what they wrote and continue the story. This activity garnered rave reviews each time I used it in English classes at all levels. These things only take minutes to describe or model, and with teachers sharing with teachers, there's a heightened chance that someone will borrow from another.

Beyond the sharing of tips and tricks, modeling a monthly method has a larger goal of focusing our time when we come together on what we purport to value the most: teaching. Too often we focus on policies and procedures, such as the new hat rule; the old dress code; or the new format for this, that, or the other thing. The monthly method also keeps you as the assistant principal engaged in teaching, but it doesn't make you the leader of the band, so to speak; you're more like a rhythm guitarist who's just happy to be there kickin' out the jams with the singer and lead guitarist. Let the teachers be the stars for a while, then pinch hit and share when they're asking you to step up as well. Ensure, however, that those modeling have a clue about what they're doing. Plug in an academic year's worth of those of your choice before others get involved. You may find for some that you need a bit of tactful prior review, so ensure you always know what will be presented and that you're on board with it.

Connect With Co-Teaching

Arguably, a great way to be relevant in terms of your teaching expertise is to stay current in full view of your teachers and staff. I realize you're busy enough with all you do in your role; however, it is important that you connect with a faculty colleague at least once per semester and co-teach something that would do well in tandem. Sometimes this can be a multiday commitment, but it doesn't always have to be. Connect with a colleague in the way that best works for you and what you have on your plate. It could very well be in your area of certification and license, but perhaps not. Either way, you're putting yourself out there in a way that will establish and maintain credibility with both staff and students. Students as well want to see that you haven't lost touch with the classroom action when you're giving them advice on how to navigate it.

In terms of a successful co-teaching experience, keep a few things in mind. First, your job is not to win a popularity contest when you're in the classroom. You're not trying to offset any negative perceptions of you in your role as disciplinarian or the one who came down on all the athletes just before sectionals for going to a party the weekend before. This is not to right a perceptual wrong, so don't be the fun one, don't be the nice one, and don't be the easy one. You're there to ensure students are learning something. Be rigorous; have high standards. Put yourself into the same hot seat we demand of our teachers with respect to student performance. Be real, and represent authentically. This means you don't bring your favorite classroom game for a week; rather, you ask the teacher when would be the best time for you to help out, and you do so in sync with the pacing that your co-teacher is using.

Another thing to keep in mind is that effective co-teaching does not involve you doing one thing, then the teacher doing another, and taking turns. This is not true co-teaching; rather, it is trading off. Co-teaching best occurs when you're both immersed in the content. Yes, one can directly teach one aspect of the lesson and the other, another, but co-teaching is more like finishing each other's sentences. It is more a way to provide another approach to the same problem, so that students are getting two ways to do it, or two perspectives on the same issue, rather than one. It is really an additive experience in terms of the quality, as you are both bringing a separate best game to the collaborative experience.

Co-teaching done well demands that you spend some planning time with your teacher, so that you both know what the road map will be when you get together. This is critical in building that credibility with each other, as you designed this thing together. You both have a vested interest in the outcome because it says something about your teaching quality as a team. Be sure to debrief together after the lesson and before you go into the next day's lesson together. It's about taking responsibility for those learners who did not keep up and to create a successful experience the next day for both those students who are ready to move forward and those who still need reinforcement. In other words, it's what a singular teacher needs to do anyway, but you now do it together.

Finally, the co-teaching experience deserves to be told as a story to others during staff meetings, during a brown bag luncheon, at the coffee shop, or otherwise. Not only do you want your collaborative exploits advertised—as this is part of your hidden curriculum in the first place—you want to make co-teaching a suggested norm for those who are interested and have time to do it. Even better, imagine the possibilities if teachers from different disciplines started making time during the semester to bring together interdisciplinary or thematic groups. The possibilities are endless. I would like to again encourage you to co-teach one multiday class a semester with a colleague of your choice with what is being demanded of them. If you do so, you'll find it exhilarating and empowering for all involved.

Visit, Just Because

As school administrators, we are challenged and charged with being in the classroom more and more. Part of this is good, as we get to experience the joy of the teaching and learning process. When we find ourselves required to be in classrooms a certain number of visits, observations, or minutes within each evaluation cycle, because of mandates enacted at the district or state level and with little discretion for building leaders, problems can arise. One observation I have made is that there is so much demand for school administrators to be in classrooms and so little time for all that we do that we are pressured into making every observation count. Whether it's an informal visit, quick walkthrough, or formalized evaluation, it seems the scripting, logging, and scribing with tablet or clipboard in hand is more the rule than the exception.

I suggest something completely different that may be even more important—a visit, *just because*. If it makes a teacher more comfortable, let them know you're hoping to stop by (*just because*). For those who don't care either way, I would encourage you just to drop by as your time permits. This might even be a virtual visit for a virtual or blended classroom. I recall, during my undergraduate education studies, expressing interest in visiting my old favorite high school teacher's classroom a few times per semester. He would greet me with a booming voice at the door, then after briefly introducing me to his class, he would sit me next to his desk as he continued teaching without missing a beat. I continued visiting even after becoming a teacher, and my favorite visit was just after I got my assistant principalship. You can imagine the looks on students' faces when an assistant principal from hundreds of miles away stops by the old hometown to see his favorite teacher teach. During my career, I found myself drawn to particular teachers' classes simply because of the way I felt being there. I was proud that this level of warmth, rigor, challenge, and inspiration was occurring. I really wouldn't want to be anywhere else, and I let the teachers and students know it. This gesture and my attention added value because it was sincere.

Then came an era of heightened accountability, which wasn't without its positive attributes, but it also scripted much of what building administrators must do in terms of number of visits, duration of visits, and even the feedback provided for each visit. It was a true struggle to carve out time to visit, *just because*, but I made it happen. And I suggest you do too.

Visiting classrooms just because requires you to do so without making obvious that you are carrying anything to write with. Now this doesn't mean you can't have a smartphone in your pocket or small tablet of paper somewhere in your belongings as well, but you do not always want to come with tablet or laptop. You want everyone to know you are there, *just because*, and that you are intentionally spending time during your busy day to take pride and joy in what they are doing. This goes for the teacher and students both. Walk around; talk to the students. If in a virtual setting, ask the teacher if you can be placed in breakout rooms or small-group meetings if the technology allows. Ask if you can get system privileges to move around among the breakout rooms or online groups. This way, you can simulate walking around as best you can. Ask them what they are doing and how they are doing with it. Give a thumbs-up to the teacher, and thank them for allowing you in. Be sure to mention to them that you are there, just because—whether you heard something was going on that was really cool, or whether you knew you could put yourself in a good mood because of the great teaching they always demonstrate—put them at ease that they are not being evaluated but rather valued.

At the end of the day, drop in their mailbox a handwritten thank-you card. Not much needs to be on it—just a few words in appreciation of their sharing a bit of their day, and their students, with you. Your taking time, just because, is really a gift that your schedule allows, and one that can be intentionally scheduled if you and your assistant find that a brief respite between flurries of activity is just what the doctor ordered for you.

The How: Strategy to Use With You

You may be placed in a situation where you are asked by your principal to conduct teaching evaluations on staff members who have many more years' experience in teaching than you had before moving into your role. This can be daunting whether you're seasoned or new, but especially if you were a junior member of the staff in the same school building. In keeping with the importance of teachers as valued instructional leaders, you will need to prepare thoroughly for these opportunities, as well as navigate the before, during, and after very carefully. The goal is to move instruction in a positive direction no matter at what level, and you cannot do so without recognizing and mentioning areas that can grow. Having tact, finesse, and resilience while doing so is an understatement. The strategy I suggest here, developing pedagogical humility, will also be very helpful.

You may find it helpful at times to demonstrate pedagogical expertise in the course of your instructional supervision and evaluation, especially if you are a new administrator. After all, if you are too vulnerable, the wolves are going to attack you, especially if you have to check a box that is anything less than excellent. Yet, beware of the narcotic of needing to either know it all or find something to point out. If you perceive this about yourself, or if you let others demand it of you, you are only setting yourself up for an eventual fall. You can head this off at the pass.

Do so by embracing and communicating a certain degree of pedagogical humility. A helpful metaphor is as follows, and I encourage you to use it with teachers. Teachers are the surgeons. They are the ones directly involved in patient interventions and treatments that will promote health and wellness. School administrators are not and should not be expected to be the best pedagogical surgeons in the building. Teachers are. School administrators, rather, are like chiefs of staff. As such, they have their own expertise—in your case, leadership studies—and they may have had experience as doctors practicing as well (as teachers), yet they do not bring greater expertise in a chosen discipline than those working most closely with the clients. That would be the teachers.

This isn't to say that chiefs of staff shouldn't run hospitals or judge the quality of surgery. They darned well should. They are charged with ensuring that operating rooms are well equipped, that qualified surgeons are hired, and that health care quality is evaluated with input from all stakeholders. They are on the front lines of ensuring institutional licensing and accreditation. As part of that, they conduct performance evaluations of staff. This is analogous to your role as an assistant principal. You are deputy chief of staff for your principal. Your principal has delegated some administrative responsibilities. This is your reality, and you embrace it.

Now, how do you get others to embrace it too? Pedagogical humility helps. Let teachers know that you are not necessarily the best teacher, but you are no slouch either. Your foray into co-teaching and modeling a monthly method will help sell this point. Yet you know that you have much you can learn from them. Having said that, this does not negate the fact that you are a helpful arm in clinical observation, and as an administrator, teacher, and learner yourself, you are fully equipped to observe and help them unpack their lessons, highlighting some things that worked really well and others that could have been done differently. Yet, all the while, maintain that you are humbly respectful of their expertise and can learn from them in the discussion. You'll find your best teachers will enter into a co-learning dialogue with you, and those who are of lesser quality will try to shoot down what you say with professed expertise as a big part of their own defense mechanisms. In these circumstances, just keep listening, nodding, and using the word *and* more than the word *but*, and then write what you believe must be written, keeping students' interests in mind. They may receive this with anger and tell some of their underperforming friends, but you can be confident that you have maintained humility and were in the right space to have that professional dialogue with them.

Toolkit for Tomorrow: Next Steps

These next steps provide some suggestions for how you can put the ideas in this chapter into action.

- Leave your laptop or tablet in your office this next week and visit two teachers, just because. Ensure you let them know you're there because you wanted a bright spot in your own day, and thank them for having you.

- Connect with your best teachers and ask them what book they have read recently that has inspired them to try out some new strategies. Order that book, and let them know once you've finished reading that you really appreciate the tip.

- Take a close look at how you and your principal are spending time in your staff meetings, and have a private conversation about whether there is enough focus on the reason why you are here in the first place—student learning.

- In keeping with the theme of focus, think hard about the three most important things you must see when you visit classrooms in terms of quality teaching and learning, and make them visible to yourself as reminders when you conduct observations and evaluations. This might include preparing a piece of paper or electronic document with some target words written at the top to focus your mind's eye, such as Student Engagement, Feeling Tone, Teachable Moments, or other items important to you that you wish to see stand out. This will help you make sense of the variety of things you jot down and be helpful for your teacher in follow-up conversation.

- Do the professional development activity on page 168, which will help you ponder the complexities of the people you work with and teach every day. We're in the people business. It is through people that all academic success occurs. First and foremost, students are our customers, clients, and products. It behooves us to become experts on them.

Professional Development: A Deeper Dive—Taking Time for Teaching and Learning

Instructions: Psychologist and consultant Nate Regier has inspired me to develop a visual model to simplify the complexity people bring to the school experience each day. We really cannot shed our baggage at the schoolhouse gate, as some might think. In this professional development activity, I am asking that you read a brief passage and become familiar with the layers that your students bring with them, as people, to school. Afterward, I'll ask you to take one student whom you are having a particularly difficult time teaching as an assistant principal and generate new ways of thinking about this student that might provide you some inroads for a connection.

First, review the following visual.

Factors of Who We Are

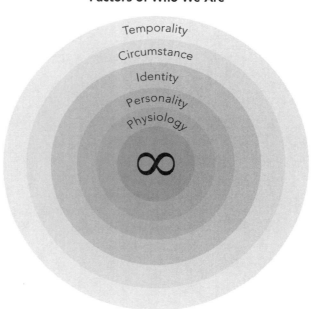

Source: Adapted from N. Regier, personal communication, July 27, 2008.

The illustration depicts the layers (or factors) of our humanity. Those of us who are spiritual might contend that the center of who we are is an essence or soul at our core. That is represented by the infinity symbol.

At or near our core, we also have our *physiology*. It comes to school each and every day. Physiology is rather fixed and fairly stable in all of its imperfections. Think about it. I am probably not going to be dunking any basketballs anytime soon, but taller people, including my son, would have a fighting chance.

Close to our core and a big part of who we are each day is our *personality*, which begins developing initially at or near our birth and becomes layered over time through experience (Kahler, 2008). Personality includes the way we see the world, preferences in how we work and interact, how we communicate, what motivates us, and even those needs we have that exist in Maslow's (1987) hierarchy.

page 1 of 3

Moving outward on the illustration past *identity* for just a minute, we have our personal *circumstance* a bit farther from our core, yet still important to who we are. This has to do with whether we are rich or poor, experience happiness or heartache, and those sorts of things. It could be our socioeconomic status or ZIP code. Circumstance influences who we are through what we have or don't have.

Regier once discussed with me that *identity* helps us navigate the span between *personality* and *circumstance* (N. Regier, personal communication, 2007). Situated between the two, identity includes things like our self-concept, self-esteem, and self-efficacy. I like the way he thinks about it. He once used a computer metaphor and called it our operating system, bridging our hard drive and software (N. Regier, personal communication, 2007).

Temporality means that over time, we change. So as we can see from the illustration, people are complex. Yet, this complexity is really simple to think about, if we let it be.

Quite simply, the layers students bring to school each day are complicated. Adults bring as many layers as the students. Within our structures, emotional hijacks can take place. "Such emotional hijacks are triggered by the amygdala, the brain radar for threat, which constantly scans our surroundings for dangers" (Goleman, 2013, p. 36). Fight or flight.

Use the following template to deconstruct the layers your most difficult student is bringing to school, and then reconstruct some supports or assets you can offer to help with any emotional hijacks that are taking place.

Factors or Layers of the Student's Humanity	Key Question for You	Deconstruct what you see here: What is going on with the student in terms of the key questions in each of the areas below?	In this space, jot down an idea, support mechanism, or asset you or the school can offer to help with reconstructing a layer of this student's life that is not providing what it should for connectedness and school success.
Intangible or Spiritual Factor or Layer (∞)	Does this student connect with anything intangible that either helps with school connectedness or hurts?		
Physiological Factor or Layer	Are the student's physiological needs being cared for outside of school?		
Personality Factor or Layer	What are the personality differences or communication differences between this student, teachers, and even you?		

page 2 of 3

Factors or Layers of the Student's Humanity	Key Question for You	Deconstruct what you see here: What is going on with the student in terms of the key questions in each of the areas below?	In this space, jot down an idea, support mechanism, or asset you or the school can offer to help with reconstructing a layer of this student's life that is not providing what it should for connectedness and school success.
Identity Factor or Layer	How are this student's self-concept, self-esteem, and self-efficacy?		
Circumstance Factor or Layer	Are there factors outside of school that are difficult for this student to deal with or incongruent with what is expected at school? What is being reinforced, and what is not?		
Temporal Factor or Layer	Has this student changed over the time you have known each other? If so, how?		

References

Goleman, D. (2013). *Focus: The hidden driver of excellence*. New York: HarperCollins.

Kahler, T. (2008). *The process therapy model: The six personality types with adaptations*. Little Rock, AR: Taibi Kahler Associates.

Maslow, A. H. (1987). *Motivation and personality* (3rd ed.). New York: Harper & Row.

CHAPTER 10
SUPPORTING SCHOOL
IMPROVEMENT AND ACCOUNTABILITY

I was standing by a fax machine one beautiful spring day after a few hours of school discipline and family intervention, thinking of how fortunate I was to be a small-school administrator in a school that began as a consortium enrolling students who struggled in area school districts and transferred to our own. I was alongside valiant colleagues who championed empowerment and student agency, and we were beating the odds with respect to turning around academic achievement before students graduated, even for those who arrived late in their high school careers.

I heard the beep of an incoming fax and pulled it off the machine for my assistant. Something caught my eye; in fact, it was the name of our school, listed among others on a special state agency news release. We appeared along with a handful of other schools who were showing deficiency in reading achievement among other markers for student success. And because of an alphabetized listing, we were *first*! Oh my goodness, how could this be? Don't they understand that we enroll students for the first time in our school in their freshman and sophomore years, sometimes even as juniors, shortly before the state standardized tests? In other words, we haven't had them since kindergarten. They transferred from different places. I was hard-pressed to comprehend the abject unfairness of it. It felt ridiculous. We needed to make a call and get this fixed!

Students were, in fact, appalled when the news got out. They wanted to take a road trip to the state capital and demonstrate. You can imagine our working overtime to quell their concern. Staff were hurt and angry, as you might imagine. Many viewed our program as a long-standing alternative education program and that, as such, it should get a pass from the spotlight. That day began some of the most significantly meaningful personal and professional learning for me that I have had in my career. It brought me closer to the assumptions I had about at-risk students, and even about the term itself, which I now find a bit unfavorable, preferring *at-promise students*, a term I heard first from the Reaching At Promise

Students Association (RAPSA, https://rapsa.org), a nonprofit organization helping educators work with students who have difficulty in school. It brought me closer to what was possible, and shortly thereafter, the situation invited me and my team, which included our students, to do something about it. Within a few years, we served as a model of deft school improvement and mindful school accountability and were forevermore better because of the wake-up call.

This chapter includes information on facilitating meaningful use of data and stories for school improvement and accountability. After discussing the what and the why of data, I'll move on to how they are important for you in your role with strategies for use with students, staff, and yourself.

The What and the Why

School improvement and accountability exist on *your* end of the pact you make with your students, families, and community. I would argue that self-accountability is even more important than external accountability, and that external accountability really is not an intrusion if you're doing things well from the inside out. Test scores are more an intrusion when your eye is on teaching to the test rather than teaching to the learning. As an assistant principal, you can facilitate the meaningful use of data and story with your teachers, staff, and students. Use your numerical *data* as your outline or a sketch of what is going on; the *story* of what you are doing and what students are experiencing allows you to fill in your sketch with more depth and detail. It is then that you have a picture that will help you look at yourselves, what you are providing, and what students need. Make no mistake about it. Data are your first step in holding up a mirror. You must understand how you can get yourself and your staff excited about using data, then how to get good at using data, and then finally how to lock in both as muscle memory over time.

Arguably one of the best resources in getting excited about using data is Edie L. Holcomb's (2017) book, *Getting More Excited About Using Data*. Holcomb (2017) notes a plethora of data sources that go far beyond standardized or school-administered tests, including the following.

- Performance checklists

- Student participation in extracurricular activities

- Student behavioral data

- Climate and perception surveys

- Focus group conversations

- Interviews with staff, students, parents, and the community

- Observation logs

- Journal entries

- Staff qualifications

- Professional development participation

I wanted to list these things at the outset because they readily demonstrate how you and your staff can use this information to paint a picture of what is going on in your school and how it might impact student success. In reviewing these items, you can build excitement about what you might find and what you might do next because of them.

Getting excited about data happens only if everyone can feel safe in reviewing them. School administration can work over time with teachers and staff members to ensure a culture in which this is true. Holcomb (2017) also notes that excitement occurs when you're not going it alone, when you can see student faces in the data, when it is easy to get, when you have time to deal with it, and when you have appropriate administrative support. Assistant principals can be on hand to help their principals know, understand, and leverage some of these key points so that staff will not feel the work is drudgery, irrelevant, or a waste of their time and energy. One example that I have seen in many schools is to provide a teacher collaboration room that features a data wall on which to share classroom and individual student data. Important in these efforts are wraparound teams that can take collective responsibility for teams of students so that, again, no one feels they are doing so on an island.

TIP

Encourage your teachers to put faces to their data—individual student images (kept private)—so that teachers never forget a data point is someone's child, and each data point is one of their students who arrives each day. Even with 95 percent student success in terms of meeting standards, someone gave birth to or takes care of the remaining 5 percent, and those students have hopes and dreams as well.

You are also in a position to help your school, your staff, and yourself get really good at using data. What I have found is that the clearer you make the processes, the more you build a certain amount of muscle memory and even data efficacy. Getting good at using your data involves a pact that no one's time is wasted. Someone on staff must be able to take charge of providing a road map of where you are and where you are going—to provide a connection among curriculum, pace, and delivery. Don't leave teachers on an island to figure this out; get someone whose talent is in this area to serve as the guide—often an instructional coach or someone from the central office.

Offering this clarity and a road map will allow your teachers to spend time digging into the meaning of data more deeply. Paul Bambrick-Santoyo (2019) notes the importance of locking in deep analysis in data meetings. These are based on interim assessments administered after a few months of teaching that show more a trend of what was learned rather than an immediate snapshot post-observation of one of your classroom visits as an assistant principal. Designate someone who really can discern what data are saying to sit down with your teachers and look at things scientifically—focus on what students learned instead of what teachers taught. But don't blame the teachers; rather, immediately do something about it to fill the learning gaps. Again, reteaching should be as natural and expected as teaching.

TIP

Find and appoint someone to serve as air traffic controller for your school's data, with your teachers serving as pilots. You need a data geek who can actually talk to people and connect with them. Ensure this person is real and credible.

Finally, work to lock in the effective use of data as muscle memory over time. Bambrick-Santoyo (2019) notes the importance of a regimen for data health: an active leadership team; ongoing professional development; building by borrowing, which is the notion of learning from the highest-achieving teachers and schools; common interim assessments four to six times per year; immediate, simple, and deep analysis, as noted previously; six-week action plans; and, of course, reteaching.

Along the way to getting both excited about and good at using data and striving to improve your school, challenges are bound to arise because of external forces that perpetually exist for schools. Invariably, something will come down from your state department of education, state legislature, or general assembly that will provide you yet another moving target. It may seem inevitable that you won't be able to compare student achievement or growth from one year to the next because of some psychometric nuance or another. Your role is key in helping your staff and even your principal see change as simply the natural order of things and that these changes may even be good ones despite the immediate challenges.

Some will not react as well to change, and you might even get resistance to ongoing school improvement out of frustration. But keep in mind, as J. Stewart Black (2014) shares in his book, *It Starts With One: Changing Individuals Changes Organizations*, it is simply a fact that "the old right thing is now the wrong thing, but you are still very good at it. In fact, you may now be world class at the wrong thing" (p. 26). Learning to do the new right thing comes with challenge at first, and even your best folks don't want to underperform in front of their friends and colleagues. Black (2014) notes that, when moving to the new way of doing things, you may even experience a *change penalty*, or temporary, negative effects resulting from a change, and this is to be expected. Examples of change penalties include implementation dips or even temporary, negative ripple effects (could be in performance, morale, and so on) of implementing something new. Change penalties are often offset by more good things to come because of the change. It's just that you have to have the resolve to put up with the change penalties in the meantime, and this often involves keeping in mind the needs of the people along the way charged with making those changes. As noted author Simon Sinek (2014) shares, "Lead the people, not the numbers" (p. 166); just keep moving forward and striving to improve your school.

TIP

Forgive in advance the folks who resist school change efforts. If they were to be honest and vulnerable, they would probably just tell you they are a bit insecure with what's being asked of them and do not want to be embarrassed in front of their friends and colleagues.

One thing to note as you work toward school improvement and accountability is that your efforts do not exist in a vacuum. They exist in science. It behooves us to understand and capitalize on that science, according to the authors of *Learning to Improve: How America's Schools Can Get Better at Getting Better* (Bryk, Gomez, Grunow, & LeMahieu, 2016) and *Improvement Science in Education: A Primer* (Hinnant-Crawford, 2020). What we often see in education is a combination of add-on interventions to try to improve things and abandonment of what we try too early (Hinnant-Crawford, 2020). The abandonment sometimes occurs because we often pilot a new approach and try to generate evidence that it's working before it's had a chance to work. When it doesn't work, we try something else, sometimes something completely different.

TIP

Keep in mind that every time we are asked to get better at doing something, someone has studied the actual *process of getting better* and can probably provide a perspective. Often, our struggles in getting better have to do with our not taking time to learn the science behind the process.

Improvement science is more like a focused learning journey in a networked community (Bryk et al., 2016). In this community, we understand that "a science of improvement is the scientific study of how to improve" (Hinnant-Crawford, 2020, p. 26). And we use it to guide our efforts. Improvement science involves doing things in a problem-specific and user-centered way rather than just general interventions for a wide audience; it also involves ensuring you measure everything about your change, not just student achievement outcomes, and it involves leveraging the power of your work through networked communities (Bryk et al., 2016; Hinnant-Crawford, 2020). Through all of this, you and your staff will begin to develop collective efficacy, which has a profound influence on student learning (Donohoo et al., 2018).

Supporting school improvement and accountability through facilitating the meaningful use of data and story, embracing change with moving targets, and utilizing improvement science in education are important because they allow you to build a courageous culture in your building for performance excellence. We all know that organizations that stay still fall behind. We see this in many sectors, and schools are no different. According to authors Karin Hurt and David Dye (2020) of *Courageous Cultures: How to Build Teams of Micro-Innovators, Problem Solvers, and Customer Advocates*, what often happens in cultures that are not courageous is a diffusion of responsibility, where everyone will assume that someone else will take care of the problems that everyone sees. Collective responsibility is key. Hurt and Dye (2020) also note a tendency toward *safe silence*, which is when folks don't think leaders want their ideas, no one asks, there is a lack of both confidence and skill to share effectively, and folks don't think anything will happen, so they don't contribute. This will certainly not be the case when you ground improvement and accountability efforts in improvement science.

TIP

Data and *story* are much like science and art, where a *both–and* approach in explaining the human condition is much more telling and explanatory than *either–or*. Use both–and in your school improvement efforts.

In fact, in creating a courageous culture through your improvement efforts, you will find many benefits, including establishing clarity around what you are doing together, generating curiosity in what you find and what you can employ, galvanizing the genius in your team and the systems you have created, and establishing an infrastructure for courage over time through your good work together (Hurt & Dye, 2020).

Consider as well what benefits will come about for your students, which I describe using the metaphor of the Skyhook, a military extraction method to rescue combatants from the battlefield and often from behind enemy lines. It involves a harness and self-inflating balloon with lift line. An airplane with a hook attached would fly low over the person getting retrieved, and would engage hook and line, thereby flying away with the person retrieved. Mission accomplished; that is, if the person being rescued was able to get safely to the extraction point.

Students are in that same position. They can only be extracted (raised to the next grade level or graduated) if they're safely at their extraction point (learning enough to show readiness), and that is precisely the job of your school. If they are not at their extraction point for each next grade level or upon graduation, they'll not be safely prepared for the ride. Note what research says about education and longevity. Researchers Marc Luy and colleagues (2019) have been compiling information on levels of education in countries around the world for many years and have found strong associations between life expectancy and level of education. With a better education, not only will the students be better off but so will we! Today's students will be tomorrow's leaders, legislators, and society's problem solvers after we retire.

School improvement and accountability efforts are extremely important for an additional reason: they are our obligation, because *we can do this thing*. As Charles Duhigg (2016) shares with us in his book, *Smarter Faster Better: The Secrets of Being Productive in Life and Business*, there is a formula for success, and what I have shared so far is much of what is in that recipe. Getting excited about data has much to do with a new way of approaching our motivation. Duhigg (2016) notes, "Motivation is more like a skill, akin to reading or writing that can be learned and honed" (p. 19). He finds a prerequisite to motivation is feeling we are in control of our actions, and the strategies you can use for getting good at using data and improvement science allow for just that.

Your role as an assistant principal is to guide, at times facilitate, and provide support for a collective effort that respects the talents of staff and fosters collective efficacy in bringing about a result. Duhigg (2016) talks of managing the how of the team, not the who, and the six principles of improvement science are laser-focused on just that. In fact, they are some fairly monumental hows that can guide your entire effort. Another way you can be smarter, faster, and better in your efforts is to establish a focus, taking control of your attention and building mental models (Duhigg, 2016) that put you firmly in charge of the improvement taking place. Black's (2014) model of change allows you to do just that, setting aside the noise of trepidation and understanding that change penalties and reteaching demands are simply new ways of normalizing the getting better experience. Finally, with the use of disciplined inquiry in improvement science, we're continually making modifications in our efforts based on contingencies discovered, which aligns with Duhigg's (2016) notion that our best decision makers are those able to envision what may happen next, as we imagine various futures based on the choices we make and actions we take. Again, we can do this! The recipe lends itself to success, and thus we have an obligation.

The How: Strategies to Use With Students

The following strategies—empowering students through advisory and training (not teaching) to the test—are effective ways to lay the foundation for your work with students.

Empower Students Through Advisory

While often used as an adjective, *advisory* in the sense I am presenting is used as a noun to refer to a school's daily or weekly advisory period. Activities in advisory span the gamut of study hall, homework catch-up, team-building activities, personal exploration lessons, sleeping, and just socializing with friends. In terms of your own school improvement through a heightened focus on learning, I suggest a primary goal of your advisory is empowerment of students to take charge of their academic lives. Spearhead this as the assistant principal, if your principal concurs, and be very clear that empowering students in advisory involves first giving students the keys so that they can drive their own data.

We've heard of data-driven leadership. I have a problem with that. If the data are driving, who is doing the leading and managing? I am a bit more comfortable with the term *data-informed leadership*, because then good leaders are doing the leading and good managers are doing the managing. Yet I'm still left with the question, Who are the ones driving the data? Data have no volition; they can't self-start. They are simply data: vessels that teachers and students fill through mutual performance. So, what really makes sense is that students learn in school how to drive their data. Driving their data involves four main things: (1) information, (2) prescription, (3) metacognition, and (4) volition.

Students in advisory should be empowered first with all of the information that your school gathers in its data digs, collaborative team meetings, wraparound teams, and instructional coaches and guidance counselors. Basically, if the adults know something about the performance or performance numbers of their students, make the students aware of this, individually, in advisory. Even the youngest students can handle performance truths that adults tactfully and developmentally deliver. These data should be communicated in a way that students understand, and they should know whether they need to work harder to meet performance standards or if they are already there and can seek out enrichment.

Students in advisory should be empowered with prescription, so that they know as teachers do how they can get their data and numbers from where they are to a higher place. Often students are simply the recipients of the interventions we provide, rather than students of the strategies themselves and why they are purported to work. Your advisory teachers—teachers or staff members who supervise advisory period, guide students accordingly, and facilitate activities therein—need to be teaching the students what the adults know about the battle plan and whether or not what you all are going to try is a good bet. Students should be able to answer questions from their own parents about why they are being asked to attend this session or that or why they are spending part of their day with this teacher or that. They should know that such-and-such teacher is the most effective in the building at helping students who are struggling with, for example, number sense and order of operations or persuasive essays and reading prompts. We should let students in on the method to our madness so that they get why they are doing what they are doing.

Students in advisory need to be empowered through metacognition. Advisory should be a hub of learning about how students learn best and why this is so. They should know about summoning prior knowledge, organizing their thoughts, mnemonic devices, self-questioning, use of cognitive maps, and multimodal (visual, auditory, and so on) repetition. Students need exposure to grade-level-appropriate, academic content details of brain research on how to get themselves into a good physiological, mental, and emotional place for learning. They need mindfulness techniques and discussions of growth mindset and grit. They need to know about themselves as learners, to become scientists of how students do school best.

Students in advisory need to learn about their own volition and agency in moving their learning to the next level. They need to learn that when they predict the grades they will receive on a test or how well they will complete an assignment, and then when the teacher challenges them to beat their predictions and they try, these are some of the most powerful influences in their success, as John Hattie notes with a huge effect size of 1.44 (Hattie, 2009). You need to empower students through advisory, and make the best possible use out of that time for them.

Train (Not Teach) to the Test

Quite simply, schools that teach to the test waste their own valuable resources and students' time as they're mired in lower-level cognitive tasks, imprisoned in pacing guides that leave many behind, and tethered in a swath of publisher promises that broad coverage is good and will do the trick. It is a cruel hoax that has lasted for decades, in a maniacal race to avoid punitive consequences in an ill-thought-out system of accountability that brings few A games to the table and has perpetuated inequalities in the United States and worldwide (Briggs, 2013).

Ethically, we can do better, and we must. We must teach not to the test but to the learning we wish for students. That is our moral, ethical, and professional obligation and one that will best carry students forward with success in life. But I'm not so naïve as to say that if we teach to the learning, the test will take care of itself. I just don't believe that.

Indeed, it is the testing conditions themselves that often stifle the performance of our very bright students. From personal experience, I have worked where students were required to use an online calculator for test computation when many students were not even exposed to the computer interface prior. And even if so, online calculators are hard to manipulate and can get in the way of what you are doing on the screen. There was another instance where I heard students were not provided scratch paper, but instead small boards to write on with erasable markers. This certainly could be a barrier as well. I even heard when students filled up one board, they had to take the board to the proctor and get another. From all vantage points, that doesn't make sense. It begets failure, and this has nothing to do with academic preparation but rather with testing barriers.

That is why I am a proponent that we must *train* students to the test, not teach to the test. If there are nutty, illogical testing-day calisthenics they must participate in, let's get them prepared. If there are specific multiple-choice strategies they can employ, because of either being penalized for incorrect answers or not being penalized for incorrect answers, let's give them the best road map for success. If there are time-management strategies they can use, then let's show them what will give them the best advantage. These are things that can be trained, and we are in a position to do just that, with proactive knowledge and a careful study of the test's theater of operation. Let's ensure that through training to the test, our students are forewarned and thus forearmed for success.

The How: Strategies to Use With Staff

The following strategies—letting data paint your picture and inform, changing what the adults do first, and confronting those who are barriers—are effective ways to lay the foundation for your work with staff.

Let Data Paint Your Picture and Inform

Here, I ask that you take a step back, remove yourself from the rush of daily activity, and allow something powerful to paint a picture of what's really going on: data. Data can be used to determine whether or not you move forward upon what you have done, or whether to pause, circle around, and re-energize your efforts. First, take a look at data on attendance and discipline and break them down by all the relevant demographics: grade level, gender, race, ethnicity, free and reduced price lunch status, special education status, 504 status, gifted-and-talented status, involvement with extra-curricular activities, family makeup, and so on. The big question is, Does disproportionality exist? Determine this by taking the typical percentage of students in one demographic category as a pro-portion of your entire student population, then determine their number and type of attendance and disciplinary infractions. If the relative percentages do not closely mirror the actual percentages in the school population within those demographics, you have a problem.

Often, disproportionality exists with respect to students who are minoritized, marginalized, receiving special education services, or all. Student behaviors are borne out of frustration in class, and when they are not understood with cultural humility, they can be targeted for office referral. Disconnects can exist because of the quality of teaching and the needs of these students, resulting in them avoiding school. Sometimes this happens because students know if they go to school, they'll get in trouble. Disproportionality is troubling. Disproportionality must be unearthed and addressed. Look for disproportionality in other things too, such as enrollment trends in certain classes and pro-grams. What about extracurricular activities? How about grades in courses? Ask yourself, "Which teachers are having more success with whom? Which students from what teachers are being sent to the office and for what offenses?" Students often get in trouble in classes with teachers who have the worst class control; things get out of hand because the adult doesn't have things together. It is interesting to look at how data on student success evolve when you ensure teacher connectiveness, cultural humility, and creative pedagogy.

TIP

Find one teacher or staff member in your school who is a data geek and also very student centered. Ask this person to partner with you to gather all of these data, and slice and dice (disaggregate) them in a way that would make for interesting conversation. Present these data to your principal, counselors, and fellow teachers.

Change What the Adults Do First

Students like to get a positive school report card and an acceptable school letter grade. Policymakers and state officials want the best outcomes. We all want the same thing—successful students. Yet, our well-intentioned efforts have drifted over time. When the test scores come in, what do we often do? Often, we require students who are deficient to do more—more mathematics . . . more reading . . . more time on task, even, I am sorry to say, during lunchtime. And if this results in less recess or social time, we are willing to make that sacrifice. But *more* doesn't let students be kids.

World-renowned problem solver and consensus builder Bob Chadwick of Consensus Associates once said to me over breakfast, "Ryan, to go fast, sometimes you have to go slow" (B. Chadwick, personal communication, July 2001). That's what we need to do here. Go slow. Push the pause button. What about a different approach that dials back the pace and results in a deeper conversation? This might take a bit of time, done right, but that's OK. If you prioritize this time to pause, reflect, and work with some superstars who are the best experts in the school—your friends and colleagues, teachers and staff—you'll reap dividends. It is an opportunity for good conversation. It is time for the adults to talk about what they are doing that they can do differently. And it can be a lot of fun.

First, ask yourself, "If students did not get the scores we hoped, what school experience did we provide?" What have we *built*? This means the experience that you deliver each day. And what was it *designed to do* in terms of student learning and test success? In your school, do these two things—learning and test scores—complement one another? Your conversation needs to be about what was tested on the test (generally) so that you can compare whether or not you covered the material in the first place. Class by class, teacher by teacher, adult by adult. Sometimes this is frustrating because you don't get much feedback from the testing companies.

TIP

Unless you have changed what the adults have done, please do not call the parents or guardians of students and ask if they would support your taking away elective classes or recess from their students to work on mathematics and reading. Key here is protecting students' childhood and adolescence while the adults learn to do their jobs better.

What you do not want to do is to have a three-day summit, disproportionately focusing on the mathematics and reading teachers, talking about this demographic or that, planning to double-dip in the tested areas, unbundling state standards, examining scope and sequence, tethering yourself to yet another pacing guide, grouping and regrouping, and doing data digs until your eyes bleed. Keep it simple with all content areas as part of the solution. Ask yourselves simply if the type of instruction you're using in all areas supported success on the test. Ask bravely, "Did we do our jobs? How can we do them better next time?" The conversation might well start with whether folks like where they are assigned and if everyone is teaching in their wheelhouses.

Educators must teach with two goals, (1) learning and (2) test taking, in order to arm their students for success. Tests are a natural part of life, no matter where you go. So, get good at addressing testing. This is probably a good time to say there is no shame in talking about teaching students for the sake of learning while also building skills in test taking. The following questions can help guide a school team.

- Classroom level:
  - What *did* we teach, and not? Why?
  - Whose students did well, and whose didn't?
  - What strategies worked and didn't?
  - When students struggled, what then did we do?
  - What did we teach students about test taking?
  - Did we allow for students to be kids?

- School level:
  - Was there anything we were asked to do that was a waste of time?
  - Was there anything we felt compelled to do because of materials we purchased or a provider contract we have?
  - Was there anything we were doing because of mandates that made us inefficient?
  - Are we tethered to a curriculum, method, or series that is just not working?
  - Did we have enough resources? If not, what do we need?
  - Did we make time for students to be kids?

Once these discussions take place, make things visual. Put what you find on a wall in the staff lounge or breakroom where students, parents, and visitors do not go. Leave it up. Schedule small-group conversations around it. Draw connections to see where you might be falling short. Dare to bring up difficult topics, like *Have we been letting students be kids?* Require yourselves as adults to change things, *before* you ask students to forego important parts of childhood or adolescence.

Too often in schools, we do not allow ourselves time to think, talk, and change what the adults do first. We *team* all day long, yet often in a rush, thinking that we must change what the students are doing for a better result. We have some of the best minds and hearts in the business, who together can accomplish anything if we hold a mirror up to ourselves.

Confront Those Who Are Barriers

At times, we find that student issues pale in comparison with those of the adults. The degree to which you are involved with the teachers and staff in your building on their not-so-good days varies depending on the wishes of your principal; however, in many cases you will be doing so directly in tandem with your boss. This strategy is intended more as a way of thinking for you to approach adult problems in your school rather than an exact science. It is derived from a theoretical principle vetted in research that has much intuitive appeal to educators far and wide with whom I have discussed. I'll present it here for you, in order to help you confront those who are barriers.

Noted author Richard Koch (2017) in his book *The 80/20 Principle: The Secret to Achieving More With Less* has described the power of the Pareto Principle, which notes that roughly 80 percent of the effects upon anything in an organization come from 20 percent of the causes, or people. Originally derived from the field of economics, this principle can be applied to human behavior as well. I use this idea as a platform for a way of thinking, not an exact science, yet something powerful I have designed for assistant principals and school leaders to consider when they are dealing with colleagues who just aren't doing their part, as well as those who are. I call it the 20/20/20 theory; it is a way of handling situations with a right-sized approach and generally a positive outlook on those with whom we work. Here's how it goes.

Among faculty and staff in any school, you will find in most cases, 80 percent are doing their jobs effortfully and with pride. Conversely, you will find that roughly 20 percent are comfortable with the way things are going in the status quo and do not wish to expend extra effort on school improvement or change, even if they know it will benefit students. Through their inaction and unwillingness to move beyond comfort, they influence (according to the Pareto Principle) 80 percent of the stagnation, or, said differently, the challenge of moving forward positively toward better student learning (Koch, 2017). Of course, extrinsic forces such as bureaucracy, mandates, and societal influences also factor in. This 20 percent of those comfortable is a ballpark estimate; it's not an exact science. The interesting point I'll make here is that many administrations attempt to deal with all of these people who are resting comfortably with various carrots and sticks. I will suggest that you hold that thought; it is wasted energy.

Think of this metaphorically as a Russian doll: when you open the top of the doll, a smaller doll appears. Of those 20 percent who are comfortable, you find appropriately 20 percent of those who are counterproductive—the smaller Russian doll. This is the 20/20 part of my theory. This works out to be around 4 percent of the total population of your colleagues on faculty and staff (20 percent of the 20 percent). These counterproductive folks are dragging others down and tend to be more connected, so that their influence creates a bigger pull downward than the original 20 percent who were simply comfortable. Many administrations initiate progressive and corrective measures for those who are counterproductive and end up chasing their tails. I would encourage you to think whether you have seen this occur in the past, and avoid making this mistake. Even though conventional wisdom might tempt you otherwise, do not do anything right away to these counterproductive folks, as holding off and conserving your energy is key to confronting those who are barriers.

Of those who are counterproductive, 20 percent are really catastrophic in terms of the harm they are creating while working with you (an even smaller Russian doll). This is the 20/20/20 part of the theory, and in doing the math (20 percent of the 4 percent), it works out to be less than 1 percent of your adults at school. This is where the problem really lies. This is your bull's-eye. The challenge for administrations who are chasing around the 4 percent mentioned previously (counterproductive, 20 percent of the 20 percent) is that the catastrophic folks are cagey enough to use those circumstances to provide themselves some cover. In some instances, they set up the more easily swayed members of the counterproductive group who get confronted by the administration, and the really pernicious ones avoid administrative attention.

My suggestion is that the catastrophic folks deserve swift and decisive administrative action, while you intentionally hold off on the counterproductive intervention to give you the space, clairvoyance, and energy to focus where you need to focus. Probably through principals or with their help, those catastrophic folks need a closed-door meeting (heads up to the superintendent) and handling with speed and dispatch, with clear understanding that the behaviors that are harmful must stop or they risk a charge of insubordination. The details of this should be vetted with a school attorney and, of course, any collective bargaining agreements that exist. The point is that the catastrophic folks should be getting the consequences, not a larger group. This is critical in confronting those who are barriers in your school.

If you are fortunate, after you are done meeting with them, those who are catastrophic will go out and tell all of their counterproductive friends what just happened to them to get sympathy or allies. This is great advertising for you, as those in the counterproductive group will not want to get similar attention. Some may even be inspired over time to make it back into the comfortable.

TIP

When you deal with those who are catastrophic, have your ammunition at the ready, but come with a heart that wants to help. Let them know you are there for their success. And be there for their success. Come with a plan that they can accomplish if they want to invest, yet keep those consequences handy if they show they wish not to cooperate.

Regarding those who are counterproductive, they need a bit of attention as well, just with a softer touch. This is key in confronting those who are barriers. Work with your principal, and examine what is emboldening them to be counterproductive; look at the root causes of what may be creating their entitlement. Typically, it is an easy-gig courseload, or some status arrangement they have enjoyed for quite some time, or a higher-paying extracurricular activity where they think they're untouchable. Examine those favorite things that embolden, and ask yourself, "Do these things really move them more toward the positive, or do they incentivize counterproductivity?" If the latter, then take away one of these things from these staff members each semester or year until they shape up. Then if they are more well behaved and contributory over time, gradually give some of these perks back (but only if they're good at those things).

For those people who are comfortable, I suggest you don't do a thing. You're too busy, and they'll see what's going on. They'll stay comfortable and out of fire, and you can live with those numbers if they're around 20 percent for you. Or, they might move to the productive 80 percent, which would be nice, and here's why. For those who are productive and contributory—in the 80 percent—work with your principal to offer them the lion's share of resources, opportunity, and authority among faculty and staff. They are the ones who will take those things and garner the most positive mileage for student unconditional positive regard and opportunity, and in doing so, you'll find your resources, opportunity, and authority are well allocated.

The How: Strategy to Use With You

Becoming serious about school improvement and accountability means generally two things: (1) getting your house in order so that you get the results you desire and (2) speaking the language of those who are determining whether you are doing your job or not. This is the language of governmental agencies, accrediting bodies, and the sort. This chapter's strategy for you involves becoming familiar with those who have you under the microscope, so that you can better articulate to them what's good about what you do on behalf of students. I call it spending time on the other side.

Often, to best help your students taking standardized tests, you can get inside the minds of the test developers to see how they approach things, and how they make meaning of what they believe students should be tested on. The best way that I have found to do this over the years is by spending time with the developers themselves. You and your colleagues can participate in a variety of activities as item-analysis panelists, content-area specialists, or referent-group participants. Often, advertisements are placed through state department of education websites and listservs for professional volunteers for these panels, or through state school leadership associations. Watch for these invitations, and sign up. Also, you could even contact the publishers directly, as often one large publisher secures contracts with each state governmental entity for those stateside assessment services. Program-level referent groups are often convened to help state governments, departments, and agencies weigh in on current issues, so ensure that you share contact information with agency officials when attending conferences. A good first impression can often secure you an invitation to the next problem-solving session. As an assistant principal, I would suggest you scan your department of education website for opportunities to serve on these panels and provide input and analysis when the sausage is being made, so to speak.

Additionally, you might contact your local or state office of assessment and accountability and offer up your building or district as a pilot for new versions of tests or assessments coming your way. Avail yourself of training as a test scorer or rater for statewide or national testing services, and perform these duties voluntarily when the opportunity visits. In short, do everything you can to get a glimpse of what the Wizard of Oz sees from behind the curtain, so that you have the intel on how test developers are approaching the next round of assessments and how state officials are defining performance. One key area to serve is when cut scores and standards for success are being developed. This is an opportunity to share the voices of your teachers and students on what is fair and what isn't. Additionally, tests and assessments are often evaluated in terms of potential implicit bias against marginalized students or groups. Ensure you are in those conversations as well. Your spending time on the other side will reap knowledge, and with school improvement and accountability as currently defined, knowledge is power. Use that knowledge to advance fairness and equity.

Toolkit for Tomorrow: Next Steps

These next steps provide some suggestions for how you can put the ideas in this chapter into action.

- Ask your guidance counselor what data are available that you could provide individually to your students so that they are self-aware about where they are and where they need to be in order to set goals.

- Note whom you have put in charge of sharing student performance data with your teachers, and have an honest conversation with your principal about whether or not this person can get your teachers excited about data, whether or not teachers feel safe discussing data, and whether or not you have anyone on the team who can provide teachers specific ideas of what to do to get better learning outcomes.

- Make a list of all teachers in your school who are comfortable, counterproductive, and catastrophic, and compare those proportions to the number of all your teachers. This will help you see what your relative percentages would be in your school, as compared to the 20/20/20 theory presented earlier. Design a plan with your principal on what to do with the catastrophic category, which is likely to amount to less than 1 percent of your staff.

- Complete the professional development activity on page 186, which asks you to move through the alphabet to keep in mind some things about data and gives you an opportunity to take notes and record ideas for moving forward. I'm going to ask you to disregard the notion of data-driven leadership or performance. After all, if data were driving, who is doing the leading and managing? Additionally, students should drive their own data.

Professional Development: A Deeper Dive—Supporting School Improvement and Accountability

This professional development activity first came to my mind when exploring book topics with my friends and colleagues Todd Whitaker and Donovan Garletts. While we did not move forward with publication or development of the ideas, I want to offer them my thanks for helping me wrap my head around looking at solutions to school data challenges, from start to finish, or, in this case, from A to Z (T. Whitaker and D. Garletts, personal communication, March 12, 2019).

Instructions: As an assistant principal, you can improve your school by keeping in mind school data from A to Z—or, rather, keeping twenty-six things in mind. As you read through the list, jot down some notes in the right-hand column of how you might integrate each into your own school or repertoire.

Letters From A to Z	Things to Keep in Mind	Implications or Ideas for My Own School
A	**Attitude** An aversion to data exists in our profession. This has to do with attitude—borne of the way educators have fielded local, state, and national criticism of test scores, rather than true learning. Instead of reacting with an attitude against others who de-professionalize our work, we might better reset our attitude through the things we do that are working, such as teaching for deeper learning.	
B	**Belief System** Underneath the techniques and strategies of educators and students using data that promote success lies a powerful belief system that influences much that we do. Embedded in these beliefs is our self-appraisal of our capacity to use data to improve performance. To believe in ourselves requires that we experience success through wins, large and small, as well as rebound from intermittent defeats. It involves vulnerability in sharing with others when we are worried so that the team can uplift the individual. We must have the strength to be honest in our beliefs.	
C	**Child-Centeredness** The eyes of a child hold the wonder that is key to our future, where mountains are moved, challenges are conquered, and the world becomes a better place. Let us ask ourselves, "Is school keeping wonder alive with all this focus on data? Is childhood at the center of the equation?" Let us not replace recess with remediation or sacrifice childhood for cut scores.	

Letters From A to Z	Things to Keep in Mind	Implications or Ideas for My Own School
D	**Decision Making** An ethical and responsible use of data-informed decision making is when we change what we expect the adults to do in schools before we ask students to change anything about the way they are engaging with school. In short, we do not want to take the childhood out of school through cessation of elective or recess or play time as a knee-jerk reaction to short-term student academic progress. Once we use decision making to reflect upon the efforts of adults, we can appropriately ask students to put forth extra effort and sacrifice their social time.	
E	**Expectations** Educators concerned with national pressures of data and accountability have made arguments for the use of growth assessments for students who are below grade level, in terms of evaluating the work of educators. They argue that selfless educators who accept our most underperforming students need to be judged on the quality of education that takes place on their watch, not that which came prior. While this might be true, we must not let the soft bigotry of low expectations influence us. Students need to leave school at a certain level of achievement in order to move forward successfully. Growth alone will not do it.	
F	**Forgiveness** In our efforts to use data to improve our schools, we find some colleagues who push back on what we do. Our most successful educators forgive them in advance and find value in their perspectives, as those opposing current efforts may have a good point or two. Every time data show something to us, it has the possibility of painting someone or something in a positive or negative light. It can be scary for some who still have good ideas, and thus they deserve a kind ear.	

Letters From A to Z	Things to Keep in Mind	Implications or Ideas for My Own School
G	**Grading Practices** Grades as a focal point in data have been a fact of life in schools and are sometimes, and sometimes not, used well in determining student aptitude and achievement. We can glean new ideas from different assessment practices in schools to promote student learning. Students who receive As in a school with subpar teaching are at a disadvantage when they work alongside students who receive lower grades in more rigorous and relevant schools. Ask yourself, if your teachers were to unveil the details of how their grades were calculated at a breakout session of a teaching excellence conference, would you be proud to say you work with them?	
H	**Health** Schools spend so much time looking at, worrying about, and defining their letter grades as preeminent forms of data; it is often at the expense of the well-being of staff and students. Might we evaluate a school's organizational health instead through a lens that assesses the health of those contributing to the mission in the first place—the staff? The sum of the individual health in the building defines organizational health, and this total impacts student performance.	
I	**Intuition** When our teachers have gut feelings about the needs of students, they are still relevant. Intuition is data, in terms of what educators can conceive and, at times, potentially measure. Teacher feeling, teacher reflection, and teacher guesstimation (educated, of course) have value, in terms of next steps, when options for students are uncertain and answers to data escape us. Let us re-engage what makes us human in this technical equation of performance-based decision making. Try things if you have a feeling they'll work.	

Letters From A to Z	Things to Keep in Mind	Implications or Ideas for My Own School
J	**Joy** Walking into schools and discerning whether there is a love of learning amidst the data in teaching and learning is obvious within minutes of any visit. Joy has an impact on student performance, not so much through a feel-good approach but rather through a brain-research approach. It has more to do with neurochemical responses to incoming stimuli and what happens next. When the eyes of students are smiling, learning is alive, and nothing is impossible.	
K	**Karma** In an era where bureaucratic pressures have led to top-down, data-based decision making, heroes are those who use data to inform what they do in spite of the pressure for data to drive what they do. Karma is alive in our profession—what goes around comes around. Good fortune created through forward-looking, data-informed decision making, coupled with a willingness to help each other and pay it forward, can position a school to progress with no regrets in terms of adult contributions and student performance.	
L	**Leadership** In our best schools, leadership with data is present at all levels, and in all different folks, whether principals, teachers, staff, students, parents, or volunteers. Leadership is the ability for those with vision to encourage and inspire those around them to travel from where they are to a better place. Our best leaders who use data to make decisions look over their shoulders every once in a while to see if anyone is following.	

Letters From A to Z	Things to Keep in Mind	Implications or Ideas for My Own School
M	**Main Things** Whatever your main thing (reason to be an educator) is, do you keep it in mind when using school data? Further, do you reach more deeply into yourself and draw from your own main thing when unpacking your data? Be true to yourself. You cannot allow data to move you away from why you went into this profession in the first place. Data should allow us to move closer to our core, rather than farther away. Knowing your main thing allows you to keep your eyes on what is important within the data—what should be prioritized because of them. Doing so can actually carve out the necessary time to take control and foster more fun while learning because you are being true to yourself.	
N	**Number Sense** Numbers in our data have roles, sometimes known to us, sometimes undercover. They have secret identities: they can paint pictures, speak languages both familiar and foreign, suggest the obvious or outlandish, and influence us to do things that are logical or, sometimes for those driven by them, counterintuitive. Number sense has to do with how we define data, how we reimagine them, and how we then use them. They are superpowers if we use them and can also be our Kryptonite. They can have addictive tendencies and provide a false sense of importance for some who purport they alone can crack the code. Numbers can be beautiful, ugly, and both. Numbers can be estimated but should not be underestimated.	
O	**Ownership** Someone in the school must provide for the care and feeding of data and steward the process to pull the data, decipher the data, discuss the data, and use the data. This takes two main skills: (1) data literacy and (2) communication. And not all educators possess both naturally. Data ownership requires an air traffic controller, or owner, without metaphor. When data ownership is just and authentic, everyone in the school will be able to articulate the why, as well as why they are grateful to have this service performed.	

Letters From A to Z	Things to Keep in Mind	Implications or Ideas for My Own School
P	**Personality** If you are to help teachers build capacity in academic performance through data, you must factor in personality in order to be successful. What this means is that if you are to connect with your front-end users of data, you must speak their language, the language of personality (some say, "in channel," much like the age-old CB radio). This includes adaptive communication—that is, how you say what you say. Often, the people sharing data with teachers and staff are simply not connecting in terms of personality. They are out of touch and off-channel. You must ensure this is not the case, or teachers will tune them out.	
Q	**Qualifications** From the onset of employment, teachers and staff need clear descriptions of the qualifications they must bring to the job in order to use data in teaching and learning. They need also to have the qualifications to help teachers and staff decide what to do next once the results are in. This is more than student groupings and pacing guides; it includes sharing ideas that best allow our educators to explore what is possible in their instruction and intervention after being informed. It involves the qualification of being a diagnostician of learning and of student brain development. More so, if those conducting trainings cannot connect with students themselves, then they are not the ones who should be conducting the trainings.	
R	**Regimen** If your school was a training regimen in the use of data to inform performance, would it promote muscle memory—the kind that allows adults and students to come into school each day, be confident that they know their data routines, and have some fun along the way? Further, do your classrooms have systemic routines in data management and use those to teach the why of data's utility as students are engaging in them? What can a smart and student-centered regimen do for you and your data?	

Letters From A to Z	Things to Keep in Mind	Implications or Ideas for My Own School
S	**Stewardship** Our best educators are stewards—they provide for the care and feeding for all in our learning communities. This is especially true in terms of helping with performance management through data. Data stewards have the abilities to equip and inspire students and colleagues to use data results to influence and carry out their mission, toward that of a vision for their success, which is in and of itself a performance expectation. Data stewards pay attention to the needs of people first, and they prioritize the realities of the moment. It's all about context, and feeling, and those fuzzy things that make our business a people profession. Stewardship is also about taking responsibility for student learning, stating, "If students are not learning, it is our fault," and convincing colleagues of this too.	
T	**Taking Time** We only have so much time in a day. We must ensure that when we use data in the precious time we have, it is used in a much more important context of connection. I have seen teachers who, before the pressures of accountability, spent their time in small talk with students during lunches in their classrooms or during recess, and are now spending time instead with focused tutorials and remediation workshops. We know that students want to know that we care more than they want to know what we know. This calls to mind the expression, "Enjoy the little things, for one day you'll look back and realize they were the big things." Students in this harried world of being tugged hither and yon, being shuttled from one prescribed task to the next, need a bit of our time, unmeasured.	
U	**Unlearning** It can be troubling to hear reports of students who want to be teachers discouraged by those from whom they seek advice, including their own teachers and parents. Too much focus on data and accountability, some say. The reality is that there is plenty to celebrate and plenty that teachers and school leaders can do creatively for students. We still own the how of teaching, and this is where the power lies. Thus, we have to resist the temptation to buy in to disillusionment. We must unlearn the noise so we can inspire ourselves anew, promote achievement, and move on.	

Letters From A to Z	Things to Keep in Mind	Implications or Ideas for My Own School
V	**Validation** Our best schools use examples from data to answer the question, Why? They are hungry for data and keep notepads when watching the news, listening to the radio, or scanning the internet. Students value the learning that takes place when adults can validate why it is important. Data help! Our best teachers employ a needs-centered approach to instruction. Through this, they validate the good in all students. Misbehavior is a teachable moment. Students' needs are data; they can be measured, weighed, and valued before they are asked to complete academic tasks or reach goals that data provide. Our best educators know students are in a better place when they feel validated. With proper effort and emphasis, teachers are validated as well.	
W	**Walking the Walk** What educators do with data, and how they do it, is watched, embraced, and adopted by students and even their families. Bystanders notice us. Our behavior is a byproduct. Foster in your team an understanding of the power involved in what you do with data day to day, so that when the next standardized testing window visits, all are mindful that what you project is not a byproduct of disdain for a test but rather a love of opportunity. Our beliefs, values, and assumptions rise to the surface, positively or not so much, as we strive to best employ data-informed instruction.	
X	**X-Factor** Some call it an X-factor of performance in discerning what our data say. Others replace a teacher's last name for the X, because many of us still believe that programs, products, and proscriptions will not improve student performance and learning . . . but people certainly can. People are the ones who turn data into opportunities. Your X-factor is where miracles are made. As you leverage the power of data toward enhanced school performance and student achievement, ensure your path to performance is through the good people who are showing the way. Ensure that X marks the spot; the people should make the data rather than the data making the people.	

Letters From A to Z	Things to Keep in Mind	Implications or Ideas for My Own School
Y	**You** In terms of a data-informed school culture, where is your focus? In a profession that touts altruism and adult sacrifice, I would hope it is first on you. When on an airplane, readying for takeoff, how often do you hear that you should put the oxygen mask on someone else first? The answer is never. Safety and best practice ensure that in order to help another, you have to have a clear head, with oxygen flowing and your own needs met first. The same holds true in schools, yet it runs counter to conventional belief and the way many of us have been trained. We have heard repeatedly throughout the years, "Students first," and some of us act this way to a fault, at the expense of our own health and well-being. The adults in your school should come first, and that starts with you, so that you all can ensure the students come most.	
Z	**Zone** We've heard of being in the zone as we perform, collaborate, or compete. The same holds true in schools. Once you learn how best to drive school data and how you can leverage data in school performance and decision making, don't rest on your laurels. Keep it up! And that will require you to be in the zone. Whether it is the zone of peak performance, the zone of proximal development, or the end zone of performance touchdowns, the zone is integral to any discussion of getting to the top of your game and staying there. It involves a look at yourself, others, and then the system so that changes start from the inside of you and then become powerful in others as well.	

☑ CONCLUSION
ALL OTHER DUTIES AS ASSIGNED

All other duties as assigned include doing everything that principals either dislike or smartly realize they have difficulty with. It could be that there are simply too many things to get done and they must be divvied up, but typically they're just not the principal's favorite things—that's for sure. They can include anything from facilitating the town hall meetings when the new reproductive and health education curriculum must be presented, to patrolling the neighborhoods in your personal vehicle during lunchtime, to representing the school with a personal swim in a fundraising dunk tank, and even to doing the chicken dance on the school rooftop if the school reaches its semester attendance goals. When your principal says so, you're up, you're on, and you're it. Yet, you know all of this. It is the last line on most job descriptions, as this book is aptly titled.

What you might not realize is that there is someone else assigning all other duties, and that's you. I'm going to leave you with three that I have found in retrospect were critical to my success—to the enjoyment I had at the time of serving as an assistant principal and now today in reflection: (1) understanding people, power, and politics; (2) being loyal and true to you; and (3) finding one's looking glass.

Understanding People, Power, and Politics

Yours is the people business; some might even say *the people's business*, because it is their sons and daughters that you are more frequently serving on any given day than your own. With people, additional layers of situational complexity exist the higher you go on the professional educator's food chain. Much of what school leadership requires is an understanding of people, power, and politics (B. Balch, personal communication, July 23, 2021) and, for me, recollections of the teaching of educational leadership professor Robert Boyd of Indiana State University. So console yourself that, sometimes, the political connections of those above you on the organizational chart will sometimes get a bit frustrating, such as when you're ready to dole out some serious consequences and your principal or superintendent calls and asks you to give a pass for reasons that are entirely political and their own.

Hardwired as I am for justice, equity, and fairness, I had a bit of difficulty with this at first and would go long in defense of what I felt was the right thing to do. Truth be told, I was dialed back a few times by a wise mentor of a principal who reminded me that there were others looking at our decisions with wider lenses—and with more factors to consider. Now, of course, there are lines that we cannot cross even if asked to, and we must stand our ground and assume the responsibility. We must expose wrongdoing when it's present, and we all have healthy and appropriate boundaries that we must maintain. Where this advice is well spent and well meant is in those situations where you are with so much back-and-forth, and with so much granular involvement, that it might take a person a bit removed from the play-by-play to ensure that the ripple effects of your actions are considered. This is when you must trust that others can see the ripples of people, power, and politics that you may not and when you need to understand that the world does not revolve around your ego. Just deal with it, accept things, do what you're asked (or directed) to do, and move on.

Being Loyal and True to You

Loyalty to your principal is sacrosanct. It may be argued you were hired with that in mind as one of your highest virtues. Key in this relationship is that while you are being loyal professionally, you are also feeding your own loyalty to you personally. You have to be true to you. Start by getting familiar with your principal's beliefs, values, and ways of doing things before your hire, if you can. Just like a marriage, the courtship is typically an attractive time, where everyone is on their best behavior and some of the little things are either covered up or overlooked. It is as fruitless to try to change your principal once in a professional relationship as it is to try to change a spouse once married.

Thus, it is important that both in matchmaking and beyond, you are loyal and true to you. Your actions have real consequences; they are weighty at times. If not handled in sync with what you believe is right, just, and appropriate—if not handled in a way that you would wish for your own loved ones or children—then it is probably not a situation where you are being self-loyal and true. Be loyal and true to you in the following five areas of the assistant principalship.

1. How you make tough decisions when there is no win–win option

2. How you decide on a course of action when you really cannot bet one way or another on what will happen next

3. How to proceed with a general lack of information available

4. What to do and how to do it when your actions will impact adversely whether the people at work will continue to like you

5. What to do when you're being asked to do something that on the surface just doesn't seem like you would recommend it

In the latter, it may be that you make some tough decisions to stand on principle and adversely impact your job security.

Finding One's Looking Glass

There's an Irish proverb that says, "The best looking glass is the eyes of a friend." I recall a particularly challenging day in my assistant principalship when, after school, I drove about an hour out of town to attend a weekend graduate class. Settling on a barstool at a trendy pub for a dinnertime meal and beverage, I saw my own reflection in the mirror behind the bar. I then recalled this proverb, which my dad had once shared with me. That particular weekend was powerful, not only due to the content I learned but especially during the breaks we took. We were early career school administrators, and our progression through coursework of our educational specialist degrees brought with it an informal cohort. We were friends. I was fortunate to find a looking glass in which to share and receive some guidance with someone safe whom I trusted.

Who is your looking glass? Who is your source of trust, support, and affirmation? Who, from time to time, calls you out on your misgivings? Many of us have spouses or significant others who provide the reflection we need; others have friends or colleagues who fit the bill. The important thing is that we have someone who will be nonjudgmental yet honest, tactful but firm, and, as we discussed earlier in the book, who will walk with us on a journey of being open, resourceful, and persistent in examining what we do and in being who we are.

I close this book with a heartfelt thanks for taking time to examine the assistant principalship, a prime and pivotal calling—not just a job but a mission . . . not just a position but a true labor of love. Those who are quiet, others who are loud, many who are unruly, and a few who are compliant—all whose lives you have influenced positively—are thankful, or at minimum better off, to have you in your role.

☑ APPENDIX:
QUICK REFERENCE—
STRATEGIES

TABLE A.1: List of Strategies by Chapter

Chapter	Strategy	For Whom?	Page Number
Chapter 1: Deciding You Want to Be an Assistant Principal	Maximize Your Visibility	Students	Page 11
	Act With Compassion	Students	Page 11
	Read Between the Lines	Students	Page 12
	Decide Through Integrity	Staff	Page 14
	Strive for Effectiveness	Staff	Page 15
	Practice Self-Care	You	Page 15
Chapter 2: Making Time for Management	Make Class Calls	Students	Page 26
	Inspect, Maintain, and Repair	Students	Page 27
	Identify and Empower Your Instructional Experts	Staff	Page 28
	Step Into Your Casting Manager	Staff	Page 30
	Embrace and Empower Your Gatekeeper	Staff	Page 32
	Distinguish the Urgent, Important, Both, and Neither	You	Page 33

continued ▶

Chapter	Strategy	For Whom?	Page Number
Chapter 3: Fostering a Positive School Culture and Climate	Take the Temperature (of School Climate)	Students	Page 43
	Develop Nuanced Observation	Students	Page 44
	Connect the Dots in School Culture	Staff	Page 46
	See a New Why in Resistance to Change	Staff	Page 46
	Become a Daily Pathfinder	You	Page 49
Chapter 4: Developing Relationships	Learn What's on the Outside	Students	Page 65
	Speak the Language of Personality	Students	Page 67
	Use the Techniques of Reciprocation, Commitment and Consistency, and Scarcity for Positive Influence	Students	Page 71
	Meet, Then Move	Staff	Page 72
	Foster Interaction Safety	Staff	Page 74
	Recalibrate Your Position	You	Page 76
Chapter 5: Protecting and Promoting Priorities and People	"Play Catch" Each Morning	Students	Page 83
	Be a Moment Maker	Students	Page 84
	Play the Name Game	Students	Page 85
	Have Regard for Regard	Staff	Page 87
	Value the Personal in the Professional	Staff	Page 88
	Start Your Days With SODA	You	Page 89

Chapter	Strategy	For Whom?	Page Number
Chapter 6: Leveraging Firm and Fair Discipline	Leave Nary a Stone Unturned	Students	Page 99
	Work From the Fringe Forward	Students	Page 102
	Design Doorways of Dignity	Students	Page 105
	Focus on Factors That Prevent	Staff	Page 107
	Empower Staff to Save and Adopt	Staff	Page 109
	Mind Your Backside	You	Page 110
Chapter 7: Capitalizing on Teachable Moments	Teach for Tenacity	Students	Page 117
	Share Ownership in the Lesson	Students	Page 118
	Facilitate Effective Conflict Resolution	Students	Page 119
	Leverage Compassionate Accountability	Staff	Page 123
	Use the Power of the Circle	Staff	Page 124
	Prep Like Teachers Do	You	Page 126
Chapter 8: Safeguarding an Equitable Education for All	Level the Playing Field	Students	Page 137
	Cultivate Your Counterspace	Students	Page 138
	Protect Safe Zones and Lifelines	Staff	Page 141
	Do Difference Differently	Staff	Page 142
	Move to the Edge of Discomfort	You	Page 143

continued ▶

Chapter	Strategy	For Whom?	Page Number
Chapter 9: Taking Time for Teaching and Learning	Empower Through Teacher Cadets	Students	Page 158
	Establish a Learners' Lounge	Students	Page 159
	House a Student Success Center	Students	Page 160
	Model a Monthly Method	Staff	Page 162
	Connect With Co-Teaching	Staff	Page 163
	Visit, Just Because	Staff	Page 164
	Develop Pedagogical Humility	You	Page 165
Chapter 10: Supporting School Improvement and Accountability	Empower Students Through Advisory	Students	Page 177
	Train (Not Teach) to the Test	Students	Page 178
	Let Data Paint Your Picture and Inform	Staff	Page 179
	Change What the Adults Do First	Staff	Page 180
	Confront Those Who Are Barriers	Staff	Page 181
	Spend Time on the Other Side	You	Page 183

REFERENCES AND RESOURCES

Agrawal, J., Barrio, B. L., Kressler, B., Hsiao, Y., & Shankland, R. K. (2019). International policies, identification, and services for students with learning disabilities: An exploration across 10 countries. *Learning Disabilities: A Contemporary Journal, 17*(1), 95–114.

Alexander, K., & Alexander, M. D. (2012). *American public school law* (8th ed.). Belmont, CA: Wadsworth.

Alexander, K., & Alexander, M. D. (2018). *Law of schools, students, and teachers in a nutshell.* St. Paul, MN: West Academic.

Alexander, K., & Alexander, M. D. (2019). *American public school law* (9th ed.). Belmont, CA: Wadsworth.

Allen, J. G., & Weaver, R. L. (2014, October). Learning to lead: The professional development needs of assistant principals. *NCPEA Education Leadership Review, 15*(2), 14–32.

Allen, R. L., & Liou, D. D. (2019). Managing whiteness: The call for educational leadership to breach the contractual expectations of white supremacy. *Urban Education, 54*(5), 677–705.

Amiot, M. N., Mayer-Glenn, J., & Parker, L. (2019). Applied critical race theory: Educational leadership actions for student equity. *Race, Ethnicity, and Education.* Accessed at https://doi.org/10.1080/1361332 4.2019.1599342 on September 13, 2021.

Ary, D., Jacobs, L. C., & Sorenson, C. (2009). *Introduction to research in education* (8th ed.). Belmont, CA: Wadsworth/Cengage Learning.

Austin, G., O'Malley, M., & Izu, J. (2011). *Making sense of school climate: Using the California School Climate, Health, and Learning (Cal–SCHLS) survey system to inform your school improvement efforts.* Los Alamitos, CA: WestEd.

Bambrick-Santoyo, P. (2019). *Driven by data 2.0: A practical guide to improve instruction.* San Francisco: Jossey-Bass.

Barroso, A., & Brown, A. (2021, May 25). *Gender pay gap in U.S. held steady in 2020.* Accessed at www.pewresearch.org/fact-tank/2021/05/25/gender-pay-gap-facts on January 9, 2022.

Bernstein-Yamashiro, B., & Noam, G. G. (2013, Spring). Teacher student relationships: Toward personalized education. *New Directions for Youth Development, 2013*(137), 1–124.

Black, J. S. (2014). *It starts with one: Changing individuals changes organizations.* Upper Saddle River, NJ: Pearson Education.

Black, J. S., & Gregersen, H. B. (2002). *Leading strategic change: Breaking through the brain barrier*. Upper Saddle River, NJ: Prentice Hall.

Bolman, L. G., & Deal, T. E. (2017). *Reframing organizations: Artistry, choice, and leadership*. Hoboken, NJ: Jossey-Bass.

Boogren, T. H. (2018). *Take time for you: Self-care action plans for educators*. Bloomington, IN: Solution Tree Press.

Books, S. (2011). What we don't talk about when we talk about "the achievement gap." In R. Ahlquist, P. Gorski, & T. Montano (Eds.), *Assault on kids: How hyper-accountability, corporatization, deficit ideologies, and Ruby Payne are destroying our schools* (pp. 35–50). New York: Peter Lang.

Braden, G. (2011). *Deep truth: Igniting the memory of our origin, history, destiny, and fate*. Carlsbad, CA: Hay House.

Bradley, D. F. (2007). A unique tool for closing the gap. *Journal of the Alliance of Black School Educators*, *6*(2), 20–31.

Briggs, S. (2013, June 25). *The perils of standardized testing: Six ways it harms learning*. Accessed at www.opencolleges.edu.au/informed/features/the-perils-of-standardized-testing on March 25, 2021.

Bronk, K. C., & McLean, D. C. (2016). The role of passion and purpose in leader developmental readiness. *New Directions for Student Leadership*, *149*, 27–36.

Bryk, A. S., Gomez, L. M., Grunow, A., & LeMahieu, P. G. (2015). *Learning to improve: How America's schools can get better at getting better*. Cambridge, MA: Harvard Education Press.

Buckingham, M., & Coffman, C. (1999). *First, break all the rules: What the world's greatest managers do differently*. New York: Simon & Schuster.

Carr, P. R. (2016). Whiteness and White privilege: Problematizing race and racism in a "color-blind" world, and in education. *International Journal of Critical Pedagogy*, *7*(1), 51–74.

Case, A. D., & Hunter, C. D. (2012). Counterspaces: A unit of analysis for understanding the role of settings in marginalized individuals' adaptive responses to oppression. *American Journal of Community Psychology*, *50*(1–2), 257–270.

Chadwick, B. (2012). *Finding new ground: A transformative approach to resolving conflict with individuals, family, community, church, education, business, and government*. Terrebonne, OR: One Tree.

Cherkowski, S., Kutsyuruba, B., & Walker, K. (2020). Positive leadership: Animating purpose, presence, passion, and play for flourishing in schools. *Journal of Educational Administration*, *58*(4), 401–415.

Cialdini, R. (2021). *Influence, new and expanded: The psychology of persuasion*. New York: Harper Business.

Clayton, G., & Bingham, A. J. (2018). The first year: Assistant principals in Title I schools. *Journal of Educational Leadership and Policy Studies*, *1*(2), 1–17.

Colburn, L., & Beggs, L. (2020). *The wraparound guide: How to gather student voice, build community partnerships, and cultivate hope*. Bloomington, IN: Solution Tree Press.

Collignon, G. (2017). *The art of adaptive communication: Build positive personal connections with anyone*. Hot Springs, AR: Kahler Communications.

Collignon, G., & Legrand, P. (2016). *Understand to be understood: By using the process communication model*. Hot Springs, AR: Kahler Communications.

Collignon, G., & Legrand, P., & Parr J. (2012). *Parlez-vous personality? Process communication for coaches*. Hot Springs, AR: Kahler Communications.

Crowe, K., & McDowell, E. (2017). *There is no good card for this: What to say and do when life is scary, awful, and unfair to people you love*. San Francisco: HarperOne.

Daggett, W. R. (2016). *Rigor/relevance framework: A guide to focusing resources to increase student performance.* Accessed at http://daggett.com/pdf/Rigor%20Relevance%20Framework%20White%20 Paper%202016.pdf on September 23, 2021.

Danielson, C. (2012, November). Observing classroom practice. *Educational Leadership, 70*(3), 32–37.

Danielson, C. (2016, May). Creating communities of practice. *Educational Leadership, 73*(8), 18–23.

Darling-Hammond, L., & Cook-Harvey, C. M. (2018a). *Educating the whole child: Improving school climate to support student success* [Research brief]. Accessed at https://learningpolicyinstitute.org/sites /default/files/product-files/Educating_Whole_Child_BRIEF.pdf on April 22, 2022.

Darling-Hammond, L., & Cook-Harvey, C. M. (2018b). *Educating the whole child: Improving school climate to support student success* [Research report]. Palo Alto, CA: Learning Policy Institute.

Donlan, R., & Gruenert, S. (2016). *Minds unleashed: How principals can lead the right-brained way.* Lanham, MD: Rowman & Littlefield Education.

Donlan, R., Hampton, E., and Regier, N. (2017, November/December). Effects of Process Communication Model (PCM) training. *Training Magazine, 54*(6), 6.

Donohoo, J., Hattie, J., & Eells, R. (2018, March). The power of collective efficacy: When teams of educators believe they have the ability to make a difference, exciting things happen in a school. *Educational Leadership, 75*(6), 40–44.

Duhigg, C. (2016). *Smarter faster better: The secrets of being productive in life and business.* New York: Random House.

Duncan, R. (2018, November 28). *Conflict without casualties: Finding value in disagreement.* Accessed at www.forbes.com/sites/rodgerdeanduncan/2018/11/28/conflict-without-casualties-finding-value-in -disagreement/?sh=30d613091d73 on February 15, 2021.

Dweck, C. (2012, November). Mindsets and human nature: Promoting change in the Middle East, the schoolyard, the racial divide, and willpower. *American Psychologist, 67*(8), 614–622.

Dweck, C. S. (2016). *Mindset: The new psychology of success.* New York: Penguin.

Dweck, C. S., Walton, G. M., & Cohen, G. L. (2014). *Academic tenacity: Mindsets and skills that promote long-term learning.* Seattle, WA: Bill and Melinda Gates Foundation.

Eells, R. J. (2011). *Meta-analysis of the relationship between collective teacher efficacy and student achievement.* Accessed at https://ecommons.luc.edu/cgi/viewcontent.cgi?article=1132&context=luc _diss on September 14, 2021.

Fathima, M. P., Sasikumar, N., & Panimalar Roja, M. (2012, April). Memory and learning—A study from neurological perspective. *Journal on Educational Psychology, 5*(4), 9–14.

Field, A. (2009). *Discovering statistics using SPSS* (3rd ed.). Thousand Oaks, CA: SAGE.

Fisher, D., & Frey, N. (2013). *Better learning through structured teaching: A framework for the gradual release of responsibility.* Alexandria, VA: Association for Supervision and Curriculum Development.

Fullan, M. (2019). *Nuance: Why some leaders succeed and others fail.* Thousand Oaks, CA: SAGE.

Fullan, M. (2020). *Leading in a culture of change* (2nd ed.). Hoboken, NJ: Jossey-Bass.

Gabrieli, J. (2020, May). Picturing the brain. *Educational Leadership, 77*(8), 52–57.

Gackowiec, P. (2019). General overview of maintenance strategies—concepts and approaches. *MAPE, 2*(1), 126–139.

Gaisford, C. (2020). *How to find your passion and purpose: Four easy steps to discover a job you want and live the life you love.* Sante Fe, NM: Blue Giraffe Publishing.

Gallup Press. (2016). *First, break all the rules: What the world's greatest managers do differently* (Updated ed.). New York: Simon & Schuster.

Gilbert, M. (2020). *Saying it right: Tools for deft leadership.* Lanham, MD: Rowman & Littlefield.

Gilbert, M. B., & Donlan, R. A. (2016). *Personality pattern inventory.* Accessed at https://link.springer .com/referenceworkentry/10.1007/978-3-319-28099-8_60-1 on September 14, 2021.

Goldring, E., Rubin, M., & Herrmann, M. (2021). *The role of assistant principals: Evidence and insights for advancing school leadership.* Accessed at https://www.wallacefoundation.org/knowledge-center /pages/the-role-of-assistant-principals-evidence-insights-for-advancing-school-leadership.aspx on September 14, 2021.

Goleman, D. (2013). *Focus: The hidden driver of excellence.* New York: HarperCollins.

Goodwin, B. (2018). *Student learning that works: How brain science informs a student learning model.* Denver, CO: McREL International.

Grissom, J., Loeb, S., & Mitani, H. (2015). Principal time management skills: Explaining patterns in principals' time use, job stress, and perceived effectiveness. *Journal of Educational Administration, 53*(6), 773–793.

Gruenert, S., & Whitaker, T. (2015). *School culture rewired: How to define, assess, and transform it.* Alexandria, VA: Association for Supervision and Curriculum Development.

Gruenert, S., & Whitaker, T. (2022). *Leveraging the impact of culture and climate: Deep, significant, and lasting change in classrooms and schools.* Bloomington, IN: Solution Tree Press.

Harris, T. A. (2004). *I'm OK—You're OK.* New York: HarperCollins.

Hattie, J. (2009). *Visible learning: A synthesis of over 800 meta-analyses relating to achievement.* London: Routledge.

Hattie, J. (2012). *Visible learning for teachers: Maximizing impact on learning.* London: Routledge.

Heifetz, R., Grashow, A., & Linsky, M. (2009). *The practice of adaptive leadership: Tools and tactics for changing your organization and the world.* Boston: Harvard Business Press.

Hinnant-Crawford, B. N. (2020). *Improvement science in education: A primer.* Gorham, ME: Myers Education Press.

Holcomb, E. L. (2017). *Getting more excited about using data* (3rd ed.). Thousand Oaks, CA: Corwin Press.

Holmes, K. (2019). Neuroscience, mindfulness and holistic wellness reflections on interconnectivity in teaching and learning. *Interchange, 50*(3), 445–460.

Hope, M. A., & Hall, J. J. (2018). "Other spaces" for lesbian, gay, bisexual, transgendered and questioning (LGBTQ) students: Positioning LGBTQ-affirming schools as sites of resistance within inclusive education. *British Journal of Sociology of Education, 39*(8), 1195–1209.

Hunter, M. (1982). *Mastery teaching: Increasing instructional effectiveness in elementary, secondary schools, colleges, and universities.* Thousand Oaks, CA: Corwin Press.

Hurt, K., & Dye, D. (2020). *Courageous cultures: How to build teams of micro-innovators, problem solvers, and customer advocates.* New York: HarperCollins Leadership.

Individuals With Disabilities Education Act, 20 U.S.C. § 1400 (2004).

Jamaludin, A., Hung Wei Loong, D., & Pei Xuan, L. (2019). Developments in educational neuroscience: Implications for the art and science of learning, *Learning: Research and Practice, 5*(2), 201–213.

Jarrow, C. (2019). *Time management ninja: 21 tips for more time and less stress in your life.* Coral Gables, FL: Mango.

Junco, R. (2012, September). No A 4 U: The relationship between multi-tasking and academic performance. *Computers & Education, 59*(2), 505–514.

Kahler, T. (2008). *The process therapy model: The six personality types with adaptations*. Little Rock, AR: Taibi Kahler Associates.

Karpman, S. B. (2014). *A game free life: The definitive book on the drama triangle and compassion triangle by the originator and author*. San Francisco: Drama Triangle.

Keels, M. (2019). *Campus counterspaces: Black and Latinx students search for community at historically White universities*. Ithaca, NY: Cornell University Press.

Kelleher, I., & Whitman, G. (2020, May 28). *Every educator needs to know how the brain learns*. Accessed at www.ascd.org/el/articles/every-educator-needs-to-know-how-the-brain-learns on January 26, 2022.

Kendi, I. X. (2016). *Stamped from the beginning: The definitive history of racist ideas in America*. New York: Bold Type.

Kendi, I. X. (2019). *How to be an antiracist*. New York: One World.

Koch, R. (2017). *The 80/20 principle: The secret to achieving more with less*. New York: Doubleday.

Kotter, J. P. (2012). *Leading change*. Boston: Harvard Business Review Press.

Lacoe, J., & Manley, M. (2019). *Disproportionality in school discipline: An assessment in Maryland through 2018*. Washington, DC: Regional Educational Laboratory Mid-Atlantic.

Lauen, D. L., & Gaddis, S. M. (2016). Accountability pressure, academic standards, and educational triage. *Education Evaluation and Policy Analysis, 38*(1), 127–147.

Leana, C. R. (2011). *The missing link in school reform*. Accessed at www2.ed.gov/programs/slcp/2011 progdirmtg/mislinkinrfm.pdf on September 23, 2021.

Loewen, J. W. (2018). *Lies my teacher told me: Everything your American history textbook got wrong* (2nd ed.). New York: New Press.

Loveless, T. (2016). *The 2016 Brown Center Report on American education: How well are American students learning? With sections on reading and math in the Common Core era, tracking and Advanced Placement (AP), and principals as instructional leaders*. Accessed at www.brookings.edu/wp-content /uploads/2016/03/Brown-Center-Report-2016.pdf on September 23, 2021.

Luy, M., Zannella, M., Wegner-Siegmundt, C., Minagawa, Y., Lutz, W., & Caselli, G. (2019). The impact of increasing education levels on rising life expectancy: A decomposition analysis for Italy, Denmark, and the USA. *Genus, 75*(1).

Marzano, R. J. (2017). *The new art and science of teaching*. Bloomington, IN: Solution Tree Press.

Marzano, R. J., Warrick, P., & Simms, J. A. (2014). *A handbook for High Reliability Schools: The next step in school reform*. Bloomington, IN: Marzano Resources.

Mascareñaz, L. (2021). *Evident equity: A guide for creating systemwide change in schools*. Bloomington, IN: Solution Tree Press.

Maslow, A. H. (1987). *Motivation and personality* (3rd ed.). New York: Harper & Row.

McTighe, J., & Willis, J. (2019). *Upgrade your teaching: Understanding by Design meets neuroscience*. Alexandria, VA: Association for Supervision and Curriculum Development.

Miller, F. A., &. Katz, J. H. (2018). *Safe enough to soar: Accelerating trust, inclusion, and collaboration in the workplace*. Oakland, CA: Berrett-Koehler.

National Association for Gifted Children. (n.d.). *Myths about gifted students*. Accessed at www.nagc.org /myths-about-gifted-students on January 26, 2022.

National Center for Education Statistics. (2020). *Data point: Race and ethnicity of public school teachers and their students*. United States Department of Education. Accessed at https://nces.ed.gov /pubs2020/2020103/index.asp on January 9, 2022.

National School Climate Center. (n.d.). *Measuring school climate (CSCI)*. Accessed at https://schoolclimate.org/services/measuring-school-climate-csci/ on October 28, 2021.

Ndaruhutse, S., Jones, C., & Riggall, A. (2019). *Why systems thinking is important for the education sector*. Accessed at https://files.eric.ed.gov/fulltext/ED603263.pdf on September 23, 2021.

NEOS. (2014). *Self-efficacy instrument: A tool to measure domain-specific self-efficacy among three composite areas—Openness, resourcefulness, and persistence*. Newton, KS: Next Element Consulting.

New Jersey v. T. L. O., 469 U.S. 325 (1985).

Nichols, H. (2021). *Finding your blind spots: Eight guiding principles for overcoming implicit bias in teaching*. Bloomington, IN: Solution Tree Press.

NWEA. (2018). *Assessing soft skills: Are we preparing students for successful futures?* Accessed at www.nwea.org/content/uploads/2018/08/NWEA_Gallup-Report_August-2018.pdf on February 3, 2022.

Oleszewski, A., Shoho, A., & Barnett, B. (2012, May). The development of assistant principals: A literature review. *Journal of Educational Administration, 50*(7), 264–286.

Oqvist, A., & Malmstrom, M. (2016). Teachers' leadership: A maker or breaker of students' educational motivation. *School Leadership & Management, 36*(4), 365–380.

Page, M. L. (2016). LGBTQ inclusion as an outcome of critical pedagogy. *International Journal of Critical Pedagogy, 7*(1), 115–142.

Paris, D., & Alim, H. S. (Eds.). (2017). *Culturally sustaining pedagogies: Teaching and learning for justice in a changing world*. New York: Teachers College Press.

Pauley, J. A., Bradley, D. F., & Pauley, J. F. (2002). *Here's how to reach me: Matching instruction to personality types in your classroom*. Baltimore, MD: Brookes.

Payne, A. (2018). *Creating and sustaining a positive and communal school climate: Contemporary research, present obstacles, and future directions*. Washington, DC: National Institute of Justice.

Pearson, P. D., & Gallagher, M. (1983). The instruction of reading comprehension. *Contemporary Educational Psychology, 8*(3), 317–344.

Pederson, J. S. (2009). Myth 17: Gifted and talented individuals do not have unique social and emotional needs. *Gifted Child Quarterly, 54*(4), 280–282.

Perkins-Gough, D. (2013, September). The significance of grit: A conversation with Angela Lee Duckworth. *Educational Leadership, 71*(1), 14–20.

Pollock, K., Wang, F., & Hauseman, C. (2017, June). *The changing nature of vice-principals' work: Final report*. Accessed at www.edu.uwo.ca/faculty-profiles/docs/other/pollock/pollock-opc-vp-report-final.pdf on January 17, 2022.

Regier, N. (2016). *Conflict without casualties: A field guide for leading with compassionate accountability*. Oakland, CA: Berrett-Koehler.

Regier, N. (2020). *Seeing people through: Unleash your leadership potential with the Process Communication Model*. Oakland, CA: Berrett-Koehler.

Regier, N., & King, J. (2013). *Beyond drama: Transcending energy vampires*. Newton, KS: Next Element.

Rehabilitation Act, 29 U.S.C. § 701 (1973).

Rimm-Kaufman, S. E., & Jodl, J. (2020, May). Educating the whole learner. *Educational Leadership, 77*(8), 1–9.

Ritchhart, R. (2015). *Creating cultures of thinking: The 8 forces we must master to truly transform our schools*. San Francisco: Jossey-Bass.

Robinson, H. M. (1965a). *Ventures*. Northbrook, IL: Scott Foresman.

Robinson, H. M. (1965b). *Vistas*. Northbrook, IL: Scott Foresman.

Rogers, C. R. (1957). The necessary and sufficient conditions of therapeutic personality change. *Journal of Consulting Psychology, 21*(2), 95–103.

Rogers, C. R. (1989). *On becoming a person: A therapist's view of psychotherapy*. New York: Houghton-Mifflin.

Rogin, M. (2022). *Change starts with me: Talking about race in the elementary classroom*. Bloomington, IN: Solution Tree Press.

Roorda, D. L., Koomen, H. M. Y., Spilt, J. L., & Oort, F. J. (2011, December). The influence of affective teacher–student relationships on students' school engagement and achievement: A meta-analytic approach. *Review of Educational Research, 81*(4), 493–529.

Roth, J. A., D'Agostino, T., & Brown, C. J. (Eds.). (2010). *2010 desktop encyclopedia of American school law*. Malvern, PA: Center for Education and Employment Law.

Rudasill, K. M., Snyder, K. E., Levinson, H., & Adelson, J. L. (2017). Systems view of school climate: A theoretical framework for research. *Educational Psychology Review, 30*(1), 35–60.

Ryan, J., Pollock, K., & Antonelli, F. (2009). Teacher diversity in Canada: Leaky pipelines, bottlenecks, and glass ceilings. *Canadian Journal of Education, 32*(3), 591–617.

Schimmel, D., Stellman, L. R., Conlon, C. K., & Fischer, L. (2015). *Teachers and the law* (9th ed.). Upper Saddle River, NJ: Pearson.

Schmoker, M. (2011). *Focus: Elevating the essentials to radically improve student learning*. Alexandria, VA: Association for Supervision and Curriculum Development.

Semrud-Clikeman, M. (2010). *Research in brain function and learning: The importance of matching instruction to a child's maturity level*. Accessed at www.apa.org/education-career/k12/brain-function on January 11, 2022.

Shaked, H., & Schechter, C. (2014). Systems school leadership: Exploring an emerging construct. *Journal of Educational Administration, 52*(2), 293–811.

Shaked, H., & Schechter, C. (2016). Holistic school leadership: Systems thinking as an instructional leadership enabler. *NASSP Bulletin, 100*(4), 177–202.

Shaked, H., & Schechter, C. (2020). Systems thinking leadership: New explorations for school improvement. *Management in Education, 34*(3), 107–114.

Sinek, S. (2014). *Leaders eat last: Why some teams pull together and others don't*. New York: Penguin Group.

Soland, J., Hamilton, L. S., & Stecher, B. M. (2013, November). *Measuring 21st century competencies: Guidance for educators*. Accessed at from http://asiasociety.org/files/gcen-measuring21cskills.pdf on February 3, 2022.

Starck, J. G., Riddle, T., Sinclair, S., & Warikoo, N. (2020). Teachers are people too: Examining the racial bias of teachers compared to other American adults. *Educational Researcher, 49*(4), 273–284.

Thomas, M. S., Crosby, S., & Vanderhaar, J. (2019). Trauma-informed practices in schools across two decades: An interdisciplinary review of research. *Review of Research in Education, 43*(1), 422–452.

Thoreau, H. D. (1854). *Walden; or life in the woods*. Boston: Ticknor & Fields.

Tinker v. Des Moines Independent Community School District, 393 U.S. 503 (1969).

Tomlinson, C. A., & Sousa, D. A. (2020, May). The sciences of teaching. *Educational Leadership, 77*(8), 14–20. Accessed at www.ascd.org/el/articles/the-sciences-of-teaching on November 17, 2021.

Tschannen-Moran, M., & Tschannen-Moran, B. (2014, February). What to do when your school's in a bad mood. *Educational Leadership, 71*(5), 36–41.

Tyler, A. C. (2016). "Really just lip service": Talking about diversity in suburban schools. *Peabody Journal of Education*, 91(3), 289–308.

United Kingdom Department for Education. (2021). *School teacher workforce*. Accessed at www.ethnicity-facts-figures.service.gov.uk/workforce-and-business/workforce-diversity/school-teacher-workforce/latest on January 26, 2022.

U.S. Department of Education. (n.d.). *Title 34 education: Subtitle B regulations of the offices of the Department of Education*. Accessed at www2.ed.gov/policy/rights/reg/ocr/edlite-34cfr104.html on November 19, 2021.

van Dijk, W., & Lane, H. B. (2018). The brain and the US education system: Perpetuation of neuromyths. *Exceptionality, 28*(1), 16–29.

Venture. (n.d.). In *Merriam-Webster's online dictionary*. Accessed at https://www.merriam-webster.com/dictionary/venture on September 16, 2021.

Vista. (n.d.). In *Merriam-Webster's online dictionary*. Accessed at https://www.merriam-webster.com/dictionary/vista on September 16, 2021.

Vygotsky, L. S. (1978). *Mind in society: The development of higher psychological processes*. Cambridge, MA: Harvard University Press.

Waack, S. (n.d.). *Collective Teacher Efficacy (CTE) according to John Hattie*. Accessed at https://visible-learning.org/2018/03/collective-teacher-efficacy-hattie/ on January 20, 2021.

Warren, R. (2012). *The purpose driven life: What on earth am I here for?* Grand Rapids, MI: Zondervan.

Washington Post. (2000, July 10). *George W. Bush's speech to the NAACP*. Accessed at www.washingtonpost.com/wp-srv/onpolitics/elections/bushtext071000.htm on January 26, 2022.

Whitaker, T. (2014). *Shifting the monkey: The art of protecting good people from liars, criers, and other slackers*. Bloomington, IN: Triple Nickel Press.

Whitaker, T., Good, M. W., & Whitaker, K. (2019). *Classroom management from the ground up*. New York: Routledge, Taylor & Francis Group.

Whitaker, T., Miller, S., & Donlan, R. (2018). *The secret solution: How one principal discovered the path to success*. San Diego, CA: Burgess.

Whitaker, T., Zoul, J., & Casas, J. (2015). *What connected educators do differently*. New York: Routledge, Taylor & Francis Group.

Whitley, S. F. (2020, Winter). A brief primer of three major counseling theories for use by school-based personnel. *Journal of the American Academy of Special Education Professionals*, 146–159.

Wilfong, S. (2021). *The mattering model: The foundational elements of mattering for K–12 teachers* (Doctoral dissertation). Indiana State University, Terre Haute.

Wilfong, S., & Donlan, R. (2021). *How mattering matters for educators*. Accessed at www.ascd.org/el/articles/how-mattering-matters-for-educators on February 3, 2022.

Wingfield, A. H. (2015, September 13). *Color blindness is counterproductive*. Accessed at www.theatlantic.com/politics/archive/2015/09/color-blindness-is-counterproductive/405037/ on November 1, 2021.

World Health Organization & World Bank. (2011). *World report on disability*. Geneva, Switzerland: World Health Organization.

Yell, M. L. (2019). *The law and special education* (5th ed.). New York: Pearson Education.

☑ INDEX

The Deliberate and Courageous Principal
Rhonda J. Roos
Fully step into your power as a school principal. By diving deep into five essential leadership actions and five essential leadership skills, you will learn how to grow in your role and accomplish incredible outcomes for your students and staff.
BKG013

Trauma-Sensitive Leadership
John F. Eller and Tom Hierck
Lead a foundational shift in the way your school approaches student behavior. Using straightforward language, the authors offer research-based, practical strategies for understanding and supporting trauma-impacted students and providing a safe environment for them to learn.
BKF911

The Wraparound Guide
Leigh Colburn and Linda Beggs
Your school has the power to help students overcome barriers to well-being and achievement—from mental health issues to substance abuse to trauma. With this timely guide, discover actionable steps for launching and sustaining wraparound services embedded within your school that support the whole child.
BKF956

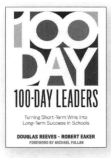

100-Day Leaders
Douglas Reeves and Robert Eaker
Within 100 days, schools can dramatically increase student achievement, transform faculty morale, reduce discipline issues, and much more. Using *100-Day Leaders* as a guide, you will learn how to achieve a series of short-term wins that combine to form long-term success.
BKF919

Responding to Resistance
William A. Sommers
Educational leadership is never conflict free. In *Responding to Resistance*, author William A. Sommers acknowledges this reality and presents school leaders with wide-ranging strategies to decisively address conflict involving staff, students, parents, and other key stakeholders.
BKF955

Solution Tree | Press *a division of* Solution Tree

Visit SolutionTree.com or call 800.733.6786 to order.

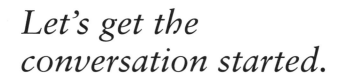